CW00350371

FROM PERS

TO PRIV.

FROM PERSONAL LIFE
TO PRIVATE LAW

JOHN GARDNER

OXFORD
UNIVERSITY PRESS

OXFORD
UNIVERSITY PRESS

Great Clarendon Street, Oxford, OX2 6DP,
United Kingdom

Oxford University Press is a department of the University of Oxford.
It furthers the University's objective of excellence in research, scholarship,
and education by publishing worldwide. Oxford is a registered trade mark of
Oxford University Press in the UK and in certain other countries

Published in the United States of America by Oxford University Press
198 Madison Avenue, New York, NY 10016, United States of America

British Library Cataloguing in Publication Data
Data available

Library of Congress Cataloging in Publication Data
Data available

ISBN 978–0–19–881875–5 (Hbk.)
ISBN 978–0–19–885185–1 (Pbk.)

PREFACE

This book—none of which has previously appeared in print—is
a descendant of my eponymous Quain Lectures, delivered at
University College London in 2014. One of those lectures was
itself descended, in part, from a public lecture hosted by the Law
and Philosophy Institute at Rutgers University in 2012. (The
logistics of that lecture furnished an extended illustration of its
thesis, retained here: see Chapter 3, section 3.) At the time of the
2014 lectures, of which there were three, I was drawn to the idea
of publishing them with only small improvements, still in their
easy-going lecture style. That was a pipe dream. Returning to the
lecture texts over the following months I saw that they contained,
in very sketchy form, ideas the full development of which might
take a decade or more. This book is not that full development.
It is a compromise between my instinct to get to the bottom of
a problem and my instinct to keep the problem engaging for my
audience. It includes, mainly in Chapters 2, 3, and 5, some fragments of the lecture texts. But the main features inherited from
the lectures are these: a relatively informal prose style (where
possible!); illustrations that tend towards the literary or the autobiographical; and relatively few footnotes. Alas, that has not pre-
vented the total number of words from growing threefold since
the 2014 drafts, and the complexity of argumentation increasing
proportionately with it.

Much of the expansion and enhancement is owed to discussions with colleagues and friends, and to comments and questions at classes and seminars and workshops. There were intensive
seminars following the lectures at both Rutgers and UCL. As
the lectures slowly turned into the book, draft chapters were
put to the test in Oxford, Los Angeles, Nottingham, Ithaca,
and Jerusalem. It is not possible to list all those who played their
part in improving the book through contributions on these occasions. I am reduced to offering wholesale thanks to all who
participated. However, I can point to specific contributions
from the following people, for whose generous efforts let me
offer special appreciation: Annalise Acorn, Aditi Bagchi, Chris

Bennett, Yifat Bitton, Leo Boonzaier, Ben Brown, Jenny Brown, Daniel Butt, Marta Pantaleon Diaz, Hasan Dindjer, Julia Driver, James Edwards, Cécile Fabre, Andrew Gold, Kate Greasley, Les Green, Ori Herstein, Gerry Johnstone, Greg Keating, George Letsas, Ian Loader, Jules Holroyd, Doug Husak, Tim Macklem, Andrei Marmor, Sandra Marshall, Mihaela Mihai, Rob Mullins, Linda Radzik, Joseph Raz, Arthur Ripstein, Connie Rosati, Craig Rotherham, Sam Scheffler, Seana Shiffrin, Sandy Steel, Jenny Steele, John Tasioulas, Fred Wilmot-Smith, Grégoire Webber, Alexandra Whelan, Jake Wojtowicz, and Ben Zipursky. Without the input of these people, this would have been a shorter, more prompt, and more readable book. But it would also have been a book far less worthy of publication. For the many deficiencies that no doubt remain, I take full responsibility, especially where, as so often, I failed to take good advice. That remark will resonate especially with my long-suffering editors Alex Flach and Emma Taylor, for whose numerous contributions I am also very grateful indeed. They, as well as Ben Brown and Jake Wojtowicz, kindly read and commented on the whole final draft, which was a service well beyond the call of duty.

Those reluctant celebrities of legal philosophy—Henrik (19), Annika (15), and Audra (8)—have starring roles in some of my examples (see, for example, Chapter 3, section 5). For this project, they and their ever-patient mother Jenny have been my most assiduous and effective teachers. In our house there is always plenty of personal life going on, from the ardent to the zany. May that be true in your house too, and may the joyless shadow of private law never (or only very rarely) be cast upon it.

John Gardner
30 September 2017

CONTENTS

Introduction

They murdered his wife. They destroyed his future.
Now they have to pay.[1]

1. Three themes, and then a fourth

Even knowing nothing of the author's work, it would not take long for a commuter at Brighton railway station to work out that Wilbur Smith's new novel belongs to the *Death Wish* subgenre. The backdrop shows a silhouetted lone figure, striding into a vast barren landscape below an ominous sky. 'Now they have to pay' is not intended to suggest that the man is delivering an invoice. He is out for blood. *Predator* promises to be a tale of ruthless, savage, and, no doubt, extremely gratifying revenge.

Remove it from its place in a publisher's publicity campaign, however, and the haiku-like teaser could bring something different to mind. It could represent—in very condensed form—a summons, a statement of claim, the pleading used to begin court proceedings in what I will call 'private law' cases. What is alleged on behalf of the claimant is a wrong against him ('they murdered his wife') and a loss to him associated with it ('they destroyed his future'). What is claimed, in light of the wrong and the loss, is a remedy ('now they have to pay'). Wrong, loss, remedy—the litigation equation, the trinity of torts, the alchemy of *assumpsit*.

It is intriguing that the language of private law—the language of debt, repayment, rectification, and so forth—is also the language of revenge. How is it that a three-line synopsis of the no doubt gripping *Predator* could equally be a three-line synopsis of the inevitably tedious *Plaintiff*? Here is one link between the two. Private law exists, in part, for the sublimation of vengeful feelings. It is a central plank of the argument for having any law, private or otherwise, that it cools heated reactions to actual and

---

[1] Advance publicity for Wilbur Smith, *Predator* (HarperCollins 2016).

From Personal Life to Private Law. John Gardner © John Gardner 2018. Published 2018 by Oxford University Press.

alleged wrongdoing, that it substitutes its laborious rituals and distractions for the horrors of the blood-feud, the vendetta, the duel, the lynching, and so forth. Strong arguments *against* private revenge, then, provide strong arguments *in favour of* private law. The two have an inverse relation. But a more intriguing question is whether, to make a strong argument in favour of private law, one first needs to muster a strong argument in favour of revenge. Is there a direct (non-inverse) relation between the two? Some people think so. Getting one's own back in the avenger's sense, they think, is the authentic moral blueprint for getting one's own back in the restitutionary or reparative sense. The hero of *Plaintiff* rightly takes his lead from the hero of *Predator*, albeit thankfully with a cooler head and more measured expectations.[2]

This strikes me as implausible, for two related reasons. First, the sense in which the hero of *Predator* gets his own back is obscure. It is surely metaphorical. His wife plainly does not return from the dead. His satisfaction when he avenges her death is not, one assumes, a resumption of the very same feelings that he had before she was killed. His execution of the murderer is not literally the extraction of a payment, for he does not literally receive it. The key plotline is not of his finding new love and reinstating connubial bliss. For him, nothing goes back to how it was. Whereas there is an ordinary literal sense, to be explored in some detail in this book, in which the hero of *Plaintiff* does get something back. As his lawyer will explain, he is entitled in law to a sum of money from the wrongdoer, calculated to restore him to 'the same position as he would have been in if he had not sustained the wrong for which he is now getting his compensation or reparation.'[3] He still does not get his wife back. But if her earnings were paying for the penthouse and the safaris, he gets damages to cover the loss of those. True, his losses are covered only 'so far as money can do it', and in the circumstances that may not count for much.[4] But, with

---

[2] See Scott Hershovitz, 'Tort as a Substitute for Revenge' in John Oberdiek (ed), *Philosophical Foundations of the Law of Torts* (Oxford University Press 2014).

[3] *Livingstone v Rawyards Coal Company* (1880) 5 App Cas 25, at 39 (Lord Blackburn).

[4] *Robinson v Harman* [1848] 1 Exch 850, at 855 (Baron Parke).

that proviso, what he gets back from the wrongdoer, he literally does get back.

Secondly, it is very hard to justify revenge. Actually, it is hard to justify even extremely mild punishment. For both revenge and punishment involve the intentional infliction of suffering or deprivation. If the person on the sharp end does not suffer and is not deprived, the act of revenge or punishment has failed. It is extremely hard to explain why anyone should aim to bring extra suffering or deprivation into the world, especially in the name of putting right suffering or deprivation already brought about.[5] Happily, one need not do so with remedial measures of the kind that are characteristic of private law. Any suffering or deprivation of the defendant here is but a side-effect of reparative and restitutionary measures. Such measures are designed, not to add new losses, but to reallocate losses which, thanks to the defendant, are already *faits accomplis*. To make them succeed, the defendant need not bear any new suffering or deprivation, or indeed any suffering or deprivation at all. If he is insured, so much the better; the deprivation will be spread thinly and will ideally go unnoticed by everyone, so there will be no suffering. Could the justification of such relatively innocuous measures in which there need be no new deprivation, let alone suffering, possibly depend on the justification of more noxious measures by which extra suffering or deprivation is created? I doubt it.

This book has nothing much to say about the justification of punishment, let alone about the justification of revenge. *Predator* will not be our concern. Nor, for the most part, will *Prosecutor*, a third instalment in our imaginary trilogy (in which the hero of *Predator* is finally arrested and indicted with the help, let us suppose, of the scrupulous killjoy hero of *Plaintiff*). I spent many years thinking and writing about philosophical issues in criminal law, while always remaining very unsure about how to justify punishment, even when it takes the form of withholding pocket money from youngsters or giving someone the cold shoulder at a party. One big reason why I stopped working on philosophical issues in criminal law (around 2008) was that I had reached the point at

---

[5] See my discussion of Hart's difficulties in the introduction to HLA Hart, *Punishment and Responsibility* (2nd edn, Oxford University Press 2008).

which, in my view, I could not proceed further without a more
secure sense of how to justify punitive responses and, indeed, a
more secure sense of how to justify the mysterious 'blaming' attitudes which seem to underlie punitive responses.[6] What are they
all about? I was not sure where to start. Strangely, for a philosopher of criminal law, I was not even sure that punitive responses
and blaming attitudes *can* be justified.

Even now the same doubts remain. One big reason why I took
up more serious work on private law (from 2008 onwards) was
that I saw more prospect of making both moral peace and philosophical progress with private law's (as it seemed to me) less toxic
remedial apparatus. In particular, those mysterious blaming attitudes did not seem to be of the essence. I vaguely hoped that
I might come back to criminal law some day, armed with some
transferable insights from the study of private law. In Chapter 4
of this book there are some hints of possible directions for further thought about punishment.[7] But all that, I must confess, is
incidental. It is not the topic of the chapter. Rather, I am trying
to get to the bottom of a puzzle about so-called 'general damages' for torts and breaches of contract. The puzzle concerns the
longing to repair the irreparable. So, you see, I have come to grasp
over the years that the remedial apparatus of private law is itself
extremely hard to explain and defend. I had underestimated the
scale of the ethical and the philosophical challenges. This book is
testimony both to the scale of the challenges and the very limited
progress I have made, so far, in meeting them. I feel that with private law I have only slightly bettered my frustrating attempts to
understand what is going on in criminal law.

The remedial apparatus of private law dominates the rather
complex middle chapters of the book, Chapters 3 and 4. They
focus on the 'now they have to pay' part of the *Plaintiff* plot.
What counts as paying in the relevant sense? Why does it count as

[6] I shared and still share the bafflement about blame expressed in Bernard
Williams, 'Internal Reasons and the Obscurity of Blame' in Williams, *Making
Sense of Humanity* (Routledge 1995). I do not share Williams' diagnosis; the puzzle
remains even without Williams' misguided 'internalism' about reasons.

[7] Some of them have been fruitfully explored by Chris Bennett in *The Apology
Ritual* (Cambridge University Press 2008), although not to the point at which my
puzzlement evaporates.

paying? And why are 'they' (the ones who committed the wrong) the right ones to be doing the paying? Chapters 2 and 5, meanwhile, are concerned with the 'they destroyed his future' part of the narrative. Chapter 2 explores the importance of how wrongs turn out—their outcomes—while Chapter 5 tries to understand how and why the losses of the person wronged are the main outcomes that matter in private law contexts. The 'they murdered his wife' part of the story—what is wrongdoing? why does it matter so much?—runs through the whole book. Chapter 1, however, pays special attention to an aspect of wrongdoing that is of particular salience in private law: wrongs, or some of them, are committed against particular people. What does that mean? And why is it so important to the rest of the story of private law? Why does it matter, for the plot of *Plaintiff*, that the person who was murdered by 'them' was *his* wife?

This whistle-stop tour misses out Chapter 6. Chapter 6 explores the part of the story that is left implicit in Wilbur Smith's publicity tercet. Let me make it explicit now:

They murdered his wife. They destroyed his future.
Now they have to pay. *And he is the one who gets to make them pay.*[8]

In *Predator*, it is personal execution; in *Plaintiff*, it is by resort to an elaborate institutional process. Either way, why is so much left up to the person who was wronged? Why so much power for that person, and so much elbow-room in how it is exercised?

In some ways, Chapter 6 counterbalances the rest of the book, which is mainly about the ways in which timeless themes of private law are also timeless themes of personal life. In that chapter we encounter some timeless themes of private law that are more reflective of its specialized institutional arrangements. When

---

[8] The added fourth limb is sometimes called the 'civil recourse' aspect of private law, following Benjamin Zipursky, 'Rights, Wrongs, and Recourse in the Law of Torts', *Vanderbilt Law Review* 51 (1998), 1. The third limb contributes what is sometimes called the 'corrective justice' aspect. That these are aspects of private law, not competing models, is argued in my article entitled 'Torts and Other Wrongs', *Florida State University Law Review* 39 (2011), 43. This book develops the point. In fact, it goes further and rejects the quest for a model, where that is taken to mean that an explanation of one aspect of private law must also explain other aspects, on pain of being insufficiently theoretical.

they are carried back over into personal life these themes tend to be ill-fitting. But the ill-fitting themes are not the ones that you might expect them to be. It is not, as many think, that coercion and authority have less of a role in personal life than they have in the law. It is discretion—latitude to treat people your way, whether or not it is the right way—that has less of a role in personal life than it has in the law. You may find that a surprising discovery. It goes hand in hand, however, with a sub-text of the book as a whole. The timeless themes of private law, the four themes from *Plaintiff*, are not distinctively, or especially, liberal themes. They have less to do with the value of personal freedom than many have tended to imagine (although it is fair to say that replacing *Predator* with *Plaintiff* does have some distinctively liberal benefits). That is why the timeless themes of private law are so timeless, whereas liberal civilization has its beginning, middle, and—one hopes not too soon—its end.

2. Personal life

The expression 'personal life', which I have used several times already and which figures in the book's title, may strike you as pleonastic. If I am a person, then surely all of my life is my personal life? Maybe that is too literal-minded. These days, people tend to use the expression 'personal life' to mean something akin to 'intimate life' or 'private life'. Sometimes they are referring euphemistically to their romantic dalliances and sexual liaisons. But no less often they mean, more broadly, the part of their lives that they share with family and close friends. An implicit contrast is often being drawn with the part of their lives that is occupied with work or career, for which the expression 'working life' or 'professional life' is often reserved. There is already something vaguely disturbing about the way in which these are idiomatically cast as different *lives*, rather than as different parts or facets of a single life. With Alasdair MacIntyre, one may be tempted to worry about the way in which

modernity partitions each human life into a variety of segments, each with its own norms and modes of behaviour. So work is divided from leisure, private life from public, the corporate from the personal. So both childhood and old age have been wrenched away from the rest of human life and made over into distinct realms. And all these separations have been achieved so that it is the distinctiveness of each and not the unity of the life of the individual who passes through those parts in terms of which we are taught to think and feel.[9]

This book does not follow MacIntyre in his hysterical diagnosis of our contemporary condition ('the liquidation of the self')[10] or in his nostalgic prescriptions. You will not find me yearning for some imaginary golden age in which there was (scope for) greater unity in people's lives. But the book is supposed to encourage a turn towards greater unity in how we *think* about people's lives, especially but not only in how they interact with law and politics. It is supposed to nudge those thinking about modern private law, in particular, towards the position that Liam Murphy calls 'monism'. For monists, 'all fundamental normative principles that apply to the design of institutions apply also to the conduct of people.'[11] As Murphy elaborates:

Monism is of course compatible with the existence of specifically political principles of a nonfundamental kind, such as the principle that taxation should be levied according to taxpayers' 'ability to pay'. What monism rejects is any defense of such a principle by appeal to a fundamental one that does not also apply directly to people's conduct. It should therefore be clear that monism does not have the absurd implication that all morally defensible legal principles are ipso facto valid moral principles. In rejecting the distinction Rawls draws between politics and morality, I am not rejecting the distinction between law and morality. Thus it might be appropriate to enact legislative or constitutional provisions that are not plausible moral principles.[12]

This passage calls for careful interpretation. In one way, monism *does* have the implication, *pace* Murphy, 'that all morally defensible legal principles are ipso facto valid moral principles.' Actions which the law defensibly classifies as wrongs are, if nothing else, *mala prohibita*. They are made immoral by the fact that they are defensibly made illegal. The absurd implication that Murphy is

---

[9] MacIntyre, *After Virtue* (Gerald Duckworth & Co 1981), 204.

[10] ibid 205.

[11] Murphy, 'Institutions and the Demands of Justice', *Philosophy and Public Affairs* 27 (1998), 251, at 251.

[12] ibid 254.

trying to guard against is only that they are also *mala in se*: that they must already have been immoral for it to have been morally defensible to have made them illegal. And in one way, *pace* Murphy, the monist *is* rejecting 'the distinction between law and morality'. She accepts it when it is interpreted to mean that the immorality of some action, its being *malum in se*, is not an adequate defence of its being made illegal. But she rejects it when it is interpreted to mean that the defence of legal norms depends ultimately on considerations that do not bear on the defence of the actions, quite apart from the law, of the people whose actions those norms regulate. No: ultimately the only considerations that are relevant to defending the law are considerations that are also relevant to defending what people do quite apart from the law (and I would add, going beyond Murphy, vice versa).

Unlike Murphy, I will generally avoid the word 'morality' and its cognates when I am referring to these considerations. Roughly, 'personal life' is my name for what people do (as well as what they think, believe, want, etc.), quite apart from the law. In the following chapters I argue in what Murphy would call a 'monist' vein that what private law would have us do is best understood by reflecting on what we should be doing quite apart from private law, which obviously entails reflection on the reasons why we should be doing it. Actually, maybe it creates the wrong expectations to say that I *argue* for this view. Perhaps it is less misleading to say that I attempt to substantiate it, or make it credible. I attempt to reveal by example and analysis that, in defiance of its reputation for remote and impersonal technicality, for lacking a human touch, the main concerns that drive and structure private law are ordinary human concerns that also apply to you and me when we relate to each other, quite apart from the law, for example as friends or neighbours or lovers or colleagues or, for that matter, as strangers queuing for the bus or holding the door open for each other or saying 'good morning' as we pass.

Theoretical writing about private law, in my view, stands today in need of a strong dose of this kind of monism. There is a pronounced contemporary tendency to think of private law as an autonomous domain, requiring a specialized apparatus of analysis and evaluation. It is the domain of 'private right', where that does not count as a mere redescription of private law but also as a constraint on the possible ways of justifying it.[13] This 'private right' view has emerged mainly in reaction to another view, in which private law is regarded as but one more tool of public policy, to be evaluated using standard techniques from the policy sciences. Here the economists of law reign supreme.[14] But even as they rightly deny the autonomy of private law from public policy, the economists wrongly insist on the autonomy of public policy from everything else. They regard public policy as a specialized domain in which preferences alone are to rule, and they decline to condemn or even evaluate anyone's preferences, for public policy purposes, except in terms of *other* preferences. Not for them the central questions of classical ethics—What goals and relationships (and hence 'preferences') should one have? How attached should one be to them? How should one feel about their loss or abandonment? In short, what life should one lead? If the economist admits that these are sensible questions at all, he typically relegates them to a different line of business. They are not the business of the policy sciences, and hence not relevant to the analysis and evaluation of private law. And here (subject only to disagreement about the 'hence') we see where the economist of private law and her 'private right' adversary find themselves, surprisingly, on the same side. Each seeks a way of insulating the study of private law (alone or with other things) from the study of the wider human condition.

The main thing that inspired me to write this book, and that still animates many of its discussions, is the thought that there can be no such insulation except at the price of extreme, and I might add gratuitous, distortion. The big themes of private law—at

[13] This is the Kantian expression favoured by Ernest Weinrib, Arthur Ripstein, and others. See e.g. Weinrib, 'Private Law and Public Right', *University of Toronto Law Journal* 61 (2011), 191, at 199, 210; Ripstein, *Private Wrongs* (Harvard University Press 2016), e.g. at 64, 177. Similar ideas are favoured by others who do not use the same terminology. See e.g. Robert Stevens, *Torts and Rights* (Oxford University Press 2007).

[14] The ur-example is Richard Posner, 'A Theory of Negligence', *Journal of Legal Studies* 1 (1972), 29. For discussion of the wider economics-of-private-law literature see my chapter entitled 'Tort Law and Its Theory' in John Tasioulas (ed), *The Cambridge Companion to the Philosophy of Law* (Cambridge University Press forthcoming 2018).

least those selected big themes that I foreground in the following chapters—are also among the big themes of life. And how we should think about them in connection with private law is none other than the same way in which we should think about them in connection with everything else to which they are relevant—for example, when we reflect on how to bring up our children, on how to put our friendships back on an even keel, on how to respond to our failures, on how to relate to people who have disappointed us, on how to make a fresh start, and so on.

In substantiating this thought, the book makes extensive use of literary examples, some developed at length. This technique might not be to the taste of all readers.[15] I do, however, have a few modest points to offer in its favour. I have never been much of a fan of stripped-down thought experiments of the kind favoured by many contemporary moral philosophers, such as the 'trolley problem' and 'the survival lottery'.[16] But I have never been entirely sure what it is about these thought experiments that makes me so uneasy. Part of it surely has to do with the way in which they draw their users into a search for impossibly sharp distinctions, with low tolerance for the indeterminacies and ambivalences which I believe are central to the lives of finite rational beings like ourselves. But I realize now, having written this book, that I have another distinct problem with such examples. For the most part, they deliberately eliminate any hint of background story. They treat problems about what some generic agent is to do now as touched on only occasionally, and in strictly demarcated ways, by the way in which the agent came to be facing those problems, the role she is occupying, and the place that her

---

[15] For those who are particularly interested in the literary examples (or particularly uninterested in them, and so keen to give them a wide berth), allow me to list the main ones here: John Steinbeck, *Of Mice and Men*, ch 1, s 2; William Styron, *Sophie's Choice*, ch 1, s 3; Arthur Miller, *Death of a Salesman*, ch 2, ss 2–3; Steven Soderbergh, *Sex, Lies, and Videotape*, ch 3, s 2; Larry David, *Curb Your Enthusiasm*, ch 3, s 4; ch 4, s 4; ch 6 s 4; William Shakespeare, *The Winter's Tale*, ch 4, s 1; Edith Nesbit, *The Story of the Treasure Seekers*, ch 4, s 3; ch 6, s 3; George Orwell, *Nineteen Eighty-Four*, ch 5, s 3; Simon Wiesenthal, *The Sunflower*, ch 6, s 4.

[16] Philippa Foot, 'The Problem of Abortion and the Doctrine of Double Effect', *Oxford Review* 5 (1967), 5, the first exercise in what is now known as 'trolleyology'; John Harris, 'The Survival Lottery', *Philosophy* 50 (1975), 81.

actions have in the wider story of her life. Some moral philosophers prize this elimination of background story. They think
the stripping out of such distracting particularity essential to do
justice to the idea that morality binds us all unconditionally. To
avoid the dangerous charms of this slippery idea is one reason
why I avoid the word 'morality' and its cognates throughout the
book. Although (as you will see) the book gives a mixed review
to the philosophical legacy of Bernard Williams, I share his un-
ease with the modern view of morality as a specialized body of
norms that bears down upon our everyday lives from a source
beyond our everyday lives, constraining and inhibiting us in our
pursuit of what are somehow more personal reasons that would
otherwise prevail. In the picture I present, every reason is in the
relevant sense a personal reason. That they help to bring this out
is one reason why I share Williams' taste for literary examples, examples in which the participants have histories, established roles
and relationships, personalities and characters, and in which the
problems that they face are always in a way problems of what to
do now *given what has gone before*. The italicized words should resonate with private lawyers. For all they may share the passion of
some moral philosophers for impossibly sharp distinctions, they
tend also to share the instinct for what I am calling background
story. They know that the rationally important features of a narrative cannot be isolated without a narrative; a stripped-down
though-experiment of the kind favoured by many moral philosophers is simply not suitable for adjudication, or even (I would
add) for much useful reflection.

In light of what I have just said about morality, it would be reasonable to say that my Murphy-style monism is not aimed only
at those who regard private law as a domain autonomous relative
to public policy, nor only at those who regard public policy as a
domain autonomous relative to morality, but also at those who
regard morality as a domain autonomous relative to the wider
human pursuit of value. At the fundamental level, there is only
value and our engagement with it as finite rational beings. There
is only what J S Mill called 'the Art of Life'.[17]

---

[17]   Mill, *A System of Logic, vol 2* (John W Parker 1856) 527.

But take care how you read the label 'monist' here, especially now that I have thrown in Mill's name. You may associate Mill with classical utilitarianism, and hence with the hopeless quest for a 'felicific calculus'.[18] I will have no part in that quest. For in a more familiar sense, not Murphy's sense, this book has conspicuously pluralistic sympathies. It presents the world as a world of indefinitely many irreducibly different values competing for our, and hence for private law's, attention. This is another way in which the position taken here differs from those found in much contemporary theorizing about private law. One perennial selling-point of the idea that private law (or policy science, or morality) is an autonomous domain relative to the wider human pursuit of value is that, in the wider human pursuit of value, there are so many possible values to pursue. Given the finitude of human life, the pursuit of any of these values by any of us, let alone by all of us together, is inevitably to the neglect of others. We may look to law (or policy, or morality) to help us bring order to the chaos of value that we confront. But how is it to do so? Perhaps by the institutional prioritization of a certain value, or a certain cluster of values. This brings us to various familiar attempts to isolate a value or cluster of values that private law especially, or exclusively, serves: the value of equality, the value of choice, the value of wealth, the value of reciprocity, and so on. Value-pluralism, if not completely defied, is at least tamed by such a domain-specific value selectivity.

This book does not hold out much hope for the taming of value-pluralism. Everything that matters in life matters in private law, and it matters in private law much as it matters in life. This means that endless values are in play in private law. Many of them are alive in the pages of this book. You may wonder how the book can nevertheless bring any order to our thinking about

[18] The name commonly given to Jeremy Bentham's quest in his *The Principles of Morals and Legislation* (T. Payne and Son 1789) for a way of assessing the value of anything, and hence comparing it with the value of anything else, on a single scale. Bentham proposed a single pleasure-pain scale, which, as critics note, is already two scales, not one—so not quite as advertised. Arguably, Mill fragmented the scales still further, and should not be associated with Bentham's quest. For discussion of Mill's divided philosophical loyalties on this point see Martha C Nussbaum, 'Mill between Aristotle and Bentham', *Daedalus* 133 (2004), 60.

law of property mainly because of the way in which they are alive in the law of torts.

You may worry that these pragmatic common lawyer's circumscriptions of my subject matter are at odds with my references, in this introduction, to 'timeless themes of private law', a turn of phrase which may strike you as a little—shall we say?—metaphysically inflationary. But they are not so intended. I am not suggesting that private law is found at all times and all places where there are human beings, or even in all human legal systems. All I mean to suggest is that the themes recur in many legal systems across the long history of human law. Legal arrangements closely resembling the common law of torts and the common law of contract are found well beyond the common law, and well before the modern age. The themes traversed in this book are not legally parochial. Would it be going too far to say that a legal system in which one or more of the themes were not represented would not have private law? If there were no legal duty of repair owed by wrongdoers to those whom they wronged, if the duty of repair were not a duty to repair losses caused by the wrongdoer, or if there were no cause of action in the courts available to the person wronged at her discretionary initiative, would 'private law ... cease to exist'?[22] I hesitate to get tangled up in this question. It is of no consequence here. This is not a book about the very idea of private law. It is a book that assumes you know roughly what private law is, and explores some of its timeless (maybe better now to say: enduring) themes.

4. Chapter synopsis

In section 1 of this introduction I already gave some forewarning of the coverage of the chapters that follow. But here is another outline, this time in sequential order, to help you find your way through the book. Such help may be needed since the topics of the chapters do not track any of the established ways of carving up the subject favoured by lawyers or by other theorists.

Chapter 1 explores the sense in which the duties of the law of torts and the law of contract may be said to be 'relational'. It takes a stand

<hr>

[22] Ernest Weinrib, *The Idea of Private Law* (Harvard University Press 1995), 28.

against the hyper-relationalism of many writings on private law, and the hypo-relationalism of others. It does so in two moves. First, it introduces the idea of a 'strictly relational' duty, which is a duty that one has for the reason that one is in a certain relationship. It argues that even strictly relational duties need not be justified by irreducibly relational arguments. They may be justified by the non-relational value of there being relationships to which such duties attach. This first move already tells against a certain kind of hyper-relationalism in thinking about private law. The second move goes further. Private law duties, I argue, need not be and often are not strictly relational. They are only 'loosely relational'. It turns out to be tricky, but important, to capture (non-impressionistically) the distinction between strictly and loosely relational duties. The distinction is explored and refined by reflecting on the duty of care in the law of negligence, and its modern history. Finally, we consider the import, but also the theoretical dispensability, of rights talk in private law. What matter are duties owed to others, and breaches of them, also known as wrongs against others.

Chapter 2 shifts attention from the wrong to the loss that is suffered by the person who is wronged. A law of torts (or of breach of contract) that does not pay attention to such losses is oxymoronic, or near enough. But on what basis can such losses intelligibly be attributed to the wrongdoer? The chapter argues that the problem goes right to the heart of the theory of human action. There cannot be human action at all—or even a decision to act—if there cannot be human action that is part-constituted by the way it turns out. There is no reason to decide, never mind a reason to attempt, if there is no reason to achieve, succeed, bring about what one decided, etc. An explanation of action, in short, depends on an explanation of the possibility of causal responsibility. The problem faced by private law, then, is not so much the problem of explaining how losses matter as the problem of explaining where we should stop: what are the limits of our causal responsibility? The chapter does not establish such limits. But it does explain that the problem is aptly described as one of *establishing*. The limits are vague, to say the least, and private law is needed to render them less so. This is one of several ways in which private law is not only an instrument of what we should do, but also helps to constitute what we should do.

Chapter 3 turns to the case in favour of the wrongdoer repairing the losses that she caused to the person wronged. The literature on repair by wrongdoers often emphasizes reconciliation. The chapter is sceptical. Is reconciliation always desirable? More importantly, when reconciliation is desirable, why is repair by the wrongdoer of losses that were caused by the wrongdoer an effective way to achieve it? There must be an independent case for such repair that makes it a suitable strategy of reconciliation. The chapter advances such an independent case, namely the case that, by repairing the losses she caused, the wrongdoer comes closer to doing what she should have done in the first place. More precisely she conforms, as far as can still be done, to reasons that she did not conform to when she failed in her duty. These reasons support her having a fallback duty, a duty of repair. The chapter raises some questions about repair effected through representative agents (such as insurance companies and banks), and explores some attractions and limitations of money as a general currency of repair. In the process, it reveals an issue to be explored further in Chapter 6 about the ability of the wronged person to thwart the repair by spending the reparative money paid by the wrongdoer on something else entirely.

Chapter 4 continues the investigation of remedies for wrongdoing. It focuses on the deficit (or 'remainder') that is inevitably left when a fallback duty is performed according to the principle defended in Chapter 3. At best, what one did when one performed the duty of repair was only second best, as compared with not committing the wrong in the first place. Does this remainder count for anything? The chapter explores the traces that the remainder leaves in the feelings of the wrongdoer, if she is reasonable, and asks whether, all else being equal, she has reason to express these feelings. The answer is negative. But the expression of the feelings, for example in a heartfelt apology, is nevertheless rationally intelligible. This may seem a long way from the concerns of private law, but it is not. It explains what I call the 'placebo effect' that apologies may have even when not heartfelt, and that explanation carries over into the explanation of money payments in damages that are not literally reparative, such as 'general' damages for bereavement or loss of companionship. These are irreparable losses that are treated, when certain steps are taken by the wrongdoer, as if they had been repaired in conformity with the principle defended in Chapter 3.

Chapter 5 turns to the question of the measure of damages, and in particular the question of why they should be oriented towards restoring the life the wronged person would have had, had the wrong not been committed. Why not instead some better life that he should have had? Why is the measure pegged to the *status quo* (the existing direction of the wronged person's life) at the time of the wrong? The chapter raises some of the most troubling and difficult questions in the book. It invites us to consider the difference that it makes to be invested in a life already, to be engaged already with some value through one's personal goals and relationships. It also invites us to consider the difference between value that is already realized in the world and otherwise identical value that is realizable but as yet unrealized. It sketches a picture according to which it is often reasonable to want to keep things one already has, or would have had but for the wrongdoer, even in a situation in which (thanks to the wrongdoer) one now has an ideal opportunity to do things differently and better. In short: that it is easier to hold on than to let go, even when all else is equal, is not irrationality. The line of thought eventually leads to consideration of the value of security (security in other valuable things) as part of the justification for private law. The chapter ends with brief reflections on the socially conservative implications of the view defended in the chapter, which turn out to be more apparent than real. Security, including the security that private law can provide, should be more of a preoccupation of progressive politics than it is.

Chapter 6 has two concerns. One is to reflect on the special institutional arrangements of private law, in which extensive discretion is given to those who claim to have been wronged to initiate, maintain, and abandon their pursuit of a remedy through the courts. The second is to reflect, more broadly, on the role of freedom, choice, and autonomy—what might be called 'liberal values'—in the defence of private law. The chapter rejects the widely favoured idea that the case for the wrongdoer to owe a reparative duty to the person wronged *entails* that the person wronged should be the one to pursue that remedy and have control over the process by which it is obtained (or not, at that person's discretion). There is no entailment. Indeed, what the process by which the wrongdoer is brought into line should be is an open question. Is it one best answered by thinking about the plaintiff's freedom, choice, or autonomy as valuable in their own rights? No. Such things should count for little. Instead, we should think instrumentally. We should think about which institutional set-up is most efficacious in righting the wrong, least wasteful, and most sensitive to the circumstances of the case. Even when damages are awarded, and the successful plaintiff is left free to spend her award on something completely unrelated to repair of her loss, the explanation is unlikely to be that we prize, in its own right, her freedom to live as she chooses. The explanation, the chapter suggests, has more to do with the importance of ensuring finality in judicial decisions. The chapter rebukes those who export that concern, and others like it, too readily into their personal lives. That the law allows you to spend your hard-won damages on a cruise (when it was nothing like a cruise that the defendant ruined) does not make it alright.

1

Something Came Between Us

For nature, heartless, witless nature,
Will neither care nor know
What stranger's feet may find the meadow
And trespass there and go,
Nor ask amid the dews of morning
If they are mine or no.

A E Housman[1]

1. Relations of duty

Who trespassed against whom matters not to 'heartless, witless nature', as Housman says. For there is no question of anything's mattering in a world without heart or wit. In human affairs, for all their obvious pitfalls, heart and wit are very much in play. And who trespassed against whom is very often regarded as a live, even pressing, question. There are said to be duties owed by one person to another, and they are said on occasion to have been breached, or at any rate not performed, such that (it is sometimes added) the right of the one was violated by the wrong of the other. Private law is often presented as epitomizing this distinctively 'bipolar' arrangement of duty-bearer and rightholder. But plentiful examples are also to be found in life outside the law. I have a right to ask questions or make demands of my children that others lack the right to ask or make, and my children have a duty to answer or comply, based on that right of mine, which they do not owe to others. Your friends owe it to you to tell you home truths about yourself that others do not owe it to you to tell you, and might even owe it to you not to tell you. Some people even think that similarly 'bipolar' arrangements hold throughout morality, by

---

[1] 'Tell me not here, it needs not saying' in Housman, *Last Poems* (Grant Richards 1922).
From Personal Life to Private Law. John Gardner © John Gardner 2018. Published 2018 by Oxford University Press.

morality's very nature.[2] They think that morality is essentially 'second-personal',[3] coextensive with 'what we owe to each other'.[4]

That is one way to demarcate morality, if demarcating morality is what you care to do. However, being owed to another is clearly no part of the nature of duty itself. Many duties are owed to nobody. I may have a duty not to despoil an inhospitable desert, not to burn an abandoned book, or not to desecrate an ancient burial ground. Anne Waldman wants to be 'free of poetry's ornaments,/ Its duty,'[5] while Frank O'Hara considers it 'my duty to be attentive,/I am needed by things as the sky must be above the earth.'[6] It is not just by poetic license that these duties are not bipolar. They are duties literally owed to nobody—not only not owed to some single other person, but also not to some wider constituency or community, and not even to the poet herself or himself.

And why should they be owed to somebody? Duties are the concern, first and foremost, of those whom they bind. We are the ones who fall short, who are on the back foot, who must answer for what we did, if our duties go unperformed. The normative deficit, so to speak, lies on our account. For a duty, also known as an obligation, is none other than whatever a norm (be it a norm of morality, law, etiquette, golf, poetry, *'ndrangheta*, Buddhism, you name it) categorically requires the duty-bearer to do. 'Requires' means that some or all of the valid reasons *not* to do the required thing are to be discounted—if not totally ignored then at least reduced in their relative weight. A duty has some ability, in other words, to trump competing considerations, or (switching metaphor) to punch above its weight in conflicts. 'Categorically', meanwhile, means that the requirement holds irrespective of the duty-bearer's prevailing personal goals at the time when it comes

[2] See R Jay Wallace, 'The Deontic Structure of Morality' in D Bakhurst, B Hooker, and M Little (eds), *Thinking About Reasons: Themes from the Philosophy of Jonathan Dancy* (Oxford University Press 2013).

[3] See Stephen Darwall, *The Second-Person Standpoint: Morality, Respect, and Accountability* (Harvard University Press 2006).

[4] See T M Scanlon, *What We Owe to Each Other* (Harvard University Press 1998).

[5] Waldman, 'A Phonecall from Frank O'Hara' in Waldman, *Helping the Dreamer: Selected Poems 1966–1988* (Coffee House Press 1989).

[6] O'Hara, 'Meditations in an Emergency' in O'Hara, *Meditations in an Emergency* (Grove Press 1957).

to be performed. You may lack or lose interest in your duty, in other words, but your duty does not thereby lack or lose interest in you.

On the first front (the 'requirement' front) duties are to be contrasted with ordinary reasons for acting, such as the reason I currently have to make a cup of tea, the reason we all have sometimes to get some fresh air, and the reason that anyone might have to read the latest Jenny Erpenbeck novel on the train home. Yes, you ought to read *The End of Days*, but '[i]t is not true', as Bernard Williams puts it, 'that every *ought* is a *must*.'[7] On the second front (the 'categorical' front) duties are to be contrasted with hypothetical requirements, such as the requirement to carry a passport if you plan to travel abroad, or the requirement to get a haircut if you're going to look smart in the photos. Like duties these are musts, but unlike duties they are not musts that—in Ogden Nash's words—'albatrossly hang around'.[8] To get rid of hypothetical requirements, you need only change your goals.[9] Things are not so easy with duties. 'O duty,' as Nash continues, 'why dost thou continue to hound me?'

So where exactly do other people fit into our duties, when they do? How can duties be owed to someone? That is not so clear. Other people may of course figure in the content of my duty, i.e. in specifying the action that I am duty-bound to perform. Often they figure as beneficiaries of the required action. I may have a duty to keep out of my neighbour's garden, or to follow my employer's instructions, or to assist someone in danger, or to return the book I borrowed from you last week. Is that all it takes to make it the case that a duty is owed to someone? It is tempting to jump straight to an affirmative conclusion. My duty not to cross my neighbour's garden is owed to my neighbour, my duty to follow my employer's instructions is owed to my employer, and so on. But suppose we complicate the cases a little. How about a case in which my employer instructs me to help a colleague

---

[7] Williams, 'Practical Necessity' in Williams, *Moral Luck* (Cambridge University Press 1981), 126.

[8] Nash, 'Kind of an Ode to Duty' in Nash, *I Wouldn't Have Missed It: Selected Poems of Ogden Nash* (Little Brown & Co 1975).

[9] Although this can be a taller order than it sounds: see ch 5 s 2.

unpack some boxes because he sees that the colleague needs some company? My employer issues the instructions, but my colleague is the principal beneficiary. Is my resulting duty to help with the unpacking owed to my employer, or to my colleague, or both? Or suppose you promise your neighbour's house-sitter—while your neighbour is trekking incommunicado in Nepal—that you will stop taking that shortcut across the neighbour's garden that your neighbour has long tolerated your taking. The house-sitter reasonably takes herself to be acting on behalf of your neighbour. Is the resulting duty owed to your neighbour, or to her house-sitter, or both?

Such questions—which are sometimes of great importance in private law—draw attention to a second and quite different way in which another person may figure in the architecture of one's duty. Sometimes, whether or not she figures in the content of one's duty, another person figures in the *reason* for one's duty. I promise my mother, on her deathbed, to look after my brother after her death. My brother figures in the content of the duty, for my duty is a duty to look after him. My mother, by contrast, is nowhere to be found in the content of the duty. Yet she figures in the reason for my duty, a reason from which my brother is conspicuous by his absence. I have the duty because of a promise I made to my mother. If someone asks 'Are you your brother's keeper?', I have an answer that is not available to all keepers of their brothers. The answer is that I promised my mother that I would look after my brother. Thanks to the promise, I can say, '*I owe it to my mother* to do this', even though my mother does not figure in the 'this' that I owe it to her to do.

That is a rather complicated type of case. In simpler cases, the person who figures in the content of my duty also figures in the reason for it, and his figuring in the reason for the duty explains why he figures in its content. For present purposes, however, I want to ignore the content of duties so far as possible, and focus on the reasons for them, and in particular on one possible way in which other people may come to figure in those reasons. I want to focus on what I will call 'strictly relational' duties. A strictly relational duty is a duty that one has for the reason that one stands in some special relationship with the person to whom the duty is owed. By a 'special relationship' I mean, in turn, a relationship other than the relationship that we are all said to have with each other simply as persons or human beings or God's creatures, etc. A special relationship, we might say, is not just a relationship with someone but a relationship with someone *in particular*, from which others must inevitably be left out.

Special relationships in this sense include those between parents and their children, employers and their employees, hosts and their guests, doctors and their patients, lawyers and their clients, and businesses and their customers. They also include, to take some more symmetrical examples, the relationship between spouses, between sexual partners, between friends, between colleagues, between siblings, and between neighbours. Notice that not all the duties that hold between people in such special relationships qualify as strictly relational ones. We all have duties not to (for example) deceive or humiliate or manipulate each other, duties that are owed alike to complete strangers and to those with whom we stand in special relationships. These duties, owed to all, are not strictly relational.[10] Strictly relational duties are distinguished from the rest by the special reason for their existence. The special reason in question is the fact of the special relationship. Someone asks: 'Why did you get him out of that hole he was digging himself into?', to which you reply: 'He's my husband; I owe it to him to stop him making a fool of himself.' Or someone asks: 'Why did you act like you didn't know about her affair?', and you reply: 'She's my friend; one never confirms salacious rumours about one's friends.' Or someone asks: 'Why did you laugh at that dumb joke?', and your answer is: 'They're my colleagues; one always has to give one's colleagues a bit of extra latitude.'

These imaginary snippets of conversation may seem to shift our attention away from the reason why one *has* a strictly relational duty to the reason why one *performs* it. Such presentational slippage is hardly surprising. Barring exceptional cases, the reason why one has a duty doubles as a possible reason to perform it.

[10] Although breaching them in the setting of a special relationship may be worse. I offered one explanation in Gardner, 'Criminals in Uniform' in RA Duff, L Farmer, S Marshall, M Renzo, and V Tadros (eds), *The Constitution of Criminal Law* (Oxford University Press 2012).

So one can usually illustrate the former by illustrating the latter. But that is about as far as the connection goes. Sometimes it is thought that if a duty exists for reason r then ideally it should be performed for reason r. Sometimes it is thought, indeed, that if a duty exists for reason r one does not perform it except by acting for reason r. But both of these claims are false, and no less false of strictly relational duties than of any others. Parents have innumerable strictly relational duties towards their children. As parents they must feed, clothe, and house their children, protect them from danger, enable and support their education, tolerate up to a point their childish ways, not show partiality between them, help to settle their disputes, celebrate their achievements, set good examples for them, etc. Ideally, parents perform all of these duties out of love, i.e. for the simple reason that they love their children. But even with ideally loving parents, the duties in question exist for the reason that they are parents, not for the reason that they are loving. If such parents were to stop loving their children, that would make them less exemplary in the performance of their parental duties and, in that respect, less than ideal parents. But it would not change in any way what they have parental duties to do, and it would not make those duties any less strictly relational than before.[11]

The existence of strictly relational duties is sometimes doubted. Those doubts matter for what lies ahead, for (as we will see) strictly relational duties play a significant role in private law. You may say that if they play a significant role in private law then

[11] Their relational duties include, incidentally, a distinct duty to love their children. That is one of the exceptional duties of which it is not true that the reason why one has a duty doubles as a possible reason to perform it. This is a duty that parents perform, when they perform it, on the strength of facts about their children that (as they see it) tend to make their children lovable. But of course those facts are not the ones on the strength of which they have the duty to love their children. They have the duty to love their children because they are their children, lovable or not. Perhaps the fact that parents have a duty to love their children and a duty to protect their children leads some to think that they have a single duty to protect them out of love for them. Not so. That is not one duty but a composite of two, each of which can be independently conformed to and independently violated. For detailed discussion of the duty to love, especially as it is owed by parents to children see Matthew Liao, *The Right to Be Loved* (Oxford University Press 2015).

necessarily they exist, so there is no need to debate their existence. But the law may be wildly mistaken. It may also be dis-
honest. It may, in particular, assert or presuppose the existence
of reasons that do not exist. And since strictly relational duties
are differentiated by the reasons for their existence, strictly relational duties may be among the things that the law has mistakenly
or dishonestly conjured up. Many who think theoretically about
private law, especially but not only among those who attempt to
understand its workings economistically, seem to think that this
is how things are with the law. They seem to think that any appearance of strict relationality in private law should be explained
away as a kind of smokescreen that conceals quite different kinds
of reasons for the law and its users to be doing what they do.
It may, of course, be a useful smokescreen. It may help to lure
ordinary chumps like you and me into fruitful participation in
valuable objectives that might not otherwise motivate us. Our
sentimental belief in strict relationality may be a profitable asset
for the law. But it is sentimentality all the same: apart from the
Machiavellian machinations of the law and similar incentivizing
social arrangements, rationality has no room for strictly relational
duties. Or so say some theorists, who like to think of themselves
as hard-nosed myth-busters. Whether they are right, or whether
they are themselves the myth-spinners, will be one of the main
concerns of this first chapter.

2. One thought too many,
one reason too few

There is a deflationary way of giving salience to our special relationships with other people in explaining why we have the duties
we have towards them. The special relationship, it is said, is not
itself a reason for the duty. It is not itself a reason for anything. It
is only ever auxiliary to some *other* reason. It is a minor premise,
we might say, that still needs a major premise to make it count for
anything. That one is better placed to help A than to help B in an
emergency situation, for example, is a possible reason why one
would have a duty to help A over B. Maybe it so happens that one
is often better placed to help one's familiars: they are more willing
to be helped, more easily reassured, easier to communicate with,

closer to hand, etc. Across a range of cases, such things might help to lend rational salience to the (otherwise rationally irrelevant) fact of familiarity. Suppose, after an accident, one attempts to assist one's wife ahead of a similarly injured stranger. Challenged, one proffers 'she's my wife' as if that by itself qualifies as a reason, albeit maybe not a decisive one, for one's having attended to her first. The curious deflationist replies: 'I can see that that fact might matter on some occasions, but how does it matter on this occasion? Is it that, since she's your wife, you know more about her medical conditions? Or is it that her being your wife helps to fortify you in your efforts so that you will give up less easily? Or what?'

Of such 'constructions', as he pointedly calls them, Bernard Williams complains that they land the rescuer

with one thought too many: it might have been hoped by some (for instance, by his wife) that his motivating thought, fully spelled out, would be the thought that it was his wife, not that it was his wife and that in situations of this kind it is permissible to save one's wife.[12]

This remark may seem to be shifting our attention, once again, from why the rescuer has his duty to why he performs it—from justification, if you like, to motivation. But Williams makes it clear in his surrounding discussion, I think, that what he is ultimately worried about is not so much the 'one thought too many' problem as the 'one reason too few' problem that lurks beneath its surface. The 'one reason too few' problem is the problem that 'she's my wife' is being denied its status as a reason in its own right—as a reason distinct from myriad other reasons that the rescuer may have, in determining the proper application and force of which 'she's my wife' might happen to be a relevant piece of information. Even when we have counted all the facility and energy that her being his wife may confer on the husband as a potential rescuer, even when we have counted all the ways, indeed, in which her being his wife may be of auxiliary salience, there remains to be counted—Williams wants to say—the distinct stand-alone reason for him to do as he does that *she's his wife*. And this

---

[12] Williams, 'Persons, Character, and Morality' in Williams, *Moral Luck* (n 7), at 18.

reason, as Williams adds, cannot easily be marginalized. For if it exists it surely make 'demands' on him—not such that he 'must prefer any possible demand' of the special relationship over all others, but demands all the same.[13] 'She's my wife', if a reason, is surely a reason for the rescuer to be duty-bound to do as he does, and not merely a reason for him to do it.

Williams is right to resist the deflationist: there are strictly relational duties only if the fact of a special relationship is itself capable of being a reason, as opposed to merely a fact made relevant by other reasons. By these standards, however, were our imaginary snippets of conversation in section 1 not perhaps already too deflationary to be regarded as exemplifying strictly relational duties? Take 'she's my friend; one never confirms salacious rumours about one's friends.' Is this not a case where the speaker is demoting 'she's my friend' to a minor premise, made relevant only by the major premise 'one never confirms salacious rumours about one's friends'? Does the latter remark not identify the true reason, relative to which the 'she's my friend' is held to be a fact of merely auxiliary importance?

That does not seem like the correct interpretation of the snippet to me. It seems to me that, with the follow-up remark, the speaker is explaining exactly which duty she takes 'she's my friend' to be a reason for, rather than invoking another reason from which 'she's my friend' is supposed to derive its relevance and importance. My duty as a friend—the speaker is saying—is to avoid confirming salacious rumours about her, and the fact that she is my friend is itself, without more, a reason for my being under that duty.

A common mistake is to think that when some fact is held up as a reason 'without more'—as a reason in the robust way that Williams insists upon against the deflationist—that is the same as refusing to explain what *makes* it a reason. One is often taken to be stamping one's foot and saying that one has reached the end of discussion; this reason *just is* a reason. But nothing just is a reason in that inexplicable way. It calls for explanation that being a person, or being in pain, or being a lover of chocolate, or being a citizen, or anything else you care to mention, is a reason for

[13] ibid 17.

anything—for being respected by others, for taking painkillers, for eating chocolate, for having a vote, or for anything else you care to mention. It equally calls for explanation that being someone's friend is a reason for anything, including for the existence of duties of friendship. The challenge in all of these cases is to avoid eliminating the reason in the attempt to explain it. It is very common for explanations of reasons to be treated as automatically eliminative, i.e. as replacing the reason with the explanation, which is now to be regarded as the *real* reason in substitution for the reason we were originally trying to explain. Williams himself falls into this trap. He warns against 'higher-order thoughts to give [the reason that *she's my wife*] a rationale', including thoughts such as the 'rule-Utilitarian ... idea that in matters of this kind it is better for each to look after his own.'[14] Williams is suggesting that such a 'rule-utilitarian' explanation can only explain *away* the reason in question, not explain it. 'She's my wife' disappears to make way for the all-purpose utilitarian reason that 'this kind of thing maximizes utility'.

But is this disappearance inevitable? As later chapters will confirm, I carry no torch for rule-utilitarianism, or indeed for any kind of utilitarianism.[15] However, it seems to me that the rule-utilitarian with the 'higher order thought' mentioned by Williams is just as likely to be a supporter as an opponent of 'she's my wife' being a reason in its own right, and hence of the existence of strictly relational duties. A rule-utilitarian who has this thought may simply be thinking—may she not?—that a world in which marriage exists is better than (she may say 'utility-superior to') a world in which it does not. And she may simply be adding—may she not?—that marriage does not exist in any world if, in that world, the fact that A is married to B is not a reason in its own right, more specifically a reason in its own right for A to owe certain duties to B. For it is an essential feature of marriage that being married is a reason in its own right, more

---

[14] ibid 18. For a similar move against what he calls 'reductionism' see Niko Kolodny, 'Which Relationships Justify Partiality? The Case of Parents and Children', *Philosophy & Public Affairs* 38 (2010), 37.

[15] In ch 5, indeed, you will find me endorsing Williams' own principal objection to utilitarianism from his 'A Critique of Utilitarianism' in JJC Smart and Bernard Williams, *Utilitarianism: For and Against* (Cambridge University Press 1973).

specifically (but not only) a reason in its own right for married people to owe certain duties to each other. The reason and the strictly relational duties that it is a reason for can be eliminated from the world, to be sure, but only by eliminating marriage, and thereby landing us in a less good (our rule-utilitarian may want to say 'utility-inferior') world.

Our rule-utilitarian may readily echo, in other words, the simple, everyday thoughts that are so touchingly expressed by George and Lennie in *Of Mice and Men*:

> We got somebody to talk to that gives a damn about us [said George]. We don't have to sit in no bar room blowin' in our jack jus' because we got no place else to go. If them other guys gets in jail they can rot for anybody gives a damn. But not us.
>
> Lennie broke in.
>
> *But not us! An' why? Because ... because I got you to look after me, and you got me to look after you, and that's why.*[16]

The moral? If only 'them other guys' were friends with each other like George and Lennie, if only they were bound to each other just by the fact of friendship, well ... what a wonderful (some might say 'utility-optimal') world this could be.

The rule-utilitarian who thinks like this is not asking George and Lennie (or their reader) to boil everything down, rationally, to 'this kind of thing maximizes utility'. If George and Lennie do that, they are not friends. And for the utility-riches she seeks, the rule-utilitarian needs them to be friends. And for that she needs 'he's my friend' to be a reason that each of them has, both a reason why each has the duties that he has towards the other, and a possible reason to perform those duties.[17] That George and Lennie sometimes reflect on the good fortune ('utility') of their friendship, as in the exchange above, does not suggest that they regard 'he's my friend' as something less than a reason in its own right. Nor are they inviting the reader to do so. On the contrary, they are presupposing that 'he's my friend' is a reason in its own right, a reason for the want of which 'them other guys'

---

[16] John Steinbeck, *Of Mice and Men* (William Heinemann 1974), 14 (original emphasis).

[17] Here I am taking much the same tack that Robert Adams famously took in Adams, 'Motive Utilitarianism', *Journal of Philosophy* 73 (1976), 467.

have a worse time of it than do George and Lennie. Thus: 'We travel together,' said George coldly. 'Oh, so it's that way' [sneered Curley]. George was tense and motionless. 'Yea, it's that way.'[18] Our rule-utilitarian sees the value in George's stalwart attitude, and the way it plays out in things said and done out of nothing but friendship. Regarding the reason 'he's my friend', then, our rule-utilitarian is neither deflationist nor eliminativist.

3. Some doubts about strict relationality

To repeat: I am no utilitarian myself. Thinking through the utilitarian position just sketched does, however, help us to pinpoint various worries about strictly relational duties, worries that ought to detain even the non-utilitarians among us.

(a) 'He's my friend' qualifies as a reason in its own right, I said, only if it 'remains to be counted' even when we have counted all the ways in which the fact that he's my friend may be of auxiliary relevance to other reasons. Some of these other reasons may surely be explained in just the same way as 'he's my friend' was explained. Suppose I count the fact that I am familiar with you, you being my friend, as a reason to rescue you ahead of a stranger. Let's say, to spell it out better, that I count the fact that my familiarity with you will facilitate the rescue. Suppose, however, that I then add the fact that you are my friend as a further reason in its own right to effect the same rescue. Our encounter with the friendship-friendly rule-utilitarian may raise a serious suspicion of double-counting here. For perhaps one way in which a world with friendship in it is better than a world without is that a world with friendship in it is one that includes more familiarity among people—familiarity of a kind that, among other things, facilitates more effective rescues. George and Lennie suggest precisely such a facilitation. If that is the case, then surely I should not be counting 'he's my friend' *in addition to* the familiarity advantages when I come to decide whom to rescue. I should not be aggregating the two. If I do, then you, as my friend, will enjoy the benefit of the same utilities twice, once under the heading 'familiarity makes rescue easier', and again under the heading 'he's

---

[18] Steinbeck, *Of Mice and Men* (n 16), 28.

my friend'. Surely what we need, if 'he's my friend' is to count separately as a reason, is some *separate* explanation of why 'he's my friend' is a reason, meaning an explanation that points to some set of values or concerns that are not otherwise catered for in the list of reasons that count in favour of my rescuing you, my friend, before others.

The worry is misplaced. By 'remains to be counted' I did not mean 'remains to be counted by the same agent as an additional reason for the same action on the same occasion'. I meant only that the reason in question deserves its own entry in the tally of *possible* reasons. That is consistent with its being available to the agent only as an alternative, not as an addition, to some or all of the other reasons on the list. Here we may develop Williams' 'one thought too many' objection a little further. For Williams, the problem was that the reason 'she's my wife' was being lumbered with a redundant major premise such as 'wives are to be rescued first'. But presumably the same objection would extend to those who accumulated 'she's my wife' with various other reasons in making up his mind whom to rescue. They too have 'one thought too many'. Why? Because, as Williams says, the reason 'she's my wife' makes demands on its users. It puts them under a duty to save, and the fact of a duty, as I explained before, is not just to be counted on top of other reasons. It trumps some of them, sometimes by excluding them from consideration altogether. Earlier, I emphasized the fact that all duties trump at least some countervailing reasons. But some duties—those that serve values that can also imaginably be served in other ways—trump certain supporting reasons as well. They trump supporting reasons that reflect values that were already accounted for in the coming into existence of the duty.[19]

It does not follow, of course, that one does one's duty only if one excludes those supporting reasons from one's deliberations. No: one does one's duty if, for whatever reason, one does what

---

[19] In the terminology favoured by Joseph Raz, such a duty 'pre-empts' a range of 'dependent' reasons. See Raz, 'Authority and Justification', *Philosophy and Public Affairs* 14 (1985), 3. Raz is discussing authoritatively-created duties but the justificatory scheme that he outlines applies much more widely, including to various duties that exist without anyone's having created them.

one has a duty to do. The point is merely that *inasmuch* as one does one's duty for the reason that it is one's duty (and it may be that in some types of relationships doing that is itself a further duty) other reasons for doing the same thing may fall to be excluded. To give weight to those other reasons would be to double-count the same value. Thus, the fact that this is one's duty is not to be aggregated with them but substituted for them. That one's duty is often substitutive rather than aggregative in this way is one of the endemic features of rational life that lends force to Williams' 'one thought too many' reflections.

(b) I have said that the reason 'she's my wife' *puts me under* a duty to rescue. That is importantly different from what I said in other passages above, namely that 'she's my wife' is a *reason why* I have that duty to rescue. And this, you may say, brings to the surface a problem that has been bubbling under for a while. Strictly relational duties, I said at the start, are duties that one has for the reason that one is in a special relationship with another. But surely the existence of the special relationship, in the cases we have been considering, already *entails* that one has the duties in question. In Williams' terminology, 'she's my wife' already makes demands on the rescuer; it does not merely count in favour of the existence of those demands. And that, you may say, threatens to turn the set of strictly relational duties (as I defined them) into an empty set. For where A entails B, A surely cannot also be a reason for B. A relationship in which one thing is a reason for another requires a certain logical independence of the former from the latter; and in the cases we have been considering no such logical independence exists. No wonder we were worried about those snippets of conversation we imagined a few pages back, such as: 'He's my husband; I owe it to him to stop him making a fool of himself.' I said that in the words after the semicolon, the speaker is explaining what duty she takes 'he's my husband' to be a reason for. But is the truth not, rather, that the speaker is unpacking the *logical implications* of 'he's my husband'? And, to restate our worry, how can anything be said to count in favour of one of its own logical implications?

I am far from convinced that such a conjunction is impossible. Be that as it may, however, the inference from 'he's my husband' to 'I owe it to him to stop him making a fool of himself' is not one of strict entailment. It is at most one of *defeasible* entailment, such that the inference is invalidated when certain other facts hold. Suppose that he's your estranged husband, or your violent husband, or the husband whom you married in ignorance of his double life. Could that not invalidate the inference? Substitute your own invalidating factors if you dislike the ones on my list. Or, if you prefer, consider the parallel case of promises: 'I promised Alice that I would attend her opening night' clearly stands in *some* logical relationship with 'It's my duty to attend Alice's opening night.' Yet if the promise was secured by coercion or manipulation or deception it does not give rise to the duty. Similarly, if the duty was waived by the promisee. Notice that none of these is a situation in which the duty is defeated by unexcluded countervailing reasons, such that the promisor is justified in not performing it. No, these are situations in which the duty does not exist, so that the question of justified non-performance does not even arise. What is defeated is not the duty but the inference from promise to duty.[20] That is enough logical independence to create space for the idea that, so far as promissory duties are concerned, the fact of the promise is the reason for being under the duty (when there is a duty). Things are the same with other strictly relational duties: the defeasibility of the entailment from the relationship to the duty creates enough logical independence between the two for the former to be the reason for the latter when it exists.

(c) You may worry that, even though 'he's my husband' does not strictly entail 'I owe it to him to stop him making a fool of himself', the latter (if indeed a spousal duty) is partly constitutive of the relationship between spouses. To be a spouse is inter alia to have, subject to the possible vitiating factors just discussed, this very duty. That explains why, when I said of strictly relational duties that the fact of a special relationship is the reason for their existence, you naturally interpreted 'the reason' to mean 'reason enough'. No additional reason on top of the relationship is needed, for the duty forms part of the relationship.

---

[20] For further discussion see John Searle, 'How to Derive "Ought" from "Is"', *Philosophical Review* 73 (1964), 43.

But with this fact now brought into the open, you may start to wonder: can the whole be a reason in this way for one of its parts? I reply: Of course it can. 'Why do you have to face that way to pray?' 'I'm a Muslim'; 'Why do you have to cut your hair so short?' 'I'm frontman in a skinhead rock band'; 'Why have you laid down that large area of viridian?' 'It's a seascape'. In the same way, but now concerning a strictly relational duty: 'Why do you make it a rule never to confirm salacious rumours about Sue?' 'Because she's my friend. And by the way ... I don't exactly *make* it a rule. It's one of the rules of friendship. It's not for me to make or unmake those. It goes with being a friend, whether I like it or not.'

(d) The 'by the way' aside here may cause you to worry about something new. Remember that duties are categorical requirements, in the sense that they hold irrespective of one's prevailing personal goals at the time when performance falls due. Surely the requirements of friendship, and of many other special relationships, are not categorical in this sense. Are they not classic hypothetical requirements? You are required not to confirm salacious rumours about Sue *if* you want to be, or to remain, Sue's friend. You can abandon this requirement just by abandoning the goal of being a friend—in other words abandoning the friendship— which is as easy as simply violating the requirement. When you lose interest in the norms of friendship, they also lose interest in you. They do not 'albatrossly hang around' after a personal goal is over, as duties do. That being so, there is no such thing as a 'duty of friendship'.

We should be careful not to underestimate the hold that even hypothetical requirements have over us. Violating them is not usually enough to dispose of them. We readily help ourselves to relaxations of our diets and exercise regimes. When we are busy we let our standards slip in respect of household chores and correspondence. After a long day we snap at the children just as we resolved never again to do. In a hurry to get home, we buy groceries from that dodgy supermarket that we were supposedly boycotting. It does not follow from the fact that we departed from the associated requirements in these cases that we lost the goals, and hence that the associated requirements ceased to apply to us. True, since weakness of will readily breeds self-deception, there may come a point at which we have become so derelict that we are kidding ourselves in classifying our idle thoughts as goals. But that point is usually quite a long way down the line. Meanwhile, the applicable requirements continue to apply.

On the other hand, we should not deny that sometimes a violation even of a categorical requirement may be such as to bring to an end the relationship of which the requirement was partly constitutive. Breach, says the law, is one possible way of discharging a contract.[21] True, to discharge the contract it has to be a 're-pudiatory' breach and it has to be treated as such by the other party.[22] Probably, it would be more accurate to say that it is the other party's treatment of the breach that discharges the contract. Be that as it may, at the point of discharge any ongoing duties under the contract lapse (although of course remedial duties in respect of the repudiatory breach itself, and other past breaches, do not lapse—more of that in Chapter 3). Much the same is true in friendships, love affairs, marriages, and the like. You can repudiate a friendship, like a contract, with just one breach of duty, where the duty is fundamental enough or the breach is egregious enough. This is the 'sudden deathblow/as if out of nowhere', of which Sharon Olds mournfully writes.[23] Yet the repudiation can still be refused by your friend, who may hope and urge that, with your cooperation, the relationship can still be saved. Sometimes the breach (e.g. if serious and inexcusable) is such that this hope is misplaced. It showed that you are incapable of being a friend and hence that the friendship is doomed.

But even when that is so, the friendship does not lapse automatically just because of the breach. Friends, and one's duties to them, are more sticky than that. And in their stickiness they are straightforwardly categorical: they come and go with the friendship, not with your commitment to the friendship. If you lose interest in or neglect the friendship without bothering to extricate yourself from it, your friend is entitled to feel aggrieved at

---

[21] Alongside performance, variation, and frustration. Compare Ernest Weinrib, *The Idea of Private Law* (Harvard University Press 1995), who finds the idea 'absurd' (at 135) that a duty could be discharged by its breach.

[22] *White and Carter (Councils) Ltd v McGregor* [1962] AC 413.

[23] Olds, 'Bruise Ghazal' in Olds, *Stag's Leap* (Knopf Doubleday Publishing Group 2012), 67.

your derelictions, for meanwhile you still owe duties to her just as you do to your builder while he waits for you to give him the go-ahead for the next phase of work under the contract. In analogizing the two I do not mean to doubt that the line between a bad friend and an ex-friend tends to be less determinate, and hence more gradually crossed, than the line between a bad client and an ex-client. Part of the value of contracting, promising, consenting, and similar instant mechanisms for incurring and waiving our duties to each other is the extra determinacy that they facilitate as compared with frameworks, such as friendship, that tend to ebb and flow and adjust, in their detailed normative content, to what Olds, thinking of the trajectory of an ill-fated marriage, calls 'the slow-revealed comedy/of ideal and error'.[24]

(e) You may wonder why, in all of this, we have said nothing to address the most familiar objection to strictly relational duties, the one to which Williams was responding with his 'one thought too many' remarks. Morality is itself impartial and requires us to be impartial. Strictly relational duties are duties to be partial. That makes them immoral. So, morally speaking, they cannot exist.[25] This objection is surely the elephant in the room.

I have already declined to get into the business of demarcating morality. Although strange to my ears, it would be no skin off my nose if people's strictly relational duties do not get to be counted as moral ones. That would not in itself affect their role in life or their importance. But, as it happens, I have already explained how someone who believes that morality is impartial, in the sense most often given to that slogan, could nevertheless defend the existence of strictly relational duties. Remember our rule-utilitarian. She thought that the explanation for the existence of strictly relational duties was the value that the existence of those duties brought into the world. True, my friends are special to me and yours are special to you. Here we see the personal value of friendship and without it there are no friends. But the ultimate value of there being such personal value is impersonal. It is the

---

[24] Olds, 'Crazy' in Olds, *Stag's Leap* (Knopf Doubleday Publishing Group 2012), 65.

[25] For a sympathetic but critical treatment of this argument see Barbara Herman, 'Agency, Attachment, and Difference', *Ethics* 101 (1991), 775.

value of friendship in general, which does not differentiate in the slightest between your friends and mine. Rather, it calls upon *you* to differentiate between your friends and mine and it calls upon *me* to differentiate between my friends and yours. It is impersonal value, in short, that necessitates a kind of partiality at the point of implementation. But it should surely never be called 'impartial value'. Value is not the kind of thing that can be impartial. Only agents can be impartial. 'Impartial' is an implementation word; and this is a value—the value of friendship—that necessarily calls for partiality at the point of implementation.

It does not follow from any of this that at the point of implementation one should give one's own friends absolute priority over the impersonal value of friendship as it is manifested in the friendships, or potential friendships, of others. Thanks to the impersonal value of friendship, one owes special duties to one's own friends, and all duties, as I put it before, punch above their weight in conflicts. It follows that, paradoxically, one is not respecting the impersonal value of friendship if one is prepared to sacrifice one's own friendships like-for-like to save the no less valuable friendships of others. One cannot respect the impersonal value of friendship by attempting, in one's own friendships, to advance impartially the impersonal value of friendship. Yet there may be occasional cases in which, for the sake of friendship more generally, betraying a friend is the only thing one is justified in doing. To save many others from having to betray their friends, say, it may be that *in extremis* one has to betray one's own friend. (I chose here to persist with the example of friendship but the same can be said, *mutatis mutandis*, in the case of one's own children, students, patients, neighbours, customers, etc.)

True, some people have duties to be impartial. At least some of these are duties to be impartial precisely in the context of special relationships. I have already mentioned that parents have a duty to be impartial as between their children. This goes to show that it is not a defining feature of a duty to be impartial that it would have one disregard all special relationships. The parental duty to be impartial is a duty not to have favourites among one's own children. One must not love one child more than the other; if one does, alas, love one child more than the other, one must avoid manifestations of this in how one treats either of them; and even if one does not love one child more than the other one must still go out of one's way to avoid seeming to do so. Loving one child more than another is not, however, a matter of being in a further special relationship with him or her. Goethe surely goes too far in having Philine ask 'if I love you, what business is it of yours?'[26] Yet he is clearly onto something important: love is an attitude, not a relationship. So the duty of impartiality among one's children is not primarily a duty to disregard any special relationship. It is a duty to avoid (or failing that to overcome) certain attitudes that may otherwise colour one's treatment of one's children, and also to avoid treatment suggestive of those attitudes, even when one lacks them.

In *Sophie's Choice*,[27] Sophie faced the cruellest challenge to her integrity as a parent by being made to choose one of her children to die in exchange for the other being allowed to live, inevitably acting in her choice as if she loved one more than the other (whether or not she actually did). By choosing one, she failed in her duty to be impartial. She did so justifiably or at least excusably in order to perform (in the case of one of the children) another duty, namely the duty to protect her children from danger. But this was not a case of a conflict between strictly relational duty to protect and a non-relational duty to be impartial. It was a conflict between two strictly relational duties that were both, tragically, constituents of the very same special relationship. She had to fail as a parent in order to do exactly what a parent must do. If you miss that you miss the main point of the story, which is the terrible secret behind Sophie's suicidal depression.[28]

---

[26] 'Wenn ich dich liebe, was geht's dich an?' are Philine's words in Goethe's *Wilhelm Meisters Lehrjahre* (Unger Verlag 1795), 249.

[27] William Styron, *Sophie's Choice* (Random House 1979).

[28] Could we eliminate the favouritism aspect and still keep the structure of the tragedy? How about we just rest the story on the fact that Sophie had to violate her duty of protection in the case of her daughter in order to fulfil the same duty in the case of her son? Possibly. That interpretation, however, reduces the significance of the fact that Sophie herself was the one who had to make the choice, if either child was to be saved. She had no scope to delegate or leave it to chance. That fact was crucial, it seems to me, to the special nefariousness of the camp doctor's scheme to destroy her as a mother. To perform either duty of protection she had to reveal her favourite.

You may say that the parental duty to be impartial is unusual in being a strictly relational one, but I doubt whether that is so. A judge's duty to be impartial is a duty to be impartial, not as between everyone, not even as between everyone who will be affected by her decisions, but only as between the parties to each particular case that comes before her for hearing. Arguably, the fact that these are the parties to *her* case—that they are her special *protégés* in respect of the doing of justice—is the reason for the judge's duty. If so, then that duty, like Sophie's duty to be impartial as between her children, is a strictly relational one. And like Sophie's, it is primarily a duty upon the judge to avoid (or failing that to overcome) certain attitudes that may otherwise colour her treatment of the parties, and also to avoid treatment suggestive of those attitudes even when she lacks them.

Naturally, there are occasions when a judge, like a parent, faces conflicts among her duties, including among her strictly relational ones. She may have extra-judicial relationships with one or more of the very parties whose case she is listed to hear. Then her judicial duties towards the parties, whether or not strictly relational, may conflict with other duties that she owes to one or more of them, e.g. as lovers or business partners or gym buddies or fellow alumnae of Poppleton University or fellow trustees of Aid International. In such cases—with some tolerance for the *de minimis*—she has a prophylactic duty to avoid the conflict by recusing herself, rather than attempting in a Herculean way to rise above the conflict, while continuing to hear the case. Not only *nemo iudex in sua causa*, but also *nemo iudex in causa amici sui, nemo iudex in causa aviae suae*, and so on.

Such rules of 'natural justice' are often thought of as prophylactics against bias and the appearance of bias. From here it is but a short step to the conclusion that the judicial duty to be impartial is simply a duty not to be biased and not to give the appearance of bias. But that short step is a misstep. Bias is a kind of rational error. Roughly, it is being more partial than one has reason to be. If people can have strictly relational duties towards others, as I have tried to persuade you they can, then not every case of partiality is a case of rational error. There need be no bias and no appearance of bias in attending to one's strictly relational duties—in being partial towards one's own children, friends, or clients—although like any other duties they may be attended to in a biased way, treated as having more or less force than they have because of rationally unsupported predilections in favour of or against one or more of those to whom they, the strictly relational duties, are owed. It is a mistake to think that when judges are sitting in court they cease to owe their duties of friendship, collegiality, etc.,[29] and hence that every instance of judicial partiality is an instance of judicial bias. If only that were so. Judicial life would be so much easier if, by stepping into it, one could be freed of all one's other relationships and the duties that go to constitute them. How much less need there would be for prophylactic protection against conflicts of duty if conflicting duties were automatically left at the courtroom door.

4. Strict relationality in legal relations

Whether they conflict with other duties or otherwise, strictly relational duties are common in private law. I have been emphasizing judicial duties to administer justice as between the parties to private law litigation. But consider instead the private law duties that we owe to each other, those duties the alleged breach of which typically provides the cause of action, and the bone of contention, in private law litigation. Think, for example, about fiduciary duties: those owed by trustees to the trust beneficiaries, by doctors to their patients, by solicitors to their clients, by confidantes to their confiders, and so on. And think about spousal duties, breach of which was once the only ground of divorce and can still be relevant today in various subsidiary aspects of private family proceedings. And then think about contractual duties, perhaps the most ubiquitous of them all.

You may suspect that, by signing up to the view that contractual duties are strictly relational duties, I am signing up to the so-called 'relational theory of contract'.[30] On this theory a contract, at least in the standard or typical case, helps to constitute a continuing

[29] For further discussion of this mistake (focusing not on judges but on police officers) see Gardner 'Criminals in Uniform' (n 10).

[30] Most closely associated with the work of Ian Macneil. For a good conspectus see Macneil, 'Relational Contract Theory: Challenges and Queries', *Northwestern University Law Review* 94 (2000), 877.

relationship between the parties that goes beyond the contract itself, and hence that should not be identified too narrowly, or too fastidiously, with its terms. This view, however, should really be known as the 'doubly relational theory of contracts'. For more precisely stated it is the theory according to which contractual relationships are standardly nested within further relationships of a non-contractual kind, such as supplier-procurer, franchisor-franchisee, landlord-tenant, or author-publisher. Clearly this theory is consistent with, because it depends upon, the idea that a contractual relationship is a relationship even when it is not so nested. Whether nested in another relationship or not, the fact of the contractual relationship is the reason for the existence of contractual duties, which are therefore strictly relational, even on their own.

An important difference between a contractual relationship and many others is its very great plasticity. Endlessly varied duties can imaginably be created by contract. We contract-makers, if only we are armed with enough negotiating power and *savoir-faire*, can extensively customize the deontic content of our contractual relationships to suit our personal goals in making the contract. Not so with friendship or parenthood or trusteeship or collegiality: although there is room for some adjustment at the margins by the parties to such relationships, each has extensive deontic content that is not determined by the parties themselves. As we put it before, it is not for me to make or unmake the rules of friendship. There are many duties which are such that, if you do not owe them to me, you are no friend of mine, or no parent to me, or not serving as my trustee, or not a true colleague, etc., whatever I may have to say about the matter.

Yet the contrast between the more fixed content of these relationships and the more protean contents of the contractual relationship should not be exaggerated. The plasticity of contract has its limits. Leave aside the vexed question of whether there are some fixed duties towards each other that those who enter into contracts cannot but incur, however ingenious their attempts not to do so.[31] A different and more interesting limit on the plasticity of contract is this: there are some relationships that cannot

---

[31] Some hold that the duty to repair in the event of breach is one such. This view is common among supporters of the so-called 'efficient breach' doctrine.

be contractually created. With enough insight and ingenuity, the deontic content of friendship could surely be *emulated* in a contract, such that the parties would be contractually bound to act as if they were friends. But could they be contractually bound to be friends? I think not. The existence of the contract is a possible reason to perform the friendship-emulating duties in the contract, but it is not a possible reason to perform the duties of friendship *qua* friend. If one performed the duties for contractual reasons, one would be no friend. As well as telling us something about the nature of friendship (it is not reducible to its deontic content), this tells us something generally important about the individuation of duties: while two duties that have different contents are necessarily different duties, two duties that have exactly the same content are not necessarily the same duty. They may exist for different reasons, or they may have different force, or their breach may have different consequences.

This makes it possible for one and the same person simultaneously to have two different duties with identical content. One might have both a duty of friendship and a contractual duty not to confirm salacious rumours about Sue, or both a collegial duty and a contractual duty to help unpack those boxes, or both a duty as supplier and a contractual duty to pay the invoice with reasonable expedition.

The last example helps us to extend our grasp of the so-called 'relational theory of contracts'. So far, we have cast this theory as drawing attention to the nesting of contractual relationships within non-contractual ones. Now we can add that the nested contract, in such cases, may be an attempt—failed or successful—to replicate some or all of the duties that already help to constitute the non-contractual relationship. Why would

---

It is telling that those who do not regard the negotiable content of contracts as binding—who therefore do not really think of a breach of contract as a breach—are compelled by their view to hold that every contract has exactly one nonnegotiable binding term. As always, one mistake leads to another. The duty to repair is not created by the contract. It is created by the breach of contract. See ch 3 for further explanation. The best critique of the doctrine of 'efficient breach', emphasizing similar points, is still Daniel Friedmann, 'The Efficient Breach Fallacy', *Journal of Legal Studies* 18 (1989), 1.

anyone attempt such replication? Sometimes, no doubt, to provide motivational reinforcement at the point of performance.
But in many relationships, even in some commercial ones, such
reinforcement is out of keeping with the original spirit of the
relationship. While their non-contractual relationship subsists,
the parties work with each other in the hope, and often in the
reasonable expectation, that nobody will ever need to consult
the contractual terms, let alone insist upon them, never mind call
upon the support of the law to uphold them. They would regard
resort to the contractual terms, even without the invocation of
their legal effect, as already exposing a crack in their relationship.
The contract exists mainly to provide a fallback, a framework
for *modus vivendi* or orderly exit, in case the non-contractual relationship begins to break down. In marriage and romantic relationships, even the suggestion of a need for such a fallback (a
'prenup') might sometimes be regarded as already an admission
of defeat by the party suggesting it, verging on an anticipatory
abandonment of the relationship. Commercial relationships are
different. In them, fallbacks are par for the course. The aptness
of fallback arrangements may even be one of the criteria for the
relationship to qualify as a commercial one. 'There's no room
for sentiment in business' may be an analytic truth as well as an
embarrassing *cliché* and a pathetic excuse for wrongdoing. But it
does not follow that we should think of commercial relationships as reducing to contractual ones. When the going is good,
the nested contractual relationship typically remains a fallback,
designed mainly to make provision for the breakdown of the
non-contractual relationship in which it is nested.

   In modern private law, as indeed in modern culture at large,
there has been a long-standing tendency towards what might
be called contractual reductivism where special relationships are
concerned, especially but not only in respect of special relationships that can be *initiated* by the making of a contract. Special
relationships with relatively fixed deontic content—employer–
employee, landlord–tenant, bailor–bailee, and so forth—have increasingly been treated by the law as comprehensively reducible
to the contractual relationship in which the parties initially tried
to capture that relatively fixed deontic content, and hence as ever

more prone to have their deontic content rendered comprehensively plastic, because contractual, in law.

This makes it hard for the law to maintain the integrity of distinctions which, for many purposes, it still needs to draw. The law still needs to draw the distinction between employment relationships and others, for example, in its doctrines of vicarious liability, and for the purposes of various tax, insurance, and licensing regimes. But by giving succour to the idea that the employment relationship is *merely* a contractual one, it has invited erosion of the distinction between employment and its absence. It has invited the exploitation of the plasticity of contractual relationships to create hybrid arrangements, some of them designed to subvert or evade the law's residual uses of the employee/non-employee distinction. Still holding out against this contractual reductivism today are fiduciary relationships and (most) family relationships. They continue to attract the law's recognition as special relationships that have their own relatively fixed deontic content, deontic content that exists quite apart from the attempts of the parties to them to replicate (or evade) that content by contract. However, even they are coming under sustained pressure to submit to total contractualization.[32] It is easy to think of this as augmenting our freedom, allowing us to craft all our special relationships to suit our particular personal goals. Less obvious is the way in which the same developments reduce our freedom, by eroding legal recognition of and support for special relationships other than that of contracting party to contracting party.[33] You may think that where the parties to a special relationship have themselves created a contractual fallback, that is no great loss. By the time the parties are resorting to the law to uphold or unwind aspects of their special relationship, it is clearly fallback time. It is now time for contractualization to kick in. But this line of

[32] See among many critical discussions Daniel Markovits, 'Sharing *Ex Ante* and Sharing *Ex Post*: The Non-Contractual Basis of Fiduciary Relations' in A Gold and P Miller (eds), *Philosophical Foundations of Fiduciary Law* (Oxford University Press 2014); John Dewar, 'Family Law and its Discontents', *International Journal of Law, Policy, and the Family* 14 (2000), 59.

[33] The subject of Dori Kimel's book *From Promise to Contract* (Oxford University Press 2003).

thought assumes that the law's only role in recognizing and supporting special relationships is the role of upholder or unwinder when they hit the rocks. It leaves no room for the possibility that the law's recognition of and support for special relationships sometimes contributes to their availability and sustainability in other ways, for example by helping to crystallize their constitutive norms, or to affirm their social significance, or to emphasize their solemnity.

5. The duty of care

Rather than develop this critique here, however, allow me to turn to some parallel developments elsewhere in private law, this time in the law of torts. Maybe some torts are (or include) breaches of strictly relational duties. Think of the tort of misrepresentation, for example, which can be committed only in the course of precontractual dealings. Contrast the torts of defamation and conversion, which can be committed by total strangers against total strangers. The socially important tort of negligence may once have conformed to the former model. The famous legal 'duty of care', breach of which (while not the complete tort) is the ingredient of the tort after which the complete tort is named, was once regarded as existing only between people in certain enumerated special relationships—doctor and patient, lawyer and client, carrier and passenger, host and guest, parent and child, teacher and pupil, etc. The relationship was given, in each case, as the reason for the existence of the duty. The duty of care, in short, was typically presented as strictly relational. But by a gradual process, culminating in the 1932 decision of the House of Lords in *Donoghue v Stevenson*, a general rationale for the incidence of the duty emerged, supposedly revealing the common thread running through all the special relationships of which the duty had hitherto been held to be a constituent. Lord Atkin wrote:

You must take reasonable care to avoid acts or omissions which you can reasonably foresee would be likely to injure your neighbour. Who, then, in law, is my neighbour? The answer seems to be—persons who are so closely and directly affected by my act that I ought reasonably to have them in contemplation as being so affected when I am directing my mind to the acts or omissions which are called in question.[34]

The point here is that 'neighbour' is not to be given the literal (geographical) meaning that it carries in the tort of private nuisance. Rather, the word has (as Lord Atkin notes[35]) something similar to the meaning that it has in the New Testament injunction to 'love thy neighbour'. It includes all and sundry, people with whom one has no relationship apart from the very action that would constitute the breach of duty. The fact that one has a special relationship, then, can no longer be the reason why one has the duty. Lord Atkin's move is not to bring together all the special relationships that hitherto gave rise to the duty of care by explaining what they all have in common *qua* special relationships. Rather, he explains what they all have in common quite independently of the fact that they are special relationships, thereby allowing the 'special relationship' feature to drop out of the analysis. And as the 'special relationship' feature drops out, the duty of care ceases to be a strictly relational duty.

At any rate, that is a rough first shot at an explanation of the shift in legal approach that came to a head in *Donoghue v Stevenson*. On closer inspection, the explanation is not very satisfying. Lord Atkin's words nicely expose a vagueness in the way that I originally distinguished strictly relational duties from others, a vagueness which, if left uncontained, threatens to turn all the duties that we owe to others into strictly relational ones. How so? The problem is that there is a sense in which everyone is an Atkin neighbour of mine, and a sense in which only some are. Everyone is an Atkin neighbour of mine in the loose sense that everyone is a *candidate* to be owed the duty of care whenever I act; but only some, those who are sufficiently 'closely and directly affected' by some particular thing that I do, are actually owed the duty of care in the doing of that thing. Why is this special positioning relative to what I do not itself a special relationship with me, such that giving it as the reason for the incidence of the duty makes the duty a strictly relational one? And by extension why is not every

---

[34] [1932] AC 562 at 580.

[35] ibid: 'The rule that you are to love your neighbour becomes in law, you must not injure your neighbour.'

duty that I owe to another person strictly relational, just by virtue
of the fact that her being specially affected by what I do is the
reason for my duty not to do it? Does this not trivialize the idea
of a special relationship?

I have already tried to anticipate this question in the previous
paragraph by saying that the Atkin neighbour relationship is not
one that holds 'apart from the very action that would constitute
the breach of duty.' But that proposal provides little help.[36] It
is false if it is taken to mean that one does not have the Atkin
neighbour relationship with particular people *before* one acts in
breach of the duty of care that one owes them. Of course one
does: how could one reasonably foresee that some stranger will
be put in harm's way by one's act if that stranger is not *already* in a
position—namely, the Atkin neighbour position—such that this
much is reasonably foreseeable? So evidently one is already in an
Atkin neighbour relationship with one's Atkin neighbours before
one breaches one's duty towards them. That being so, how are
we to read 'no relationship apart from the very action that would
constitute the breach of duty' so as to make it true of Atkin neighbour relationships? That now seems obscure.

We can feel our way out of the fog by looking back to sections
2 and 3. The question there was how to defend the existence of
strictly relational duties. The answer was to look for value in the
special relationships that are the reasons for those duties. Special
relationships, in the sense required to give rise to strictly relational duties, are defeasibly valuable relationships, meaning relationships of types that it is valuable to have in existence, or on
the menu, even if they are not always valuable in the way they
work out in particular cases. Earlier, I spoke of value that might
be added in a 'world in which marriage exists'. That is the kind of
impersonal value that distinguishes a special relationship and that
explains its ability to give rise to duties.[37] The relationship that

[36] Compare Samuel Scheffler, 'Morality and Reasonable Partiality' in B Feltham
and J Cottingham (eds), *Partiality and Impartiality: Morality, Special Relationships, and
the Wider World* (Oxford University Press 2010), 117.

[37] Contrary to first appearances this does not precommit us to what Rawls
branded a 'teleological' view, according to which the performance of the duties
serves some independently specified value. It is consistent with a 'deontological'

holds between Atkin neighbours does not meet this condition. That is not to say, of course, that there is no value in your having or performing your duty of care towards me, when I am your Atkin neighbour. Of course there is: that someone is kept out of harm's way is analytically valuable; and inasmuch as your having a duty to keep me out of harm's way contributes (instrumentally or constitutively) to keeping me out of harm's way, the duty too is valuable. But that is not the issue. The issue is whether there is any value in my being positioned relative to you such that your action threatens to *put* me in harm's way, and such that I *need* the protection of a duty of care owed by you. Should I want to be in such a vulnerable position, cherish or sustain it when I am in it, etc.? Apart from the fact that it lands you with a duty of care towards me, in other words, is there anything to be said in favour of my being your Atkin neighbour? If not, then we are not in a special relationship in the relevant sense, and the duty of care is not, after all, strictly relational.

And that is indeed the correct verdict, the one that explains the paradigm shift that *Donoghue v Stevenson* represents in the history of the modern law of torts. The duty of care owed to one person by another in the law of negligence today is not based on the value of the relationship of Atkin neighbour that holds between them. It is based, rather, on the value in the life of the one to which breach of the duty of care by the other poses a threat. That value in the life of the one may of course include the value of her special relationships. The person to whom you owe a duty of care may well be someone's friend, someone's doctor, someone's mother, or someone's teacher. She may even be your friend, your doctor, your mother, or your teacher. Breach of the duty of care that you owe to her may imperil these or other special relationships that she has. That may be the particular way in which they pose a threat to the value in her life. Fine. The point is only that, in the law of negligence after *Donoghue v Stevenson*, your duty of care exists by reason of the threat that your actions pose to some or all of the value in her life, never mind whether the threat

view according to which the value in question lies in the performance of the duties and cannot be independently specified. See John Rawls, *A Theory of Justice* (Belknap Press 1971), 30.

consists in the imperiling of her special relationships. For yours is no longer a strictly relational duty.

You may well find the expression 'value in her life' opaque. Obviously, it does not mean the value of her staying alive. I am not thinking primarily of actions that risk another's death. I am thinking primarily of actions that imperil some valuable *aspect* or *aspects* of a person's life: her relationships and roles, her plans and projects, the pursuit and accomplishment of her personal goals, and so on. She may be put in danger of no longer being able to support her family, pay her rent, pursue her career, bear children or look after them, live in her own home, save her marriage, cultivate her garden, develop her skills as a pianist or goalkeeper, take pleasure in travel or films or cooking, take pride in herself as a parent or lover, etc. Some people like to call the things on this list, and others like them, her 'interests'. For various reasons, I will try to steer clear of this terminology. Nevertheless, I do want to endorse a claim made by many who adopt it. Sometimes, as the court decided was the case in *Donoghue v Stevenson*, the fact that some aspect of a person's life will otherwise be damaged or imperiled is reason enough for another to be under a duty in connection with the damaging or imperiling of it. When this is the reason for it, the duty in question is said to be owed by the latter person to the former. We might say that this is enough to license our calling it an interpersonal duty or a loosely relational duty. It is not a strictly relational duty because the reason for it is not the duty-bearer's special relationship with the other person but the special vulnerability of the other person to, or special dependence of the other person upon, the duty bearer's breach or performance of the duty, whether that vulnerability or dependence arises out of a special relationship or not.

Many people, including many people writing about private law, worry above all else about the sufficiency threshold for loosely relational duties. How much damaging or imperiling of which aspects of another's life is reason enough for me to find myself under a duty with regard to the avoidance or curtailment of that damaging or imperiling? Much effort is expended on the quest for a general answer to this question, or at least a general framework for answering it. I tend to think that this quest is misguided. It is fuelled by the thought that, when one person is held to owe a duty to another, some value in the life of the former is being earmarked for sacrifice in favour of some value in the life of the latter. In the language of interests: the interest of the one is being made to give way, at some point, to the interests of the other. At what point? Presumably somewhere that splits the difference between them, that treats the two equally, that gives like attention or importance to the interests of each, or such like. Our discussion of strictly relational duties revealed, however, that this is not always the right way to think about what is going on with duties owed to others. At least some duties owed to others are such that their breach destroys value in the life of the person who owes them, and not only in the life of the person to whom they are owed. In *Sophie's Choice*, for example, the interests of mother and children are almost entirely aligned. The evil scheme by which Sophie is made to breach her duties to her children is primarily devised by the camp doctor as a way to destroy Sophie's own life, not a way to destroy the lives of her children (who can just as easily, indeed more easily, be disposed of in the gas chambers without giving Sophie any say in the matter). You may think that loosely relational duties are different in this respect. But I doubt whether that is so. Arguably, to return to our earlier example, the judicial duty of impartiality is not strictly relational after all. Arguably, it is only because the parties appearing before the judge are especially affected by his decisions that he owes them the duties he does. So arguably those duties are only loosely relational. Even so, the breach of them destroys value in the life of the judge, and not only in the lives of those who appear before him. Partiality as between the parties compromises the judge in his judicial role no less than Sophie's partiality compromises her in her parental role. And just as Sophie's duty is an essential ingredient of her being a parent, so the judge's duty is an essential ingredient of his being a judge. The duty's existence is not, then, a burden to be borne by the judge for the sake of others. Its existence is also integral to the value in his own life.

So even with loosely relational duties the problem of the sufficiency threshold is not, as so often assumed, the question of when the duty-bearer finally gets to stop making sacrifices for others. The corrupt or slapdash judge is the true loser, who sacrifices value in his own life; the judge who unflinchingly performs his duties, meanwhile, is the true winner. Or at any rate, if the latter is a loser, it is not the fact that he has and performs the demanding duties of his office that makes him so. *Ceteris paribus*, these duties only create more opportunities for the judge, like the parent, to add value to his or her own life by contributing positively to the lives of others. Duties owed to others are not generally zero-sum as between the person who owes them and the person to whom they are owed.

You may say: by the time a judge or parent is being sued for breach of duty, it is too late for all that. Once we are dealing with legal duties we should think of the question as the question of who gets to be the winner at whose expense. The situation has turned into a zero-sum one. And we should think of having a duty towards the other as helping to put one on the losing side, not the winning side. I reply as I did in section 4: the law is not only there to mop up when things go wrong. For non-special relationship roles, as for special relationship roles, the law is also there to crystallize constitutive norms, to affirm social significance, and to emphasize solemnity.

I will have more to say about the norm-crystallization function in Chapter 2. However, I will have little to say about the question of the sufficiency threshold. It does not follow that I see no general puzzles about loosely relational duties. Later on, in Chapter 5, I will be coming back to what I regard as the main puzzle. It is the puzzle of why *value in someone's life* is held up for special protection, even for special attention. Why the focus on value that is already, so to speak, vested? Why not just value in general? Is such vested value somehow more valuable, and hence more in need of protection or more deserving of attention, than any other? That, it seems to me, is the deepest and most difficult puzzle about private law, as well as about life in general. That is why it needs a whole chapter to itself.

6. The relationality of rights

This talk of 'vesting' may draw it to your attention that, soon after the start of this chapter, all talk of rights petered out. At some cost in ease and elegance of expression, I have spoken throughout of 'the person to whom the duty is owed' (or similar) rather than 'the rightholder'. That is in spite of the fact that many people think of rights as having a special place in private law, to the point even of being its distinctive currency or basis.

I have kept rights out of the discussion for two main reasons. The first is that talk of rights seems out of place in connection with some strictly relational duties. Some of the awkwardness here is pragmatic. Even when friends do have rights against their friends, it is out of keeping with the spirit of friendship for them to stand on their rights, or assert their rights. It is much the same problem as the problem of the 'prenup' mentioned in section 4 above: if you are casting your differences with your friends in terms of rights, you are already calling your friendships into question. Rights talk has some adversarial overtones. Some adversariality is consistent with, and may even be called for, in friendship: 'as your oldest friend, I think I had the right to hear it from you first'; 'you have no right to treat your mates this way'; 'I have every right to be angry with you—that wasn't how I expected my best friend to react', etc. But people who talk in this (or a like) idiom about everything that comes between them as soon as it comes between them are almost certainly not friends.

Yet it does not follow from the fact that we avoid or postpone talking about something that comes between us in the language of rights that we do not have rights in respect of that thing. And it seems to me that friends do have various rights against each other just *qua* friends. As George's and Lennie's list of various benefits of having friends reminds us, many duties of friendship exist on the strength of the contribution that the duty-performing act of one of the friends makes to the life of the other. When such contributions form the basis of the duty we might be tempted say that it is both strictly relational *and* loosely relational. In any case we should think of the duty as serving not just the friendship but also the friend, and we should think of the friend as a rightholder in respect of it. In the same vein, when Williams' rescuer explains 'she's my wife' we naturally understand him to be saying that he is protecting *her*, not protecting their marriage. And that is because we think that the strictly relational duty of husband and wife to prioritize each other for protection (unlike some other spousal duties) is a duty based on the value that each spouse thereby brings to the life of the other, that being central (in turn) to explaining the value of marriage. Similarly, the duty of parents to protect their children. Children surely have a right to that protection. It does not follow, however, that every strictly relational duty that a parent owes to a child is a duty in respect of which the child has a right. Arguably, some parental duties exist because of value in the parent-child relationship that is independent of the value that the particular parent brings, by performing those duties, to the life of the particular child. One may think that, for example, of the parental duty of impartiality. Arguably one owes this duty to one's children but not by right. Why? Because arguably its existence does not depend on whether one's own children benefit from one's having and performing it.[38]

These complications represent, however, only the more minor of the two concerns that led me, for most of this chapter, to eschew all talk of rights. Of more concern to me was the fact that some people deny that the existence even of a loosely relational duty suffices for the existence of a right. According to some there must also be a power in the rightholder to determine the incidence of the duty, the justifiability of its breach, and/or the normative consequences for the breacher. The rightholder must also, some add, enjoy some permissive latitude concerning the exercise of such powers, or more generally concerning what is to be done next. For example, the incidents of the right to self-defence (it is commonly thought) include a permission for the self-defender to defend herself or not to defend herself at her discretion, and not merely a duty owed by others to the self-defender not to impede her self-defensive acts. And that same right also (to many people's way of thinking) makes the permissibility of any attempt to assist the rightholder in her self-defensive acts subject to her veto, giving her a power to determine the normative position of her assisters. Although they strike me as questionable, I make no particular quarrel here with these or similar thoughts about the right to self-defence. But they do not seem to me to be generalizable across all rights. Think about the self-defender's assistants.

---

[38] I am not suggesting here that we dispense with the so-called 'person-affecting condition' in the explanation of value. It is a long way from denying that the duty exists for the benefit of the particular child to whom it is owed to denying that it exists for the benefit of anyone. On the person-affecting condition see Derek Parfit, *Reasons and Persons* (Clarendon Press 1985), 393 ff.

Suppose they are her friends who happen to be on the scene. Their right to assist their friend in her self-defence, it seems to me, is associated with a duty owed to them by others not to impede them in their attempts to support their friend's self-defence. Yet, barring exceptional circumstances, they do not have any associated powers to alter their own or anyone else's normative position in respect of their interventions, nor any permission (discretion) not to intervene. Those who decline to exercise their right to assist their friend's self-defence are not covered by any right not to. Or at any rate, if they are not, that in no way affects the truth of the proposition that they had a right to assist their friend.

It hardly matters, however, what I take to be the necessary normative incidents of a right, and what I take to be the merely possible ones. What matters is that all the normative incidents ultimately need to be explained, and need to be broken apart for the purposes of explanation. One cannot short-circuit this process of explanation by bundling everything together under the heading of a right. In fact, one cannot achieve much by bundling everything together under the heading of a right. True, one can sometimes save words, or make more vivid connections with more familiar topics. But in the process one invites a good deal of confusion. One risks the running together of various loosely connected duties, powers, and permissions, each of which calls for its own explanation. This makes it all too easy, in turn, to inflate the sense in which duties owed to others are relational, or bipolar, or second-personal. For now one risks treating as if they were automatic certain accompaniments or consequences of the existence, performance, or breach of such duties that in fact arise only in certain circumstances, upon further argument. The theoretical study of private law, where the language of rights is common, has not been immune from these problems. In fact, they are widespread. Thanks to the elasticity of rights talk, various interconnected but distinct norms that figure prominently in private law doctrine have come to be treated as if they stand in relations of at least defeasible entailment, such that defending one of them is, in effect, defending all of them. They are taken to stand or fall as a package deal. Since the defendant's original duty was owed to the plaintiff, it is often thought, the plaintiff is the one who without (much) further ado has the permission to waive or disregard the breach of that duty as he sees fit, the one who without (much) further ado has the power to instigate and terminate legal proceedings or other modes of complaint against the defendant as he sees fit, the one who without (much) further ado is owed some secondary remedial duty or duties by the defendant, the one who without (much) further ado gets to put his remedial winnings to whatever use he might favour, and so forth.

In this chapter I have offered an account of what it means to owe a duty to another—actually two accounts, the strictly relational one and the loosely relational one. What I proposed might be described as 'minimalist'. A duty counts as owed to another in virtue of the reasons for its existence, no more and no less. No special normative consequences of the breach, or special accompanying powers or permissions for the person to whom the duty is owed, are built into this analysis. That such things are not built into the analysis does not suggest that they do not exist. But when and why they might exist are, to repeat, further questions calling for separate attention. Some of them are tackled in later chapters of this book, notably in Chapter 3 (which considers the case for the existence of remedial duties) and Chapter 6 (which considers the case for giving some control over the normative consequences of a breach of duty to the person to whom that duty is owed). To avoid the accidental prejudging of these questions and others, I tend to shy away from rights talk in this book.[39] I do so without intending to cast any doubt on the common ideas that private law recognizes and creates rights, that private-law litigation exists to determine, uphold, and eventually enforce rights, that an actual or imminent violation of rights is what a plaintiff in such litigation normally complains of, that such a complaint is in some interesting sense 'private', and so forth. I am not denying these claims but rather avoiding them as treacherous, as vague truisms that tend to conceal the puzzles of private law rather than solving them.

There is something bewildering, you may think, in the fact that I ended this chapter by warning against the blandishments of private-law relationality inflators. My original targets, you

---

[39] Although in some sections I use the word 'rightholder', for want of a better shorthand, to refer to the person to whom a duty is owed.

may recall, were their foes, the relationality deflaters and the relationality eliminators. But this *volte face* is not as curious as it looks. Theoretical work on private law, as on many other issues in moral, political, and legal philosophy, tends to be excessively polarized. Fanaticism breeds fanaticism. Depressed by utilitarianism, people are naturally tempted to become not just non-utilitarians but anti-utilitarians, siding against the utilitarians on anything and everything. Shocked by an economic analysis, people are naturally tempted to rest everything on the one thing which, to their eyes, the economists missed. Appalled by one kind of reductive thinking, people are inevitably tempted by reductive thinking of some diametrically opposed kind. But most of the truth, here as elsewhere, is not diametrically opposed to anything. Life is full of tragedies. But having to choose between hyper-relationalism and hypo-relationalism in how we think about private law, or about personal life, is not one of them.

2

That's the Story of My Life

We meet events halfway; they are part of us, and we part
of them.

Malcolm Bradbury[1]

1. The ins and outs of wrongdoing

I pointed out in Chapter 1 that acting negligently towards another, in breach of one's duty of care, is but one ingredient of
the tort of negligence. It is not yet the whole tort. To commit
the whole tort, one must also cause or occasion some legally recognized loss to the person towards whom one acted negligently.
Two rival analyses of this arrangement are possible. On one analysis, there is only one legal duty in play, and that is the duty of
care. That some loss must come of its breach is only a limit on
what lawyers call the *actionability* of the breach—a limit on the
range of cases in which the breach is a ground of legal liability.
On the rival analysis, there are two legal duties in play. There is
the duty of care owed to the plaintiff (P), and then there is the
further duty not to cause or occasion legally recognized loss to P
by breaching one's duty of care towards P. You might suspect that
I stacked the deck against the first analysis, and in favour of the
second, by saying that the breach of the duty of care is 'not yet
the whole tort', but only an ingredient of it. But I did not. A tort
is not merely a legal wrong. It is an actionable legal wrong. The
first analysis makes the causing or occasioning of the loss into a
condition of actionability that is not an ingredient of the legal
wrong. The second analysis makes it a condition of actionability
that is *also* an ingredient of the legal wrong.

On both analyses the legally recognized loss is what we might
call an *outcome* of the legal wrong, something brought about in or

[1] Bradbury, *Eating People is Wrong* (Picador 1959).
From Personal Life to Private Law. John Gardner © John Gardner 2018. Published
2018 by Oxford University Press.

by the commission of it. On the first analysis it is a *consequence* of the wrong; on the second analysis it is a *result*. A result, as many philosophers use the term[2] and as I will use it here, is an outcome of an action that is also an ingredient (also known as constituent) of that action; a consequence, by contrast, is an outcome that is not an ingredient. So, for example, my dying is a consequence of your having shot me, but it is a result of your having (thereby) killed me; that you are offended is a consequence of my having said something offensive, but it is a result of my having (thereby) offended you; that Tom is asleep is a consequence of his having taken a sleeping pill, but it is a result of his having (thereby) sent himself to sleep; that Viv has a solution to the puzzle is a consequence of her having applied her mind to it, but it is a result of her having (thereby) solved it. One brings about a result *in* doing something, we tend to say, whereas one brings about a consequence *by* doing something else.

Some people working on the nature of human action have been resistant to the very idea that actions can have results. Strictly speaking, they think, there is no such action as killing. There may be death-prone or death-dealing or even death-directed actions, but when an actual death is their outcome, it is always, strictly speaking, a consequence rather than a result of what was done. In Donald Davidson's famous version: 'We never do more than move our bodies. The rest is up to nature.'[3] I am not the first to wonder how, on Davidson's view, we even get to move our bodies. Surely, in the cases that Davidson has in mind, my body's moving is itself an outcome of something else I do, namely *trying to move it*? So why not push back further than Davidson, and say that all we ever do is *try* to move our bodies? Suppose I am exposed to some paralysing toxin (maybe I am bitten by a snake) so that my body stays put when I try to move it. Even the movement of my body turns out to be 'up to nature', so shouldn't we follow Davidson's logic to say that it is also a consequence rather than a constituent of my action? Nor need we stop there. Even trying

---

[2] Following GH von Wright, *Norm and Action* (Routledge & Kegan Paul 1963), 39–41.

[3] Davidson, 'Agency' in Davidson, *Essays on Actions and Events* (Clarendon Press 1980) 59.

can be analysed into, so to speak, an input and an output; not every time we decide to try do we actually manage to try. We may be too late or it may be too much for us; our decision to try may come to nothing. So perhaps all we ever do is, say, *see if we can try*? I'm sure you get the point. As Thomas Nagel famously put it: 'the area of genuine agency ... seems to shrink under this scrutiny to an extensionless point.'[4] Nagel's is a *reductio ad absurdam* of the Davidsonian view. The idea is that once we deny that actions can have results, we deny that there can be actions. We were hoping for something that was all input and no output. But there is no agency at all in something that is all input and no output. Agency—and action—is essentially causal. It gets *some* kind of result every time, even if not always the one sought by the agent, and even if not always one visible to the naked eye. Sometimes, all I did was set my thoughts racing or form an intention or let a funny image stay in my head. But even these actions have results: I end up with racing thoughts in the first case, an intention in the second, and a funny image in my head in the third.

You may say that I elided here the most important words of Nagel's remark. What he said, more fully, was that 'the area of genuine agency, *and therefore of legitimate moral judgment*, seems to shrink under this scrutiny to an extensionless point.' Nagel was not interested only in the theory of action and agency but also in the implications for how we are to *judge* actions and their agents. It is true that if actions do not have results, actions cannot be judged by their results, and nor can we, as their agents. But the converse is not true. We could think that actions have results, while doubting that they, let alone we, should be judged by those results. The problem that detained Nagel was not whether there can be actions with results but the problem of whether, when, and how those results are relevant to determining (inter alia) the rightness and wrongness of what we do, which he called the problem of 'moral luck ... in the way [our actions] turn out'.

The expression 'moral luck' has turned out to be a double-barrelled philosophical liability. First, the word 'moral' has left its usual trail of destruction. Bernard Williams, who coined the

---

[4] Nagel, 'Moral Luck', *Proceedings of the Aristotelian Society Supplementary Volume* 50 (1976), 137.

expression 'moral luck' for the purpose of his symposium with Nagel,[5] had hoped to prompt sceptical questions such as this:

What is the point of insisting that a certain reaction or attitude or judgement is or is not a moral one? ... [W]hat comfort [is it] supposed to give to me, or what instruction ... to other people, if I am shunned, hated, unloved and despised, not least by myself, but am told that these reactions do not belong to morality[?][6]

Alas, the expression did more to shore up the view that morality is importantly distinct from the rest of practical life than it did to call that view into question. We know that what we do is plagued by luck, people came to say, but is it really *moral* luck?

Meanwhile, the word 'luck' brought its own problems. It encouraged a focus, not on the question of what (for better or worse) we bring to the world, but on the question of how the world might wrong-foot us in the bringing of it. This flipping of the question turns out to have a distorting effect on people's reactions. When they think of luck *tout court* (as opposed to my luck and your luck) people tend to think not of a kind of uncertainty that is built into our actions but, rather, of some kind of cosmic agency—'Lady Luck', the gamblers call her—that competes with and neutralizes our agency and so cannot be in any sense built into it. It is precisely *under this scrutiny*, as Nagel recorded, that our agency seems to shrink an extensionless point. Our reaction should not be to see our agency as duly shrunken. Our reaction should be to see this as the wrong kind of scrutiny.

As Nagel's remark suggests, the problems that he and Williams treated as aspects of the problem of 'moral luck ... in the way [our actions] turn out' are less tendentiously approached as problems about the ways in which the results of our actions figure in certain assessments of them as actions. And perhaps the most persistent and familiar problem of this kind is the one nicely conveyed by John Donne:

---

[5] Williams, 'Moral Luck' *Proceedings of the Aristotelian Society Supplementary Volume* 50 (1976), 115; Nagel, 'Moral Luck', ibid, 137. Williams' essay is also in his book *Moral Luck* (Cambridge University Press 1981); Nagel's appears in his *Mortal Questions* (Cambridge University Press 1979).

[6] Williams, 'Moral Luck: a Postscript' in Williams, *Making Sense of Humanity* (Cambridge University Press 1995), 244.

And though they be not fair, 'tis much with me
To win their love only for their degree.
And though I fail of my required ends,
The attempt is glorious and itself commends.[7]

It is a sentiment echoed today by well-meaning primary school teachers and liberal parents everywhere. In action we should be judged by our efforts and intentions (conceived as the inputs), not by how our efforts and intentions pay off or play out (conceived as the outputs). I may have hurt your feelings, but I meant well, and surely that is what counts. I may not have passed the exam, but I gave it my very best shot, and surely that is what matters—that is where the real glory lies.

Yet you will notice, however, that this reading takes much of the poetic tension out of Donne's words. Donne says that my ends beyond my attempt can be 'required'. But in what sense can ends be *required* of us if we cannot ever be judged to have gone wrong, to have let ourselves down, or to have showed ourselves up, in failing to attain them? That being so, can the glorious attempt that admittedly 'itself commends' really be *all* that counts in determining how well we are faring (one might say 'faring as agents' if that were not so obviously built into the verb 'to fare')? On closer inspection, Donne does not say that the attempt is all that counts. He says it counts for something. It is some consolation. But he also points out what it is that necessitates such consolation, namely a personal failure. Is Donne perhaps offering a parodic critique, anticipating by three centuries all of those well-meaning teachers and liberal parents?

Required results, as we might now call them, are also found in many corners of the law. In the manner of Donne, the law often contrasts the completed (result-yielding) action with the attempt (be it glorious or inglorious). The criminal law requires me not to handle stolen goods as well as requiring me, in a further rule, not to attempt to handle them; it similarly requires me not to wound you as well as requiring me, in a further rule, not to attempt to do so. In the same vein, your contract may require you to use your

---

[7] Donne, Elegy XVII, 'Variety' or 'The heavens rejoice in motion' in Herbert Grierson (ed), *The Poems of John Donne, Vol. 1: The Text of the Poems with Appendixes* (Clarendon Press 1912), 113.

best endeavours to deliver a consignment on Monday, but mine requires me actually to deliver a consignment on that day. And on one analysis, you will recall, the law of torts requires me to take care not to cause loss to you, but it also requires me, under a further rule piggybacked onto the first, actually not to cause the loss (when I do so by failing to take the required care). You may think that these legal cases differ importantly from Donne's case. Donne's required results are only hypothetically required; the norm requiring them depends for its application on the prevailing personal goals of the person to whom it applies. His narrator seeks true love, and it is the requirement that he win that love in respect of which he risks failure. When the law requires results, by contrast, it does so in the categorical voice, the voice of duty. One is legally required to attain or avoid certain results, never mind one's personal goals at the time. But how could this matter? As we saw in Chapter 1, it is merely a difference in the conditions under which the respective requirements apply. Why would anyone think that the conditions of application of a requirement would affect its possible content, such that those that apply irrespective of one's personal goals cannot be result requiring? Could there be some confusion here connected with the word 'goals', that leads some to think that if a requirement does not depend for existence on my prevailing personal goals (=my projects, commitments), then its performance can have no built-in goal (=result that would make it complete)? Kant himself slipped quite easily from the thought that a duty is categorical to thought that its performance could not depend on results.[8] Maybe others slip with him?

Be that as it may, I will be interested here in persuading you that results matter, or are capable of mattering, in law as much as in love. The tort of negligence, analysed as the breach of a result-requiring duty, is admittedly a complex example. It has curious features that call for separate discussion. I put it in the foreground mainly to set aside one particular set of doubts about result-requiring duties. In my own view, many result-requiring duties (outside the law as well as inside it) are *strict* duties. They include duties actually to deliver the consignment on Monday,

---

[8] Kant, *Groundwork of the Metaphysic of Morals* (trans HJ Paton, Basic Books 1964), 61–2.

never mind whether one tried; they include duties not to handle stolen goods or to wound, never mind what one was attempting to do in the process; and so on. The putative result-requiring duty in the tort of negligence is different. To avoid breaching this duty, it is sufficient (although not necessary) that one did not breach the duty of care on which it piggybacks. That there is no *strict* result-requiring duty here helps us to cut the question of whether there can be result-requiring duties loose from the often-associated question of whether there can be strict duties. At the same time, the example helps us to pin down a common doubt about result-requiring duties, one that I hope to allay here. It is tempting to think that result-requiring duties cannot but contain some rational redundancy. Never mind what is the most we can ever do. The most we can ever have *reason* to do is to try; the rest is up to nature. If that were right, then the law of tortious negligence would give us all the reasons for action that it is capable of giving us by giving us a duty of care. Adding the second alleged duty, the result-requiring duty, could not possibly add extra rational guidance for us as potential tortfeasors, for there can be no extra reasons not to cause people loss beyond such reasons as there are to make every effort not to do so. That, think some, is the basic case against the very existence of result-requiring duties, and the basic explanation of why the tort of negligence should be given the rival analysis which I set out at the start, in which no result-requiring duty is involved.

2. The biography argument

Tony Honoré has done more than anyone else to raise consciousness of the problem among tort lawyers. He calls the problem one of outcome-responsibility. He has many important and memorable things to say about the institutionalization of outcome-responsibility in the law, and we will be returning to that topic shortly. But I want to focus first on what Honoré calls a 'deeper' point, one that he presents all too enigmatically:

[O]utcome [responsibility] is crucial to our identities as persons; and unless we were persons who possessed an identity, the question of whether it was fair to subject us to responsibility could not arise. If actions and outcomes were not ascribed to us on the basis of our bodily movements

and their mental accompaniments, we could have no continuing history
or character. There would indeed be bodies and, associated with them,
minds. Each would possess a certain continuity. They could be labelled
A, B, C. But having decided nothing and done nothing these entities
would hardly be people.[9]

This is clearly meant to be a *reductio ad absurdam*. Is it Nagel's *reductio*? It is a variation on Nagel's *reductio*, as I adapted it to bite
against Davidson. The thesis, as Honoré sets it out, is that refusing
to think of human beings as outcome-responsible, whether because one sees the problem in terms of luck or otherwise, means
refusing to think of human beings as agents at all. If we deny that
outcomes form part of what we do, we deny, by implication, that
we do anything. If our agency is not in the wider world it is not
in us either. Indeed, we would not only have done nothing; we
would by the same token have 'decided nothing'. We can presumably add that we would have intended nothing, and had no goals.
The will itself, so central to responsibility in the eyes of so many,
would be gone.

You may think that this is patent hyperbole. Surely, just as
we could imagine a much-reformed criminal law that is all attempts and endangerments, with none of what we now call
completed crimes, so we could tell a story of our lives that is
a story only of endeavour and neglect, free of any upshots or
payoffs: 'Never mind what came of my big ideas, just understand that I gave it 110% every time'; 'Forget broken hearts
and shattered lives—the point is that I paid no attention to
anyone and put no effort into anything'. Either of those could
still be the story, could it not, of a 'person ... who possessed
an identity' with a 'continuing history or character'? And, *pace*
Honoré, the story could surely still include its subject's decisions, if nothing else.

Arthur Miller's *Death of a Salesman*, for example, might still
have been read as the story of Willy Loman's eventual decision
to kill himself, even if we never heard whether he succeeded (i.e.
even with the 'Requiem' after Act II deleted). And even if the
background of Willy's eventual decision included none of the

---

[9] Honoré, 'Responsibility and Luck: The Moral Basis of Strict Liability', *Law
Quarterly Review* 104 (1988), 530 at 534.

fruits of his earlier decisions, the play could still have shown the
decisions he made, at first confidently and idealistically, but later
weighed down by encroaching exhaustion and depression. At the
same time, the play could still have made much of the actual disappointments in Willy's life, without presenting anything as the
disappointing repercussion of his own decisions. The story could
have been one of ever-less-ambitious plans hatched under ever-
worse conditions, freed of any hint of the escalating contributions made by the one to the other. It would still have been, in
another telling, the sad story of Willy Loman.

True enough, but that would be a strange and attenuated
telling. By its affected silence on the subject it could only deepen
our curiosity concerning Willy's contributions to the unfolding
of events in his own life and that of his family. Was Willy faring
as badly as he thought? Or was that partly the dazzling light of
unrealistic expectation casting a shadow, perhaps the shadow of
the black dog of depression, on respectable achievements? Did he
really fail, for example, as a father? Did he leave his eldest son Biff
'seeing what I [Willy] am'?[10] Did he live and die in vain, since his
younger son Happy resolves, in homage, to repeat his mistakes?
What, if anything, was Willy's true legacy?

Many of these questions remain unanswered in Miller's own
text as it stands. For some of them, the relevant results have
yet to materialize by the end of the play. Nonetheless, the play
puts Willy's agential impact on the world repeatedly in the spot-
light. Miller misses few opportunities to foreground endeavour's
troubled relationship with achievement, and he puts *that*, not
mere adverse circumstance, at the heart of Willy's fate:

And when I saw that [reminisces Willy early in the play] I realized that
selling was the greatest career a man could want. 'Cause what could be
more satisfying than to be able to go, at the age of eighty-four, into
twenty or thirty different cities, and pick up a phone, and be remem-
bered and loved and helped by so many different people?[11]

[10] Arthur Miller, *Death of a Salesman: Certain Private Conversation in Two Acts and
a Requiem* (Penguin Books 1961), 100.
[11] ibid 63.

How can they dare refuse? [He protests later, thinking of the post- suicide insurance payout.] Didn't I work like a coolie to meet every premium on the nose? And now they don't pay off? Impossible.[12]

Of course, the play is a scathing critique of the American dream. So the question of the potential endeavour–achievement mismatch is particularly pronounced. My point is that it does not take the special ideological context to make that question live for those interested in the story of Willy Loman's life. A story of the inner life of a decision-maker, in which all else is treated as merely unfolding around him, could be an interesting literary experiment. In a way, it is the literary experiment conducted by Camus in *L'Étranger*.[13] But, as that work shows, and was perhaps written to show, such an entity is hardly a person, and the record of his existence is hardly the story of a life.

Why is that? It is because the story of a decision-maker is by its nature the story of a would-be world-affecter; decision already aims, if you like, at its own implementation. The normal reasons for deciding to do something are also reasons to do whatever one decides to do. For instance, the normal case for deciding to stay, or deciding to go, is simply the case for staying or going (as the case may be). How does a reason for staying or for going do double service, in this way, as a reason for deciding which to do? The relationship is instrumental. By deciding to stay or deciding to go, one got closer to, or readier for, the staying or going (as the case may be). Sometimes, true enough, one has reasons to decide that are independent of reasons to do what one decides to do. Sometimes it would be better to make any decision than no decision at all. 'Stay or go,' we sometimes say, 'but just make your mind up!' Yet even here, decision is clearly answering to practical reasons, reasons in favour of and against acting. The point of deciding is still to get on and do something, normally the thing decided upon. Decision is still a means to action and normally

---

[12] ibid 100.

[13] Albert Camus, *L'Étranger* (Gallimard 1942). The title translates as 'The Stranger' or 'The Outsider' but the overtone (which the French title conveys better) is that the novel's central figure, Meursault, is estranged even from himself; he relates even to his own agency as if he were a mere observer of events.

there exist reasons to make decisions only if there exist reasons to act on them. So, as Honoré rightly observes, if there is never any reason actually to do things, if there is no rational agency beyond decision, there is no reason for decision either.

Or at least, not normally. I included this qualification right from the start of the paragraph to cover those rare cases, vaguely evocative of some composite Woody Allen character talking to his long-suffering therapist, in which some difficulty in one's life—say writer's block or a temporary stutter—will evaporate if only one manages to make a decision about some difficulty in one's life—say what typeface to use in one's draft, or what to serve the in-laws for Sunday lunch. Or perhaps, to borrow a fabulous example from Hergé's *Adventures of Tintin*, one can't get to sleep at all until one decides whether to sleep with one's beard under or over the covers.[14] Suppose that the very act of making the decision is all that it will take to overcome the difficulty; it will provide all the relief one seeks. Perhaps the making of the decision is so cathartic, indeed, that one will soon forget one ever made it, and hence fail to carry it out. So what? Naturally the decision was still made with a view to its implementation. Otherwise, it would not be a decision. Seen from the point of the decision, then, the non-implementation will represent a kind of failure. But the point of the decision was, in a way, a point of strategic self-deception (or perhaps strategic deception by one's therapist). There never was a valid reason to act as one decided to act, or indeed to care which way one acted. Beard under or over the covers? What a daft thing to pay attention to!

I hope you can agree that such cases are oddities.[15] They show only that occasionally we have reasons to kid ourselves that we have reasons for doing something such that we can at least make a decision. That proposition is not only consistent with, but in a

[14] In Hergé's *The Red Sea Sharks* (trans Lonsdale-Cooper and Turner, Methuen 1960), Allen leaves Haddock locked in his cabin with the goodnight question about his beard, which is asked precisely in order to keep Haddock awake.
[15] Gregory Kavka's famous 'toxin puzzle' (Kavka, 'The Toxin Puzzle', *Analysis* 43 (1983), 33) belongs to the same category. The category is carefully explored, although its exceptionality is underplayed, in James Morauta, 'In Defence of State-Based Reasons to Intend', *Pacific Philosophical Quarterly* 91 (2010), 208.

roundabout way supportive of, the view that we have no reasons for decision without reasons for action. And that, it seems to me is, what we need to unpack Honoré's point about action and decision. Those who have no actions beyond decision to call their own also have no decisions to call their own.

Yet this leaves us some way from establishing Honoré's main point about outcome-responsibility. It is one thing to show that, without actions to call our own, we also have no decisions to call our own. It is quite another thing to show that, without outcomes to call our own, we have no actions to call our own. Surely even without outcome-responsibility we can still glory, as Donne says, in the attempt; and we can still tell the story of such glories as the story of a life? Perhaps we can, but again it would be a strange, artificially limited story. For the argument that I just ran in respect of decisions can also be run, *mutatis mutandis*, in respect of attempts. The normal case of a reason to attempt is a reason thereby to do whatever one attempts to do. The attempt is defended as an instrument of the completed action that one is attempting. One should try to help people, normally, because one should help people. One should try not to offend people, normally, because one should not offend people. Sometimes, true enough, one has extra reasons to attempt that are independent of reasons to succeed in the attempt. Sometimes, as Donne says, the attempt 'itself commends', where 'itself' implies 'independently'. But even then the attempt, as one might put it, still aims at its own success. One cannot attempt anything other than by acting for the sake of succeeding, i.e. for a reason that one takes to be a reason in favour of actually doing whatever one attempts to do. That is what an attempt is; if one does not take oneself to have some reason to succeed, and act on it, then one is not really trying. One may be mistaken in what one takes to be a reason to succeed in a particular case, or in which success one takes it to be a reason for, but can we all really be wrong in thinking that reasons to succeed can exist? After all, if such reasons cannot exist, then even attempts of the self-commending variety that Donne describes are not rationally intelligible. For it is part of their nature that they are undertaken for reasons of a non-existent type, namely reasons to succeed.

So, as I have put the same point before, reasons to succeed have explanatory primacy over reasons to try.[16] This is true in two closely related ways. If there are no possible reasons in favour of saving people or not offending them—by which I mean, in favour of doing so successfully, complete with results—then there are not only (i) no derivative reasons in favour of trying to save people or trying not to offend people; there are also (ii) no rationally intelligible acts of trying to save people or trying not to offend people, even in the rare cases in which there are non-derivative reasons in favour of the trying per se.

This, I believe, is the cryptic Honoré argument unpacked. Honoré does not claim that one cannot tell or imagine the story of one's life as a story of decision. He claims that one cannot tell or imagine the story of one's life as a story of decision without raising the question of whether one acted on the decisions, by trying to implement them.[17] And with that thought he means to invite the next thought too: that one cannot tell or imagine the story of what one did to *try* to implement one's decisions without raising the question of whether what one actually managed to implement them, i.e. achieved what one set out to achieve. It is no idle curiosity, notices Honoré, that drives us to ask for these further particulars. It is an interest that a rational being cannot avoid having, an interest in whether the reasons for action already playing a role in the story, already implicated on the input side, were ultimately conformed to in the output. One decides in order to attempt and one attempts in order to succeed. Narrating decisions invites the question of what one attempted; narrating attempts invites the question of what one achieved. One's life story is a story of how one did, answering to reasons, and since there are reasons to succeed, one's life story is not told inasmuch as it fails to reveal how one's actions turned out. That gives us one

---

[16] J Gardner, 'Obligations and Outcomes in the Law of Torts' in P Cane and J Gardner (eds), *Relating to Responsibility: Essays in Honour of Tony Honoré on his Eightieth Birthday* (Hart Publishing 2001). Sections 2 and 3 of this chapter further develop the argument sketched in the penultimate section of this earlier essay.

[17] Nicely illustrated in *L'Étranger* (n 13). Camus represents Meursault's disconnection from the results of his actions by emphasizing his lack (or at least disclaiming) of any reasons to have performed them.

of the less daft readings of Yoda's famous rebuke in *The Empire Strikes Back*: 'Do, or do not. There is no try.'[18]

3. From biography to responsibility

Clearly we are still some way from the law. It is one thing, you may think, to regard the way one's action turns out as an integral part of one's life story, but it is quite another to regard the way one's action turns out as figuring in the content of one's legal duty, and hence as affecting the incidence of one's legal liability to pay damages for losses caused to others. Honoré's argument— let's call it 'the biography argument'—encourages us to think about how *my* wrongdoing affects the path of *my* life. But the law is interested, surely, in how *my* wrongdoing affects the path of *your* life. These different interests raise completely different problems. In an essay about the role of outcome-responsibility in private law, you may be inclined to say the biography argument is but an irrelevant detour or a colourful decoration.

We can agree that, when I am the defendant and you are the plaintiff in private law litigation, the court 'does not care whether [my] injuring you has changed my life', as Arthur Ripstein voices his criticism of Honoré.[19] An explanation for that fact is not hard to find. In the court's eyes, I did not merely have an ordinary reason not to injure you, a reason that competes in the ordinary way with all the various other reasons that I had at the time. Rather, not injuring you was my duty, or part of it. A duty, as we already know, is a categorical requirement. It binds me regardless of my personal goals at the time, and (what is more) to the exclusion of such competing reasons as my personal goals at the time may give me. Here are some examples of where duty calls, and success in personal goals is what falls to be sacrificed: 'I guess I'm going to miss my audition, because it would be wrong to leave you alone when you're this upset'; 'I was keen to try out my new recipe on our guests but I'll need to rethink, because you can't

[18] Irvin Kershner (dir), *Star Wars: The Empire Strikes Back* (20th Century Fox 1980), at 01:06:44.

[19] Ripstein, 'Private Law and Private Narratives', *Oxford Journal of Legal Studies* 20 (2000), 683 at 696.

feed this curry to someone with a nut allergy'; 'I suppose I'm not
going to make it to the stadium in time to compete, because now
I'll have to make sure everyone's alright, exchange insurance details, get the car towed away, and all that'; 'Sadly I'm not going to
make my fortune today, because I'm here as your representative
and I've got to think about this exclusively as a business opportunity for you'; 'I'll have to live with writing off my treasured
vintage car by swerving into that ditch, because I owe it to that
child not to kill her'. Some of these are cases, obviously, to which
the courts might end up having to attend. And when they do,
as Ripstein says, we would expect the courts to give short shrift
to those who whine about the personal goals (enthusiasms, voca-
tions, ambitions, investments, etc.) success in which they had to
sacrifice for the sake of doing their duty towards another.

So what would we have to say about such people on reading
their similarly whiny autobiographies? If we have any sense we
would also give them short shrift. Our reaction to them would be
similar, I hope, to reading the non-apologetic autobiography of
someone who actually failed in his duties. Bemoaning the fact that
one had to write off one's vintage car to save a child is not so very
far away, attitudinally, from simply running over the child to save
the car. Begrudging the fact that one had to devise a new menu
to suit a nut allergy sufferer is not so very far away, attitudinally,
from simply serving him the potentially lethal nuts. Such attitu-
dinal links will concern us further in Chapter 4, when we come
to discuss apologies. I mention them now because they help us to
give a more charitable interpretation to the biography argument,
one that helps to preserve its relevance to the law. Nothing in
the biography argument suggests that the story of my life, in the
relevant sense, is the story only of how my own life was affected
by what I did in the course of it. Nothing suggests that what I did
with my life means what I did *to* my life. Indeed, the story of my
life, in the relevant sense, may be very largely the story of what
I did to other people's lives, for better or for worse. If the story of
my life is going to be worth telling or hearing, indeed, that is the
kind of life it had better have been.

Return to Willy Loman. It is true that the story of his life is at
one level the story of what he does to his own life. Yes, he ruins
it. But the important part, for our purposes, is how he ruins it. It

is not by sacrificing his success in pursuit of his personal goals on the altar of duty. It is not that he is unable to make it as the big-shot salesman of his dreams because he is so busy doing right by his wife and children. If he is busy doing anything, in the scenes that portray his descent into ruin, he is busy doing *wrong* by his wife and children. He bullies Biff to the point of sending him off the rails ('I never got anywhere because you blew me so full of hot air I could never stand taking orders from anybody').[20] He cheats on Linda, and not in a classy way ('Where's my stockings? You promised me stockings, Willy!').[21] He thereby comprehensively disillusions Biff, who hitherto had belief in his father's honour, if nothing else, to hold onto ('You—you gave her Mama's stock-ings! ... You fake! You phony little fake!').[22] Even Willy's posthu-mous arrival at his goal of liberating the family from debt by his winning ways is as nothing when set against the loss he ironically inflicts on Linda by his suicide ('I made the last payment on the house today. Today, dear. And there'll be nobody home. [*A sob rises in her throat*]').[23]

Willy's ruining of his own life is principally owed, then, to his ruining of the lives of those around him. The contribution of the latter to the former is not, however, causal. It is not that he ruins the lives of others and then must face the consequences, the reckoning, the moment of truth, the sword of justice. No, he goes to his grave as vain and self-deceptive as ever, never really having faced up to anything. Insofar as Biff calls him to account towards the end ('You're going to hear the truth—what you are and what I am!'),[24] it still mainly serves to feed Willy's delusions ('that boy is going to be magnificent!').[25] Miller treats the suicide, then, not as some kind of comeuppance for Willy. There may be some subconscious longing for expiation in respect of the old wrongs, to be sure, but, as Willy tells it, it is but another fine scheme for making it big. (Biff will be 'outstanding with twenty thousand behind him'; 'it does take a great kind of man to crack the jungle').[26] The suicide is the *pièce de résistance* in the long cata-logue of ways in which Willy inflicts damage on his family by

---

[20] Miller, *Death of a Salesman* (n 10) 104.   [21] ibid 94.
[22] ibid 95.   [23] ibid 112.   [24] ibid 104.   [25] ibid 106.
[26] ibid 106.

self-aggrandizing fantasies. The contribution of this catalogue to his decline is not causal but constitutive. To use the distinction drawn at the start of the chapter, Willy does not ruin his own life *by* ruining the lives of others. Rather, he ruins his own life *in* ruining the lives of others. The scenes I mentioned portray, not what leads Willy to ruin, but rather the ruin itself.

As I warned in Chapter 1, it is a mistake to think of our duties as burdens that get in the way of our living our lives well. Although performing a duty may sometimes hold us back in some aspect of our lives by inhibiting our pursuit of a personal goal—getting a West End audition, making a fortune in currency speculation, having 'hundreds of salesmen and buyers at [one's] funeral',[27] etc.—what most reliably blights our lives is not the performance of our duties but the breach of them. It is a mistake, then, to contrast taking an interest in the wrongs we commit with taking an interest in how our lives are going. It is a mistake that makes it true but misleading to say that the court in a private law trial 'does not care whether [my] injuring you has changed my life'. True, the court does not care about the causal consequences for me of my having committed my wrong. My whining about how bad it has all been for me, or is going to be for me, falls on deaf ears.[28] Yet the court cares very much that it is my wrong, that it belongs to me, that it sits on my shoulders, that I am the one responsible. The point of the biography argument is merely to establish that there is *nothing* that belongs to me in the relevant sense, not even my intentions, if I disclaim the way my actions turn out. If I insist that the way my actions turn out is not my responsibility, then, 'having decided nothing and done nothing' I have nothing to show for myself, no life to call my own. Once the biography argument establishes that much, the role of the concept of biography in understanding responsibility harmlessly falls away. Your biography is just the story of what you do. And what matters first—in law, just as in love and loss and life—is what counts as your doing.

[27] ibid 63.

[28] Similarly, how it all fits into the story of my life. Ripstein finds in Honoré's treatment the thought that 'tort law is a way in which the state reinforces and encourages people to make sense of their own lives': see Ripstein, 'Private Narratives and Private Law' (n 19) 701. I see no trace of this thought myself.

4. Where justice comes in

In assessing how we did, how we fared, we cannot but think of ourselves (and others) as the agents of outcomes. This goes with us wherever we go. In language I favoured elsewhere, our outcome-responsibility is an aspect of our basic responsibility. Our basic responsibility is our ability and propensity, as rational beings, to explain ourselves (including our actions as well as our intentions, beliefs, desires, emotions, etc.) by giving reasons.[29] Since there are reasons to do things complete with their results—that much was established by the biography argument—actions complete with their results are among the things for which I am basically responsible. It falls to me, as a rational being, to account for my having left people bereft or offended, let the garden go to rack and ruin, poisoned people with my cooking, etc.

Since our outcome-responsibility goes with us wherever we go, it also goes into our transactions and conflicts with other people, and can be—often is—a bone of contention between us. 'You did this to me!', you assert. 'You were author of your own misfortune,' I reply. 'Actually this was the system's doing; you were both victims of that,' says the would-be peacemaker. The would-be peacemaker may not prevail. A further peacemaker may be needed to tackle the newly enlarged dispute to which the would-be peacemaker is now a party. And so on. In Chapter 3, I will raise doubts about the supposedly self-explanatory appeal of making peace. But I do not doubt that it is often a task of great importance. The law may aspire among other things to be the peacemaker of last resort, the one that makes peace among all the warring peacemakers, as well as among the original warriors. The law thereby comes under rational pressure to assign outcome-responsibility authoritatively when the assignment of outcome-responsibility is a bone of contention. It also comes under rational pressure to have rules to forestall such contention even where the

---

[29] J Gardner, 'The Mark of Responsibility' *Oxford Journal of Legal Studies* 23 (2003), 157. The idea has been further explored by Angela Smith, 'Responsibility as Answerability', *Inquiry* 58 (2015), 99, as well as in my own 'Relations of Responsibility' in R Cruft, M Kramer, and M Reiff (eds), *Crime, Punishment, and Responsibility: The Jurisprudence of Antony Duff* (OUP 2011).

contention has not yet erupted—rules to settle authoritatively in advance who is to count as the agent of which outcome and who for that reason has, in the eyes of the law, basic responsibility for its eventuation or avoidance.

The law may resist all this rational pressure, of course, and imaginably it could be right to do so. It is not true, as some imagine, that the nature of law sets no limits on the possible content of the law,[30] but it is also not true that there must be laws assigning outcome-responsibility merely because people are outcome-responsible apart from the law, and sometimes get into squabbles about it. The content of the law is shaped and reshaped by people—officials of a legal system—who must reflect, like the rest of us, on whether they are the right people, with the right tools at their disposal, to achieve what it is admittedly desirable to achieve. They may, of course, face a rational pressure to include certain rules in the law, and yet be amply justified in declining to do so. There may be powerful reasons for legal systems not to take a stand on particular aspects of people's conflicts, or more generally to avoid affirmatively regulating certain matters. The main reasons are boringly familiar.

(1) The law may be ineffective in improving how people act either because people ignore the law, or because they try to follow it but fail, or because they succeed in following it but doing so creates even bigger problems. For instance: drivers in the wrong will not admit they are in the wrong in case that is treated as an admission of legal liability, which would prompt their insurance company to decline to cover the claim. So then, by not admitting it, they are even more in the wrong.

(2) With its rather limited arsenal of rather crude techniques, the law threatens people's freedom more, or more damagingly, than some other techniques for improving how people act. The loss of freedom may be too high a price to pay for whatever improvements the law is able bring about. That explains some principles of legal toleration such as J S Mill's

---

[30] See my brief discussion in 'Law as a Leap of Faith as Others See It', *Law and Philosophy* 33 (2014), 813 at 835.

famous 'harm principle',[31] and various rights held against the authorities such as those of freedom of speech, freedom of conscience, reproductive and sexual freedom, freedom of movement, etc.

(3) The law regulates by the use of general (many case) rules and some problems are such that any such rule will fail to accommodate their rational complexity. If left indeterminate enough to accommodate that rational complexity, the rule will only add an additional threat to people's freedom by leaving them in a state of bafflement about how to stay on the right side of the law. Here lies the problem of the rule of law, and in particular the problem of how to prevent our concern for it veering into legalism (the obsession with 'legal certainty').

(4) Finally, and for present purposes most importantly, we must always remember that the law allocates the help it gives to people, and the burdens it thereby creates—including but not limited to the burdens on freedom—to particular people. So there is always the problem of how to do the allocating of such legal goods and ills, which is a problem of justice.

I have formulated these as if they were all rational constraints on the creation and use of laws, the affirmative reasons for which lie elsewhere. But item 1 on the list is simply the flip-side of the most general affirmative reason for legal regulation. The law exists to improve how people (including its own officials) will act. Indeed, the reason should be stated even more capaciously than that. The law exists to improve people's conformity with reasons that already apply to them, including but not limited to reasons to act. If the law can make it the case (or make it more likely) that I will think what I have reason to think or feel what I have reason to feel, that is a reason for the law to step in. But let's focus for now on a less troubling type of case. Suppose the law can take steps to ensure (or make it more likely) that I will do some duty that I already have—say a duty not to let my friends down or a duty to protect my children from starvation or a duty to phone my

[31] For the classic formulation see Mill, 'On Liberty' in *On Liberty, Utilitarianism and Other Essays* (ed Philp and Rosen, OUP 2015), at 13.

elderly mother at the weekend. This is without further ado a reason for the law to take those very steps.

I should emphasize that this is not because of something special about the law. It applies to all of us all of the time, in ways that Chapter 3 will make clearer. If I can help you to do right by your friends or your children or your mother, that is without further ado a reason for me to do it—to create opportunities or incentives or capacities or facilities that will help you to do right by everyone. I do not need to be in a special relationship with you for this rudimentary reason to be relevant to what I do. But I do need to be in a position actually to help. And often I am not. Often my intervention would be more of a hindrance than a help. Maybe I don't understand enough about what is going on with you, maybe I don't have time or energy to intervene properly given all the other demands upon me (including my own duties), maybe my own judgment is no more reliable than yours concerning what would count as an improvement in your actions, maybe my intervention will irritate you and entrench you in your original mistakes, etc. It is easy to see that the affirmative reason for intervention here simply entails the constraint on my acting to serve it. If what I am about to do won't in fact help you, then what I am about to do won't be what I have, *ex hypothesi*, a reason to do, namely to help you to do the right thing. So now I have, so far as we know, no reason to do it.

That is also the most common situation with the law. Why is there no great temptation to think of the law as having failed the Loman family by failing to get Willy to do his duty? Actually, the presupposition of the question is not quite true. As we witness the ways in which Linda has to struggle with Willy's narcissism we may sometimes be tempted to shout the word 'divorce' in a crowded theatre. Applying for a divorce is a private law power the successful exercise of which (even in the late 1940s) would have scaled back and simplified Willy's duties towards Linda in a way that might have made his performing them more likely. One possible way to improve a person's performance of his duties, after all, is to have him bear fewer and simpler duties. Divorce would not have made such a big difference to Willy's duties towards his sons, but it might have startled or constrained or nudged him into performing them better. Short of divorce, however, the very idea of the law being drawn into the situation (Biff suing Willy for negligently sending him off the rails, Happy being made a ward of court to protect him from growing up like Willy, Linda calling in the vice squad to deal with the stockings incident, etc.) may strike you as positively comical.

I suspect that is primarily because you are fairly sure, without having to give it much thought, that the law would be of little help in the Loman case. Leaving aside divorce, Willy would surely not have become a better father or husband thanks to anything the law might have thrown at him. The destructive conflicts between Willy and Biff would surely not have been mitigated by being litigated. Would any of the family really have lived better lives, do we imagine, thanks to the law's attempting to improve the dynamics of the family, short of breaking it up? (Interestingly, the law does step in with Biff as a young adult, when he gets into his cycle of thievery. The criminal law is treated, in a rare concession by Miller to the American Way, as having been helpful in the longer run. Seemingly, his brief jail time helped Biff to see what had become of him and why, and thus to set himself on a better—more humble—path.[32])

Of course, lack of effectiveness is not our only worry about interventions in the actions of others, whether by the law or by anyone else. That was only item 1 on our list. Even when an intervention is effective in improving what someone does, it may be destructive in all sorts of other ways because of the means used. Different techniques of intervention do their different kinds and degrees of damage in different situations, and thus yield different reasons to avoid them in spite of their effectiveness in improving the actions in which they intervene. The law is sometimes thought to be uniquely challenged in this respect because its technique is said to be exclusively and distinctively coercion. That is thought to subject it to a radically different set of constraints, maybe understated by items 2, 3, and 4 on my list. This difference is, however, exaggerated. The law may keep coercion up its sleeve as a last resort, but relatively rarely needs to resort to it in influencing what people do. Coercion is, as Hart put it, a 'secondary provision ... for a breakdown in case the primary

---

[32] Miller, *Death of a Salesman* (n 10) 104.

intended peremptory reasons [exercises of legal authority] are not accepted as such.'[33] Nor is the law the only user of this technique, namely authority coupled with the prospect of coercion in the event of nonconformity. Employers resort to the same technique all the time, and so, alas, do domestic abusers on the next rung of the ladder up from Willy Loman. The abuser tends to fold manipulation in as well, which helps him to sustain his periodic use of authority and coercion. Whereas the law relies on the myth of its unconditional legitimacy to do the same. Nevertheless, the techniques of the law are not unique. Nor do they boil down to just one. They are not even, typically, the most dangerous to our freedom. All the same, thanks to item 3 on our list of constraints, the law's techniques are relatively few and not very flexible, and that makes them rather prone to create collateral damage, and hence to call for additional constraints of the kind identified under item 2 on our list. Often the constraints under items 2 and 3 added together mean that, even though the law is capable of improving what we do, for instance by getting us better to fulfil our duties towards each other, it should decline to intervene. Sometimes that is true even when intervention is urgently needed, e.g. to tackle an escalating conflict. Sometimes the law must, in spite of the urgency, leave it to someone else to sort it out, possibly to the parties to the conflict themselves. Or sometimes the law must at least wait to intervene until called upon for help by one or other of the parties, so as to reduce the risk of disproportionate, clumsy, and premature solutions.

You may say that item 4 on our list is different. The problem of justice, you may say, is not a problem of whether the law is used to improve people's behaviour but only of how it is used. The other principles I mentioned affect whether somebody's action should be subject to legal intervention. But only when we decide that legal intervention is called for, you may say, do we arrive at the question of how to do so justly. This contention puts too big a distance, however, between the problem of justice and the others I mentioned. Sometimes, the main argument against an obscure or intolerant law, for example, is that its obscurity or intolerance

---

[33] HLA Hart, 'Commands and Authoritative Legal Reasons' in Hart, *Essays on Bentham* (Clarendon Press 1982), 254.

would be unjust to some particular people, would put too big a
burden on their freedom in particular (say), rather than eroding
people's freedom in general. Whatever else it shows, this shows
that there are some matters that should not be regulated by law
because the regulation could not be just. Some people think of
this as an absolute constraint. If some matter cannot be regulated
justly by law, regulating it by law is ruled out irrespective of competing considerations. Justice has lexical priority, at any rate in
the law.[34] This thesis is too strong. Justice does not have lexical
priority, even in the law. But some legal institutions—notably
the courts—have a special responsibility for doing justice and this
puts a considerable rational pressure on the law not to regulate
matters which it cannot regulate justly, even when it could regulate them effectively, tolerantly, and consistently with the rule
of law.

The thought that the courts have a special responsibility for
doing justice may prompt a different (and in some ways contrasting) worry about how justice is represented on my list. Item
4 should be up there with item 1, you may say, for like item 1 it
offers (in the guise of a constraint) an affirmative reason for legal
intervention. Justice is to be done and this is already a reason,
if not the pre-eminent reason, maybe even the only reason, for
the courts, and perhaps therefore for the law, to be involved in
anything. Avoiding injustice is no mere constraint. This worry,
however, betrays a misunderstanding of the relationship between
item 1 and item 4. Inasmuch as somebody can be helped by the
law to avoid breaching a duty of justice, item 1 on the list already
applies. It applies because this is a case in which their actions can
be improved by the law. There then arises the question, however,
of whether their actions can be improved by the law without the
law's perpetrating its own injustice. That is where item 4 on the
list enters the picture. There is no reason to assume that when
the law helps people to perform their duties of justice under item
1, it acts justly in doing so under item 4. Nor is there any reason
to think that, when the law acts justly under item 4 in helping

---

[34] The Rawlsian view, in J Rawls, *A Theory of Justice* (Belknap Press 1971), 3, is
that: 'laws . . . no matter how efficient or well-arranged must be reformed or abol-
ished if they are unjust.'

someone to perform their duties under item 1, the duties in question are duties of justice.

You may think that all duties owed to another are duties of justice. But consider how evaluatively limiting that thought is. Perhaps Willy's passing his wife's supply of stockings to someone with whom he is having a sleazy fling is fundamentally an injustice. It is a misallocation of the stockings. It is not surprising that the young Biff, with a typical teenage fixation on injustice, focuses on this wrong of his father's above all others. But anyone who thinks that the primary wrong in the sleazy fling itself is its injustice is putting the cart before the horse. The primary wrong is, of course, the infidelity. We may think that the infidelity was compounded by injustice because, say, a wife as wonderful as Linda does not deserve her husband's infidelity (still less with that floozy!), or because Linda has already had to put up with more than her fair share of infidelity, or because Willy has already got away with too much infidelity, etc. But, as these formulations show, the claimed injustice is a secondary wrong—it lies in the misallocation of infidelity, not in the infidelity per se. I suppose that some may be tempted to redescribe the infidelity per se as a misallocation of sexual services, or of affection, or of attention, or maybe even of fidelity. But if you put it that way to Linda, I like to think she would say that (stockings aside) what she wanted was not a share of whatever it was that Willy was offering to his girlfriend. She only wanted him not to have one. In saying that, she is objecting to his infidelity—even if some others, maybe with more teenage priorities, would object more to the injustice of having a husband that is, so to speak, wrongly allocated.

Even if you don't accept that there can be breaches of duties owed to others that are not injustices, the fact remains that the law's interventions to help avoid breaches of duty is covered by item 1 on my list, even when the breaches *are* injustices. Under item 1, the question is whether the law helped to prevent or reduce those injustices. Under item 4, by contrast, the question is whether the law managed to avoid adding its own injustices in the process of providing that help. Item 4, on this view, gives no affirmative reason for legal intervention. It sets a constraint on the ways in which the law is to make those interventions for which item 1 provides the affirmative reason.

5. The allocation of outcomes in life and in law

This returns us to the debate between Honoré and Ripstein. Here, I think, is what is most fundamentally at issue between them. Honoré takes the question of whether we are outcome-responsible apart from the law (and indeed apart from any other mode of social organization) to be the first question. In support of the view that we are outcome-responsible apart from the law (and its ilk), Honoré offers what I reconstructed as the biography argument. Yet he gives over a great deal more space to the question of whether and how it is just for the law (and its ilk) to *make something* of our outcome-responsibility, for example by having us pay for losses we cause or occasion to others. He addresses his arguments mainly to those who think there is something unjust about the law's doing this, e.g. because it unjustly compounds our moral luck. He assumes that there is a reason for the law to uphold the outcome-responsibility that we have apart from the law, and he proceeds as if the problem were to avoid the law's treating us unjustly when it acts on that reason. So he does not anticipate an opponent like Ripstein. Ripstein denies that whether we are outcome-responsible apart from the law is even relevant to the question of whether we should be treated by the law as outcome-responsible. He thinks, in other words, that item 1 on my list above is not the right place to begin. We should go straight to item 4. We should focus from the outset on the justice of the law's assignment of outcome-responsibility, which is determined without regard to whether the law helps to uphold whatever outcome-responsibility we may have apart from the law. In Ripstein's own words, 'the sort of outcome-responsibility that shows up in tort law is not simply a refined version of the sort at stake in our deepest self-understandings', i.e. as it appears in the biography argument.[35]

Why would the two domains of outcome-responsibility come apart so radically? In some of his formulations Ripstein seems to suggest that the disconnect has something to do with the

---

[35] Ripstein, 'Private Law and Private Narratives' (n 19) 694.

interpersonal character of law, or at least of private law.[36] Private
law does not simply regulate what I do but regulates what I do to
others. But this feature, as Ripstein makes clear, is ever-present in
life outside the law too. I explored that fact in Chapter 1; I also
reprised it in section 3 in this chapter. As *Death of a Salesman* illustrated, in the story of one's life one cannot ignore the ways
in which one scarred, or indeed brightened, other people's lives.
Doing well in life is already a largely interpersonal business, as
Ripstein acknowledges.[37] Indeed, acting justly is a significant part
of it.[38] People who take all the credit when things go well and
point the fingers at others when things go badly are acting unjustly and their biographies (more often autobiographies!) are
usually tragi-comic affairs. That shows that biography itself, as
well as the life of the subject of biography, is a partly allocative
activity. Ripstein points that out too.[39] He agrees that there is
justice to be done in personal life and in the recounting of it.

And yet Ripstein does hold out for the idea that where the law
of torts is concerned, holding people outcome-responsible is 'allocative in [a special] sense'.[40] This is what he means:

Our interpretation of our own [outcome-]responsibility, and our responses to it, need not be compatible, because from the first-person
perspective in which outcome responsibility is so often important,
there can be more (or less) outcome responsibility than there are outcomes ... [M]y autobiography and your autobiography need not be
compatible, any more than each of our own sense of who we are needs
to be compatible with that of the other.[41]

It is different, as Ripstein says, in the law of torts, and more generally in private law, because in that setting there is an element of
zero-sum game. It is not open to the courts, faced with a claim for
damages, to allocate the same outcome to both the plaintiff and
the defendant. For any unit of loss, either the defendant is liable
to pay damages in respect of it or the loss rests with the plaintiff.
In this setting, a 'just resolution requires that there be a single and
determinate answer.'[42]

---

[36] ibid 683 and 692.   [37] ibid 696.   [38] ibid 695.
[39] ibid 692.   [40] ibid 691.   [41] ibid 691–2.   [42] ibid 692.

Agreed. But that only returns us to a point we made in section 4. When people get into destructive conflict, peacemakers may be needed. No doubt some peacemakers succeed by fudging so that the parties are bamboozled into thinking that they have no differences. Other peacemakers may succeed by containing the conflict so that it becomes more constructive and less destructive, so that people learn to accept their differences. But the law's distinctive way of being a peacemaker is to provide an authoritative determination of the matters that are in contention. This it cannot do, when outcome-responsibility is in contention, by refusing to make an authoritative determination of where the outcome-responsibility lies. So inconsistent assignments of outcome-responsibility that are tolerable when there is no conflict in need of legal resolution are no longer tolerable in the law. If the relevant determinacy cannot be found in the raw facts apart from the law, then the law needs to manufacture its own determinacy. That is what it does with traffic light colours, income tax rates, and the choice of a system for electing a government. It is just the same where outcome-responsibility is concerned.

Ripstein also seems to concede this, although perhaps he does not think he is conceding it. He observes that: 'legal institutions are not always needed to make outcome-responsibility more determinate, because outcome-responsibility does not always need to be interpersonal.'[43] Here, 'interpersonal' takes on a technical meaning, I think. It does not mean 'a matter of what one person did to another'. It means roughly 'zero-sum'. And Ripstein is right that outcome-responsibility does not always need to be zero-sum. Yet sometimes it does. And when it does the law sometimes needs to be the one to make it so, by deciding that the changes in your life were my doing, and mine to pay for. How does this help to show, as Ripstein needs to show, that outcome-responsibility in the law has a different basis from outcome-responsibility in ordinary life? It shows the opposite. The problem to which the law provides a solution is the problem that outcome-responsibility in ordinary life is not allocated determinately enough for some purposes. So the law allocates it, where the 'it' refers to the very same outcome-responsibility that was not sufficiently allocated apart

---

[43] ibid 693.

from the law. It does not refer to some quite different thing that happens to bear the same name.

This brings us to Ripstein's third gambit. He tells us that, on the contrary, outcome-responsibility is a quite different thing that happens to bear the same name. The word 'responsibility' famously carries many senses and Honoré is changing senses in mid-argument when he moves from the constitution of one's life story to the acquisition of one's tort liabilities. The former he calls 'implication-responsibility' and the latter 'displacement-responsibility'. In the case of the latter,

[r]ather than acknowledging my deed, I must undo its effects, or take them back. ... I am [displacement-]responsible for injuring you if my injuring you was a wrongful interruption of the ordinary course of things; liability in damages is a way of making it as though that interruption had never taken place. Now if the interruption is to be understood in terms of the private stories that either of us tell ourselves, money damages would be a peculiar and ineffectual means of restoring normality.[44]

Like several other Ripsteinian references to the biography argument, the reference to 'the private stories that [we] tell ourselves' is seriously misleading. It makes it sound as though the narrative to which Honoré refers, the story of our lives, need not have any rational impetus or any rational structure. But recall that an Honoré-style narrative, as I explained earlier, was a story of reasons, of conformity to reasons and non-conformity to reasons. It was a story, as I said, that a rational being cannot avoid being interested in. The basic reasons from which others derive, as I said, are reasons to succeed, meaning reasons to act complete with the results. These include numerous reasons concerning the treatment of other people: reasons not to kill them, reasons to help them, reasons not to upset them, reasons to give them their due allocation. They are reasons actually to do these things and not merely to try to do them, or decide to do them. There may, as Donne says, be glory in the failed attempt, but that does not mean, as Donne also points out, that there is no failure in the failed attempt. How could it mean that?

---

[44] ibid 695.

In the next three chapters I will set out to persuade you that these reasons to succeed, which the biography argument puts at the centre of rational life, not only underlie the human impetus to apologize, to rue the day, to atone, to account for oneself, and so on. They not only underlie the various actions that Ripstein is willing to treat as characteristic of implication-responsibility. They also underlie the human impetus to repair the damage one did, including, in some cases, by paying for it. In other words, I will be trying to convince you, against Ripstein, that there is nothing 'peculiar' or 'ineffectual', so far as the conclusions of the biography argument are concerned, about 'restoring normality' in precisely the same way that tort law would have one restore it when one pays reparative damages. Apology and damages have the same rational impetus, although in a way they have contrasting and complementary justifications. Those will be the themes of Chapters 3 and 4: roughly, the justification of damages in Chapter 3, the justification of apology in Chapter 4. That the impetus in both cases is the impetus to 'restore normality' will be the topic of Chapter 5. That there is no Ripsteinian divide between personal life and private law—well that, of course, is the theme of all of the chapters of this book taken together.

3

It's Not About the Money

'It is not crucial what one does; it is crucial what one does next.'

Robert Musil[1]

1. The clamour for amends

Recent decades have seen multiplying and ever more vocal demands for governments, corporations, and other organizations to make amends, or to arrange for amends to be made, for wrongdoing perpetrated by them, or by their predecessors, or by people that they are thought to represent or that are thought to represent them. These demands are typically made by pressure groups or community leaders purporting to speak on behalf of those who were wronged, or on behalf of successors or descendants who claim to be blighted by the wrongdoing's legacy. The demands are typically for amends to be made under one or both of two headings; the expression 'making amends', as I will use it, should be understood broadly enough to cover both. The first form of amend-making is apology, an expression of regret that conveys an admission of responsibility. The second form of amend-making is reparation, a contribution to the cost of repairing whatever damage was done by the wrongs. Some campaigners seek only one of these; others seek both.

I have some reservations about this widespread clamour for amends. That is not to say that I am unsympathetic. We should welcome signs of growing confidence on the part of previously silenced and marginalized groups. We should also welcome the climate of openness, characterized by a greater emphasis on freedom of information, in which wrongdoing by the powerful is routinely exposed by historians and other expert investigators in nauseating but compelling detail. And we should surely welcome

---

[1] Musil, *Der Mann ohne Eigenschaften, vol 2* (Rowohlt Verlag 1933), ch 10: 'Nie ist das, was man tut, entscheidend, sondern immer erst das, was man danach tut.'

From Personal Life to Private Law. John Gardner © John Gardner 2018. Published 2018 by Oxford University Press.

the genuine moral progress thanks to which, in many of these cases, nobody any longer stoops, at least in public, to doubting whether the wrongdoing was indeed wrong. Nobody, or almost nobody, says: slavery was fine; dispossession of aboriginal populations and ensuing colonial rule was nothing to be ashamed of; apartheid was innocuous. Even if we are still not so good at seeing the error in our current ways, we human beings have in many cases come to see the error of our former ways, and that is a small something we can be proud of.

But it does not follow that we should view the clamour for amends with an uncritical eye. You may think, as I often think, that demands are being issued to the wrong people, or by the wrong people, or on behalf of the wrong people. With regimes long ago overthrown, empires long gone, corporations long since merged or restructured, and populations blended across the generations, maybe there is nobody left whose place it is to make amends and, in some cases, for similar reasons, nobody justly entitled to claim or receive them. With my own conspicuous Celtic-Viking heritage, I could not help laughing at the 2007 discussion, during a Danish official visit to Ireland, of whether the Danes had apologized, and should have apologized, for coastal raids on the Irish that took place 1,200 years before.[2] I like to think that my Irish cousins were making fun of po-faced modern pieties, as well as playing on what they took to be Danish naivety. But maybe not? After all, some of those injured or bereaved in the 1999 rail collision at Ladbroke Grove in London sought, and were apparently glad to receive, a grovelling apology offered in court on behalf of infrastructure operator Network Rail eight years later. That was in spite of the fact that Network Rail was created after (and partly because of) the collision, which took place when the tracks were maintained by its discredited and defunct predecessor Railtrack plc. Different ownership, different board, different mission, different managers, different methods of working, and a different regulatory regime. Are we so besotted with amend-making that we scarcely bat an eyelid at such absurdities? Is the idea simply

² Lars Eriksen, 'Dane guilt' *The Guardian* (16 August 2007), on the news blog at https://www.theguardian.com/news/blog/2007/aug/16/notsosorryaf.

that someone, never mind who, must abase himself to purge the taint of wrongdoing?[3]

In a related vein, one may think that the lawyer's slogan *ubi ius, ibi remedium*—where there's a right, let there be a remedy—casts a legalistic pall over modern culture, of which the rise in demands for collective or corporate amends is but another symptom. As Aristotle pointed out, it is possible to be 'a stickler for one's rights in a bad way',[4] like the person who wakes a sleeping passenger in a sparsely occupied train carriage to claim his particular reserved seat. Why not just sit somewhere else? Sometimes we should think of an old grievance as a sleeping traveller, better left to sleep. It is not always noble or righteous to seek a remedy, to confront those who wronged us, to demand justice (even when one truly has justice on one's side). To my eyes it is a sign of growing alienation from our fellow human beings, and hence of a countertrend to the moral progress I already mentioned, that so many people, and so many groups of people, nowadays react to the exposure or rec-ollection of wrongdoing with a vaguely litigious set of demands, including demands for the rest of us to back them up on pain of being tarred as accomplices after-the-fact. Of course, it is also a sign of growing alienation that people feel the *need* to be such sticklers for their rights, for it suggests that the spontaneous re-sponses of wrongdoers are often severely out of order. Denial and evasion of responsibility are the orders of the day. But that too seems to be partly a consequence of the vaguely litigious spirit of the age, in which spontaneously ameliorative reactions by wrong-doers are often seized upon as opportunities to force something more out of them (and hence are often treated by insurance com-panies as prejudicial admissions that call for a denial of cover).

So much for my doubts as an amateur cultural critic. My doubts as a philosopher have a different source. Reflection on the rise of demands for apology and reparation makes me realize how little we really understand about the rational significance of the past, about how the fact that things were already done (or

---

[3] Hugh Muir, 'Catalogue of Railtrack failures that led to deadly collision' *The Guardian* (27 March 2007). For reasons that will emerge in s 5, I have no similar difficulty with Network Rail paying the tort damages.

[4] *Nicomachean Ethics* 1137[b]34.

not done) can count as a reason, or at any rate supply a reason, for doing something else now. We therefore do not understand much, it seems to me, about the making of amends. That is in spite of a recent spate of extended philosophical treatments of the subject, including notable books by Trudy Govier, Elizabeth Spelman, Aaron Lazare, Margaret Urban Walker, Nick Smith, and Linda Radzik.[5] Indeed, it was reading these works that made me appreciate that we do not understand much about the rational significance of the past. For, although they differ greatly on the details, these authors all agree in locating the business of making amends—the business of apology and reparation—inside the larger topic of *reconciliation*. The mood of the times, reflected in a different way in each of these books, is to think that apology and reparation alike are to be understood and justified as tools for restoring or rectifying damaged relationships. That strikes me as a bad way to get started. Allow me to explain why.

2. On reconciliation

Reconciliation means putting our conflict behind us, settling our differences, healing our rift. Often that is a good thing, no doubt. It is one of the reasons why we have courts. Indeed, it is one of the reasons why we have law. But it is not true that conflict between people is in itself bad. Should we not be inclined to harbour negative feelings towards wrongdoers, and to challenge them about their actions, if putting them on the spot would do some good? Should we prefer false geniality or, perhaps even worse, true geniality? I doubt it. Conflict is bad, it seems to me, only inasmuch as it tends to draw people into cycles of mistaken belief, overblown emotion, and unjustified action. Consider the comments sections on many media websites. The format encourages instant, short, and simple reactions that often come across as aggressive, breed

---

[5] Govier, *Forgiveness and Revenge* (Routledge 2002); Spelman, *Repair: The Impulse to Restore in a Fragile World* (Beacon Press 2003); Lazare, *On Apology* (Oxford University Press 2004); Walker, *Moral Repair: Reconstructing Moral Relations after Wrongdoing* (Cambridge University Press 2006); Smith, *I Was Wrong: The Meanings of Apologies* (Cambridge University Press 2008); Radzik, *Making Amends: Atonement in Morality, Law, and Politics* (Oxford University Press 2009).

animosity, and entrench opponents. Opponents are thereby encouraged to add instant, short, and simple reactions that come
across as aggressive, breed animosity, and ... you get the picture.
It tends to become a 'Punch-and-Judy-Fest'.[6] The problem is not
the conflict as such. There are some people with whom one has
every reason to remain at odds. The problem is the escalation of
the conflict into mean-spiritedness, self-righteousness, pettiness,
intolerance, bigotry, and so on. Such escalation, I would be the
first to agree, should be avoided. When apology and reparation
help to break the cycle, by helping the warring parties to recon-
cile, and thereby stemming the rising tide of ill-feeling that afflicts
them, that is something to be said for apology and reparation.

So I can see little to dissent from in, for example, Margaret
Walker's observation that wrongdoing often

> creates a relationship charged with powerful negative feelings and bur-
> dened with losses that can continue to mar a victim's [and, we may add, a
> wrongdoer's] life ... In relationships characterized by violation, violence,
> and complacent and profound contempt, any attempt to regain or stabilize
> the trust that holds us together in moral relations will have to find a foun-
> dation in hope ... Restorative justice captures this need for renewed confi-
> dence and trust that will 'restore' us to a working moral order.[7]

Treading the same path as many others in the recent literature,
Walker goes on to connect these truisms to the rational appeal of
apology and reparation in the following way:

> In restorative justice ... material amends play instrumental and sym-
> bolic roles in the attempt to set things right between people. Reparation
> often includes restitution or compensation to make repair concrete and
> in some cases to give weight to other interpersonal gestures, such as
> apologies and expressions of sorrow, shame, [or] guilt or the wish to
> make amends. Some studies of restorative justice practice find that vic-
> tims value symbolic reparation more than its material tokens.[8]

Again, there is little to provoke dissent here. In this passage and
elsewhere, Walker paints a plausible picture of what 'victims

---

[6] Elizabeth Jensen, 'NPR website to get rid of comments' http://www.npr.
org/sections/ombudsman/2016/08/17/489516952/. (The gendered implication of
the expression 'Punch-and-Judy-Fest' is also apt.)

[7] Walker, *Moral Repair* (n 5), 209–10.   [8] ibid 210–11.

value' and hence of the everyday psychology of the making of amends. But can this everyday psychology represent the whole story, or the basic story, of what apology and reparation are about? Here are a couple of doubts expressed as questions.

(a) What about those wrongs that do not (or no longer) leave behind ill-feeling or hostility or other catalysts of conflict or conflict-escalation? Should we conclude that the case for apology and repair is missing in such cases? Does the case for reparation and apology evaporate (as opposed to merely becoming less urgent) when there is mutual indifference, mutual resignation, or mutual obliviousness? What about the case in which, far from seeking reconciliation, both wrongdoer and wronged would rather forget each other, put it all down to experience, move on without further ado, and stop dwelling on the past? Suppose they can do that, because we can give them a drug that enables them to forget each other quickly. Is there (all else being equal) nothing to be said in favour of administering apologies and repairs instead of administering the drug? If there is still something to be said for apologies and repairs, are we already forced to the rule-consequentialist gambit of putting this down to the value of having a general rule in favour of apology and repair that does not bow to every weird counter-example in which ordinary human psychology is altered, replaced, or otherwise stipulated out of the story? As you know from Chapter 1, I am not one of those who thinks that rule-consequentialist gambits are doomed to fail. Far from it. But we may well ask: Where the making of amends is concerned, are we driven to these gambits so soon?

In Steven Soderbergh's film *Sex, Lies, and Videotape*, mild-mannered but troubled twenty-nine-year-old Graham returns to Baton Rouge after nine seemingly aimless years away. By his own account a recovering 'pathological liar' who 'used to express [his] feelings nonverbally' so that he 'often scared people who were close to [him]', Graham has been drawn back in vague hope of reconciliation with his estranged college girlfriend Elizabeth, who is living nearby. Not a rekindling of their romance, Graham makes clear, but 'a sense of closure . . . a resolution of some sort'. We interpret: as part of his effort to reform his character, as the next step in his recovery, he hopes to make amends of some kind for his wrongs. New friend Ann, having insinuated herself into the role of confidante, is scathing. 'That's pathetic,' she chides. 'You just can't walk up to her and show her you've changed like it's some gift or something.'[9] In any event Graham soon discovers, from another source, that he may have held a rose-tinted image of Elizabeth at the time of their relationship, not merely a sepia-tinted one afterwards. By the end of the movie, it seems, Ann and Graham are lovers. All thought of amends, all thought of reconciliation, indeed all thought of Elizabeth (whom we never meet), has evaporated. Her ghostly presence, it seems, was needed primarily to engineer the confession–confrontation that draws the lonely-hearts Graham and Ann together, each fleeing from their respective former lives of desperate self-deception (the lies of the title).

Linda Radzik lists *Sex, Lies, and Videotape* among 'literary and filmic treatments' that leave one 'feeling skeptical' about the making of amends. 'We can become better people in the future, but can we ever make up for the past?'[10] That is a good question, and one to which I will return in the next chapter. It is also a possible question to take home from Soderbergh's film. But it is not the question that I take home. The film leaves me feeling sceptical, not about the making of amends, but about the longing for reconciliation. Soderbergh, it seems to me, deliberately leaves open whether Graham owes something to Elizabeth in virtue of his past wrongs. He lets that question peter out. He even leaves us unsure who wronged whom in that relationship, and in what ways. His point is that, whatever Graham's debt to Elizabeth, or Elizabeth's debt to Graham, all things considered it is now better left unpaid. The reconciliation envisaged by Graham is a pipe dream. Elizabeth has long since moved on. Ann, meanwhile, is there to serve a role something like that of the imaginary drug I conjured up two paragraphs ago. She is what Graham needs to allow him to move on as well, to stop living in a romanticized past and brooding on his own role in its failure.

So Soderbergh leaves us, I think, with exactly my first question: does the most basic case for apology or repair evaporate when reconciliation is a pipe dream? Or it is that in such

[9] Soderbergh (dir), *Sex, Lies and Videotape* (FF Classics 1989). All the lines quoted here are from the long climactic scene that runs from 1:19:06 to 1:31:32.
[10] Radzik, *Making Amends* (n 5) 4.

circumstances the basic case remains, the rational pull to make amends is still there, but it can be better to let it go, like the trespass of the sleeping passenger on the train? Thanks to Soderbergh, you'll notice the question now arises without the need for any weird counter-example in which ordinary human psychology is altered, replaced, or otherwise stipulated out of the story. Notwithstanding Graham's unusual fetishistic interest in making and watching videotapes in which he interviews women acquaintances about their sex lives with other partners, it really is all about ordinary human psychology. That is part of the film's intelligent charm. Odd pastime, ordinary people.

(b) Now for my second question. Why would anyone, including the person wronged, think of repair and apology in particular as suitable measures by which to secure the relevant reconciliation? What gives these particular actions their special salience, and hence their special hold over human psychology? Why not dancing, taking a day off work, learning Arabic, or doodling in red ink? Why not throwing a ball, throwing a party, throwing a tantrum, or throwing a kiss? Is it just that certain actions—reparation and apology—happen to have acquired a conventional meaning that makes them the ones that are apt to do the reconciliatory work? Or is there something about these actions, quite apart from their conventional meanings, that makes them suitable to do that work, such that their acquisition of those conventional meanings, such as they are, is no accident?

Compare duelling with swords or with pistols. At some times in some places and in some social circles, one proper response to having been wronged was to challenge the wrongdoer to a duel. The wrongdoer was regarded as bound to accept the challenge. Correctly carried out, the duel was regarded as a way of settling the parties' differences, even if it had to be posthumous on the part of at least one of them. So here is Turgenev, replying in fine 1860s Russian style to the challenge of an aggrieved Tolstoy:

I fully recognize your right to demand satisfaction from me in a duel ... I can say in all honesty that I would willingly have faced your fire in order thereby to make amends for my really insane words.[11]

---

[11] Quoted in AV Knowles (ed), *Turgenev's Letters* (Charles Scribner's Sons 1983), 97.

How exactly would Turgenev's submitting to a deadly shoot-out between the two of them have served to *make amends* for his abusive outburst? True, reparative language is often used in connection with the duel. What is at stake, apparently, is the restoration of the wronged person's honour. But that just deepens the mystery. Is there a relevant account of what honour is that does not already specify duelling as a suitable way to restore it? Is there any independent reason—independent, that is, of idiosyncratic social meanings that the practice may have in particular times and places and *milieux*—to regard duelling as a way of settling differences? No doubt some features of the duel can be independently rationalized. Yet the ritual also seems rife with arbitrary features that carry conventional meanings in a certain social setting but are mysterious apart from it. Anyone who proposed challenging a wrongdoer to a duel in Europe today, barring certain gangster contexts where *burlesque* versions of the old honour code still prevail, would be likely to be met with the bemused reaction: 'What would that achieve? Hasn't there been enough bad blood between you two already?'

A century or so hence, will they perhaps be saying the same kind of thing about our contemporary amend-making practices—about apologizing and repairing? Are these similarly arbitrary placatory rituals, rituals that just *happen* to placate (when they do placate) late modern types like ourselves? Or do they have a timeless rationale that helps us to understand *why* they placate people when they do? The question, I emphasize, is not about particular contemporary ways of apologizing or repairing. It is not about sending flowers, say, or sending a cheque to cover the cost of a new bicycle. Attempting to repair with money is sometimes regarded even now as a vulgar *faux pas*, an insult added to injury, and we can imagine that meaning taking over completely in days to come. (Recall those 'studies of restorative justice' mentioned by Walker.) The standard apologetic meaning of a floral bouquet, meanwhile, may some day wither and die of triteness. That much is easy enough to see. The question remains, however, whether the same fate could await reparation and apology as such, quite apart from any particular techniques we may have for furnishing them. If the case for apologizing or repairing in the wake of one's wrongs is only that one thereby promotes reconciliation, then it is hard to see why they too should not die out in favour of as-yet-unknown twenty-third century rituals for promoting reconciliation. Whatever works, you might say. Nothing makes repair and apology salient apart from the fact that they are, currently, what works. Nothing about them makes them especially *suitable* to work.

These two lines of questioning point in the same direction. Both invite us to look for arguments in favour of apology and reparation that are independent of their contribution to reconciliation. Only when we have such arguments can we see (a) why we might still be drawn towards apology and reparation even when we don't seek or need reconciliation, and (b) when we do seek or need reconciliation, how apology and reparation qualify as suitable actions by which to achieve it. To find answers we need to go behind the fashionable reconciliatory rationales.

Some who favour those reconciliatory rationales may say that I am missing the point of what they are saying. For Walker and Radzik, in particular, the point is explicitly not *personal* reconciliation but *moral* reconciliation. How should we understand that idea? Here is Radzik's explanation:

The kind of reconciliation [at stake here] involves the restoration of a paradigmatically moral relationship. It is one wherein the parties regard one another and themselves as equally valuable moral persons.[12]

And here is Walker's:

[W]e can understand 'restoration' ... as normative. 'Restoration' refers to repairs that move relationships in the direction of becoming morally adequate, whether or not they have been adequate before.[13]

These remarks already suggest, and the remainder of Radzik's and Walker's discussions confirm, that moral reconciliation is not really to be contrasted with personal reconciliation. Rather, moral reconciliation is, for both authors, a special *type* of personal reconciliation. It is personal reconciliation that meets some further conditions concerning its moral acceptability. My request for a case in favour of apology and reparation that is independent of

[12] Radzik, *Making Amends* (n 5) 81.
[13] Walker, *Moral Repair* (n 5) 209.

their contribution to reconciliation is unaffected by the setting of such further conditions. Even with the extra conditions we still want to know why apology and reparation are reconciliatory when they are, and why we should still care about them when they are not. Being told that we shouldn't want the reconciliation in question to reinstate an immoral relationship, and that we therefore shouldn't count the reinstatement of an immoral relationship as part of the case for apologizing or repairing, helps us to answer neither of these questions.

3. Reparation and rational continuity

In any case we should doubt the assumption, which Walker and Radzik seem to share, that all wrongdoing warranting apology or reparation eats away at our morally acceptable relationships, such that there is a need for moral acceptability to be restored. I already doubted, in Chapter 1, that all our wrongs against others are to be cast in such a strictly relational mould. But even when we narrow our attention to strictly relational wrongdoing, not all of it strikes me as eating away at the moral acceptability of the relationships in which it takes place. True, domestic abuse, bullying at work or school, and exploitation of power and trust in caring for the vulnerable do often fit that description. On the collective front, the same goes for 'ethnic cleansing', the installation and upholding of apartheid, and similar. One might perhaps stretch the description to include a wider range of heinous and culpable wrongs. But not all wrongs are culpable or heinous, and the culpable and heinous ones, it seems to me, are not the only ones that call for reparation and apology.

I first spoke on the topics of this chapter and the next—reparation and apology—on Friday 2 November 2012 in Camden, New Jersey. Because of Hurricane Sandy I had flown in late and had broken a promise to give my talk twenty-four hours earlier, on Thursday 1 November 2012. I owed my hosts and my audience profuse apologies for not having lectured on schedule, even though it was a wrong that was certainly excused and probably justified. I also owed it to them to take reparative measures. This may not be so obvious, but giving my lecture the next day *was* a reparative measure. It was a new duty that I acquired, as part of a very cordial settlement with my hosts that was designed to put my hosts and audience, so far as it was still possible, in the position they would have been in had I turned up the day before and performed my original duty. Suppose that 2 November had not been a suitable substitute day for my lecture (too much residual travel disruption, a clashing event that evening on campus, audience members too fed up to reconvene so soon, notice too short for effective advertising, you name it). Then I (or we together) would have had to come up with a further proposal for putting my disappointed hosts and audience in the position that, but for my breach of promise, they would have been in. My wrong would have called for a more elaborate repair. Even as it was, I had gone to great lengths to put things right, holding an airline agent on the phone for nearly an hour until a flight popped onto her screen that would take me into the East Coast on the Friday via a circuitous route that avoided the tail end of the storm. Interestingly, the airline agent was equally engaged in a reparative mission. The airline, after all, had cancelled my flight on the Thursday and owed a repair to me in much the same way that I owed a repair to the people at Rutgers. I doubt whether any airline agent, however patient, would have stayed on the line for nearly an hour (without hope of making a new sale) if there had been no breached duty on the airline's part to take me across the Atlantic on the previous day.

Both apology and reparation were owed, in this case, by the airline to me, and by me to my audience and hosts. Yet I can see nothing to suggest that anyone's moral relationship with anyone had been (in Walker's words) 'shaken, broken, distorted, or fouled'[14] by anything that anyone did; nor can I see any hint that (in Radzik's idiom) anyone had 'jeopardize[d]' anyone's 'deserved and ... perceived place in the moral community'.[15]

Nevertheless, my autobiographical example brings out the true, much less inflated, sense in which there is a moral deficit after wrongdoing. A duty of mine went unperformed on 1 November 2012. By the next day, even by later that same evening, it was too late to perform it. All that was available was

---

[14] Walker, *Moral Repair* (n 5) 209.
[15] Radzik, *Making Amends* (n 5) 82.

some second or third or fourth best, an imperfect fallback: a lecture on 2 November, or if that were inconvenient to my hosts then maybe a lecture at some later date, or if that didn't appeal then perhaps some other contribution to the Rutgers programme or curriculum. A duty of repair is none other than a duty to mitigate, so far as possible, one's non-performance of one's original duty. In some cases, the best way to mitigate may be to render an alternative service, in others to pay money—what common lawyers would call 'reparative damages'. You may think that my failing to lecture is unlikely to fall into the second category. But that is not so obvious. If Rutgers had already advanced expenses for my trip that were not otherwise recoverable by them, and if I had not shown up at all, I might well have regarded my reparative duty as including a duty to repay the advance, even if doing so left me out of pocket.

An easier case to imagine, perhaps, is one in which the shoe is on the other foot. Suppose, for example, that I had shown up as originally planned to give my lecture on 1 November, battling through the storm, but my hosts had by oversight failed to book and pay for my hotel room as they had promised. Then they would have owed me, by way of reparation, the reimbursement of whatever hotel bill I incurred to put myself, so far as it was still possible when I arrived, in the position I would have been in had the promise been kept. That is because paying the money back to me is the next best alternative to having paid it direct to the hotel when they were supposed to have done so.

Cases like this—cases in which some monetary quantification of the reparative damages already appears on a bill or invoice—make it seem easy to work out what is next best. But of course it is not always, or even usually, so easy. Go back to the question of what I was to do when I couldn't make it to Rutgers in time for my lecture. What was next best? Lecturing at the originally appointed time via Skype, or postponing to the next day, or postponing to the next week, same day same time, or the following year, or what? In my view, that depends on what reasons went unconformed to when the duty went unperformed. These include the reasons for the duty and the reason that resides in the fact of the duty itself. The question is: what can I still do maximally to conform to these reasons, given that *ex hypothesi* I already failed to conform to them perfectly? If it is uncertain what those reasons are, or how one should now maximize conformity with them, then it is uncertain what fallback duty one now has, and hence what would be the called-for repair. In such cases an authoritative determination, say by reaching a new agreement with my hosts, may be called for to resolve the uncertainty. If such an agreement cannot be reached, and the conflict escalates, there is even an imaginable if far-fetched role for the law—for example, in ruling and securing that I would make a repayment to Rutgers of whatever advance sum for expenses they had paid to me, notwithstanding my objection that such repayment would leave me out of pocket.

The example reminds us that often, as conflict escalates or as other aspects of the background situation change, less conformity with the *ex hypothesi* unconformed-to reasons is available, and so less repair is possible. We see this most vividly in the law relating to so-called specific performance of contracts. Specific performance, when awarded as a remedy for breach of a contract performance of which should on its terms already have been completed, is in fact a reparative remedy. *Ex hypothesi* it is too late for performance, meaning perfect performance. The builders used the wrong slates, or the china tea service was lost en route, or the tour guide did not show up. Here the courts are sometimes prepared to issue an order substituting a new, second-best, mode of performance: a belated substitution of the correct slates, a replacement shipment of china, a new date for the trip. This repair is 'specific' in the sense that it preserves as many features of the original unperformed duty as can be preserved consistently with the preservation of the duty's rationale. But, as the courts often point out, many breached contractual terms are beyond rescue by such specific means, or very quickly become beyond rescue. When the builders disappeared, the plaintiff brought in new builders to correct the litany of errors. The china tea service was a family heirloom. The same tour guide can no longer be expected to show these particular clients around now that they have fallen out with him so spectacularly over his earlier non-appearance. That being so, a less specific performance may be called for, and the payment of money damages may be regarded by the courts as the most unspecific of all. Never mind, for now, whether the courts are right about this idea of where money damages fit in. We will come back to that in a moment. Just notice that the argument in favour of money damages is the same as the argument in favour of an order of specific performance, and both are the same argument, essentially, as the argument in favour of not having breached the contract to begin with.

I call this 'the continuity thesis'.[16] It is the thesis that, when a contract was breached or any other wrong was done to another person, various reasons went unconformed to, and those reasons are still awaiting conformity. The question is always, what is the best conformity with those reasons that is still available? Whatever it is, that is now one's remedial or 'secondary' duty towards the same person. Even with my missed lecture, if I hadn't found a suitable fallback performance at once with the help of my airline, we might conceivably have reached the point at which payments of money to balance out expenses incurred would have been the best that anyone could hope for. The time might have come when the colleagues who arranged the lecture would have moved to positions elsewhere, when Rutgers would have rethought its legal theory programme, and when the rescheduling of the lecture or the rendition of substitute professional services by me would have become futile, even wasteful. Then it would all, perhaps, have come down to who should pick up the bill for that never-used hotel room.

4. The reparative uses of money

You may read me as suggesting that, when it comes to repair, money is always a counsel of despair, coming into play only if it is now too late for some more specific kind of repair. But that is not my view. No, that is the view that, a few sentences ago, I promised to come back to. Personally, I regard it as mistaken. To see what is mistaken about it, consider the following exchange from Larry David's *Curb Your Enthusiasm*.[17] Some weeks

---

[16] Gardner, 'What is Tort Law For? Part 1: The Place of Corrective Justice', *Law and Philosophy* 30 (2011), 1 at 33.

[17] 'The Korean Bookie', *Curb Your Enthusiasm* (dir. Bryan Gordon, HBO, 27 November 2005), at 11:18.

have passed since Larry rear-ended the parked car of local worthy Ben Heineman, smashing a tail light. Larry promptly (and obsequiously[18]) paid for the damage. He now spots Heineman's car parked outside Heineman's favourite restaurant with its tail light still broken. Disgruntled, he marches in to challenge Heineman. Here he is, straight after the confrontation, reporting back to his friend, manager, and perennial yes-man Jeff:

> LARRY: He said he has no intention of getting the car fixed. He gave the money to his daughter. He said she needed it for something.
> JEFF: Well that's a big ball of wrong.
> LARRY: You can't do *that*!
> JEFF: You can't *do* that!

Notice that the payment of money to Heineman was a substitute for a more specific remedy. The more specific remedy was a like-for-like replacement of the tail light. Larry could perhaps have replaced the car's tail light at the scene of the collision, if only he had happened to have the parts and the tools to hand. He could equally have replaced the tail light at any point since by buying and installing the parts, or by getting his own handyman to do it, or by taking the car to a suitable repair shop. Evidently, Larry paid Heineman to take the car to a repair shop as a substitute for taking it there himself. Presumably the amount of money Larry handed over was the same amount that he estimated (or that he and Heineman agreed) would be the repair shop's charge for the work. So the money was handed over in the full understanding, on both sides, that it was *not* the closest still-available alternative to Larry's not having smashed the tail light in the first place. Actually replacing the tail light remained the remedy by which Larry would best have conformed to the reasons that he failed to conform to when he smashed it. That Heineman did not spend the money on replacing the smashed tail light means, therefore, that Larry's attempt to do the right thing by the light of the continuity thesis has been frustrated. Hence Larry's indignation. The

---

[18] The 'accident' with the car was a ruse for getting to know Heineman and making a good impression: 'The Ski Lift', *Curb Your Enthusiasm* (dir. Larry Charles, HBO, 20 November 2005). This twist does not concern us here.

rightholder himself has thwarted Larry's attempt to fulfil his reparative duty towards the rightholder.

As usual, Larry's reaction to being thwarted is over the top.
He reacts as if there is nothing of importance at stake except
for his carrying out his reparative duty as determined by the
continuity thesis. But of course there are other factors in play.
There are conflicting considerations. Suppose that Larry had
been able, at an earlier moment, to get the tail light repaired
in a way that did not require Heineman's cooperation. When
Heineman found out that he had done so—even if Larry
promptly and ingratiatingly informed him—Heineman might
reasonably have protested about the further unasked-for interference with his car, never mind that now his car is in better
shape than before. And if the car were, thanks to typical Larry
miscalculations, to become accidentally locked up overnight
at the repair shop, Heineman could reasonably also have com-
plained about the disruption of his plan to drive to the ocean
that evening (for which disruption, indeed, further reparation
by Larry might well be owed). These thought-experiments
highlight that a reparative step that is called for according to
the continuity thesis is not necessarily called for, all things
considered. (We have already anticipated that conclusion, incidentally, in the discussion of *Sex, Lies, and Videotape*.) But
they also help us to see, more specifically, how the payment
of money might sometimes be the correct reparative step to
take, all things considered, even though there still remain alternative reparative steps that could be taken that would come
closer than the payment of money to what the continuity thesis
dictates. The payment of money may give the rightholder a
way to get the (continuity-thesis-dictated) repair done, while
minimizing her exposure to extra intrusion, interference, disruption, inconvenience, and so forth.

For anyone who knows the preoccupations of contemporary
private law theory, it may be tempting to sum these reflections up
by saying: once we take account of the value of the rightholder's
autonomy, a payment of money to the rightholder is sometimes the correct remedy, even though money is not what the
rightholder lost. For all his fanaticism, Larry helps us to see that
this is a misleading approximation. For Larry is right not to be

satisfied with Heineman's pleading of his own autonomy when asked why the car has gone unrepaired:

HEINEMAN: Considering it's none of your business … I had better use for the money.

LARRY: Such as?

HEINEMAN: If you must know I gave the money to my daughter who needs it for something far more important than fixing a car.

LARRY: What does she need the money for?

HEINEMAN: It's really none of your business.

LARRY: It's a little unethical you know, not fixing the car.

HEINEMAN: It has nothing to do with ethics. It's my money. You gave me my money. I can do with that money what I please.[19]

Larry believes, I think rightly, that Heineman is going too far in his final riposte. The money for the repair is indeed subject to some ('ethical') restrictions as to its use. There is something akin to what a lawyer would call an 'implied trust' in play. That is not to say that a rightholder's autonomy in respect of his or her use of reparative money counts for nothing. In ways to which we will return in Chapter 6, it sometimes counts for a great deal. People's lives are sometimes thrown into disarray by wrongdoing, in ways that may give them valuable opportunities for innovation, even personal revolution, that the wrongdoer should help to fund (for the sake of autonomy or otherwise). The point that matters here is merely that the use of one's autonomy, even in the cases that will interest us in Chapter 6, always answers to reason. One's own autonomy is no reason, in itself, to do the thing that one autonomously does. Asked 'Why did you do that?', those who say 'Because I was free to do it' (as Heineman finally resorts to saying) are parrying the question, not answering it. They do not yet reveal any reason for having done as they did.

Now Heineman is probably right that he wouldn't normally owe Larry an explanation for why he uses his own money in one way rather than another. In any other circumstances, his parrying rather than answering Larry's question about how he spent his own money would be unobjectionable. But this particular money,

Larry is right to think, is different. With this particular money, as we noted, Larry is being thwarted by Heineman in his attempt to do his reparative duty towards Heineman. In holding his use of this particular money to be none of Larry's business, Heineman is dropping Larry prematurely from the justificatory equation.

Look at it this way: having run into the back of Heineman's car, Larry might easily have infringed Heineman's rights in addinal ways by attempting to repair the car himself or by taking the car for repair without first consulting Heineman. But Larry needed to mitigate the wrong that he already committed against Heineman without committing further wrongs against Heineman in the process. The proximate objective of avoiding 'additional intrusion, interference, disruption, inconvenience, and so forth' was not that Heineman's autonomy should be respected in the aftermath of the collision, but rather that Larry was required to mitigate his wrong against Heineman without in the process compounding it by committing further wrongs. That applies whether the further wrongs in question would have been wrongs thanks to the value of Heineman's autonomy or otherwise. And now that Heineman thwarts Larry in the business of mitigating without compounding, Larry is not out of order in wondering, and asking, why Heineman is doing so. Heineman is going too far when he claims that this is none of Larry's business.

Of course Larry is, as usual, going about the asking in totally the wrong way, disturbing Heineman's lunch, helping himself to Heineman's pickles, generally winding Heineman up and giving Heineman several good excuses for refusing to answer Larry's increasingly importunate questions. Larry is driving a bigger wedge between them than the original collision ever did. In a way, however, that only illustrates the main point of this section. In his usual self-defeating style, Larry does end up compounding his original wrong by his insistence that his original wrong must still be further mitigated. In a way, his dealings with Heineman also illustrate the main point of this chapter. Reparation is capable of serving reconciliation, when handled reasonably on both sides. But the basic rationale for reparation—the one supplied by the continuity thesis—does not rely on the fact that reparation is reconciliatory. Rather, it explains how reparation is capable of being reconciliatory. Yet fanatical commitment to the continuity thesis (as we often find in the dog-in-a-manger climate of protracted private law litigation) can serve to drive people even further apart. 'Boy, that went well,' says Larry, summing up his own monomaniacal intervention.

5. How reparation gets personal

There are many lessons of relevance to the law in Larry's dealings with Heineman. Some of them, to which we will return in the next chapter and beyond, concern the protean and problematic role of money in making amends. But, for now, allow me to bring out a quite different lesson. Larry's maximal conformity to the reasons to which he failed to conform when he rear-ended Heineman's car—in other words, his reparative success by the lights of the continuity thesis—does not depend on his actions alone. He relies on Heineman, and through Heineman on Heineman's chosen repair shop, to finish the reparative job, by replacing the tail light. What interests us now is not whether this is an all things considered desirable delegation (I have already given a sense of why it might be), but how it is even logically possible.

How can it be that the wrongdoer's reasons to repair, under the continuity thesis, do not end their special hold over the wrongdoer now that the reparative process has been taken out of the wrongdoer's hands? This matters for the law, because the law may also take parts of the reparative process out of the wrongdoer's hands. Quite apart from its role in guiding, incentivizing, and sometimes even coercing the performance of reparative duties by the wrongdoer, the law sometimes authorizes or requires the wrongdoer's insurer, bank, employer, or successor in title, or the rightholder's bailiff, to finish the reparative job without much, if any, cooperation from the wrongdoer. For this to be logically possible, there must be a sense in which the wrongdoer's reparative reasons, and her duties based on them, are impersonal. There must be a sense in which they are not the sole preserve of the wrongdoer. The trick is to work out what that sense is, such that we do not lose sight of the different sense in which the same reasons and duties are nevertheless somehow personal to the wrongdoer. We want to know how Larry's reasons can possibly be conformed to by Heineman, or by a third-party auto-repairer, notwithstanding that they remain Larry's reasons—such that it is still his business whether or not they are ultimately conformed to.

Pinpointing the sense in which reparative reasons and duties are personal, and the sense in which they are impersonal, has given recent private law theorists plenty of headaches. Consider this influential remark by Stephen Perry:

> On the agent-relative understanding, the duties of repair that fall ... upon injurers are the only reasons for action that corrective justice generates. Corrective justice is, on this view, a principle of private, rather than public, morality (which is not to say that it is not properly enforceable by public institutions like courts).[20]

Why, we may wonder, is this not to say what the parenthetical aside at the end says that it is not to say? If the reasons that wrongdoers have to repair are genuinely 'agent-relative', if they are principles of 'private, rather than public, morality', how come they are reasons for anyone other than the wrongdoer? How come they are reasons for the rightholder, or for the courts, or for the law, to see to it that the wrongdoer conforms to them? This formulation already reveals one ambiguity in Perry's label 'agent-relative'. Possibly the reasons he is interested in are reasons that only the wrongdoer can *conform to*, but that others can equally *attend to* in contributing to that conformity. Only the wrongdoer can actually do the relevant repairing, but others can, for example, assist, persuade, encourage, or enable that repairing by the wrongdoer. Perhaps, in the terminology that I tend to favour, the reasons that Perry has in mind are personal *in respect of conformity* but impersonal *in respect of attention*.

My own view is that all reasons, by their nature, are impersonal in respect of attention. If you have a reason to listen to *Hunky Dory* or to *Court and Spark* on vinyl, I have that very same reason to source a copy for you. RCA or Asylum (as the case may be) also has the very same reason to reissue the disc, the arts editor of *The Times* has the very same reason to let you know about its availability, the High Court has the very same reason to order

[20] Perry, 'Comment on Coleman: Corrective Justice', *Indiana Law Journal* 67 (1991), 381, 390. One of the ways in which the remark was influential was in persuading Jules Coleman to overhaul his account of corrective justice in private law. See Coleman, *Risks and Wrongs* (Cambridge University Press 1992) 211–18.

you to listen to it, and so on (always assuming that these interventions will be productive in getting you listening). This is the classical view of reasons according to which any reason for P to φ is equally a reason for any action by anyone, familiar or stranger, that contributes to P's φing.[21] The trick, of course, is to understand why this attention-impersonality of all reasons should not propel each of us towards a life overwhelmed to the point of madness with endless efforts to help everyone to do whatever it is they have reason to do (which includes helping everyone to do whatever ... and so on). In this book, I have already incidentally pointed to just a few of the many rational brakes on such wild do-goodery.[22]

Building on a theme of Chapter 1, not all the reasons to help others are mandatory and categorical for the would-be helper, and they may conflict with others that are. Having a reason to help does not mean having a duty to help. That remains true even if the reason in question is the fact that the person you are helping has a duty to do whatever you would be helping her to do. There is no general duty to be helpful, let alone impartially helpful, in respect of the duties, let alone the reasons, of others.

Building on a theme of Chapter 2, not every reason to help another person automatically yields a derivative reason to *try* to help her. Many would-be helpful efforts do not help, and some positively hinder, the helpee: for instance, by stealing her opportunity to conform to a reason that is hers alone to conform to (as when our children make their first attempts to cook or swim or cycle 'all by themselves', and we keep meddling).

Building on a theme of this chapter, even if they do help, our efforts to help others may be independently objectionable. They may be intrusive, disruptive, patronizing, disempowering, or presumptuous. Sometimes this consideration may land us with a duty to stand by and let people fail, even though we could very easily have helped them to succeed (as when we see a parent at the bus stop struggling, because he is using counterproductive tactics, to cope with his small child's tantrum).

---

[21] Anthony Kenny, 'Practical Inference', *Analysis* 26 (1966), 65.

[22] For more on these themes, see Derek Parfit's treatment of the 'pure do-gooder' in Parfit, *Reasons and Persons* (Clarendon Press 1984), 24–43.

In the coming chapters you will find further challenges, including in Chapter 5 what you may well regard as the master challenge to the idea that everyone should devote his or her life to the better conduct of other people's lives. But none of them undermines, and indeed all presuppose, the truth of the classical view: that all reasons are impersonal in respect of attention.

Exploring the classical view properly would take us well beyond what could reasonably be attempted in this book. Arguably, exploration of the classical view is the principal task of moral philosophy as a whole. For present purposes, the main importance of the classical view is this. If reasons were not impersonal in respect of attention, it would be hard even to begin defending the authority of private law to do what it does. For, in the eyes of the law, the fact that a wrongdoer breached his primary duty (committed a tort or breach of contract) is a reason for his having a secondary duty of repair, and that same reason doubles as the law's reason for recognizing and getting him to perform that duty of repair. Moreover, in working out what exactly the wrongdoer's duty of repair might be, the law relies on the further reasons why, in the eyes of the law, he had his primary duty. In line with the continuity thesis, in other words, the law treats those reasons that (according to the law) the wrongdoer has to take reparative steps as its own reasons to mandate (and in the process to lend determinacy to: see Chapter 2) the reparative steps to be taken. Maybe one could come up with an explanation of how all this is possible that leaves it the case that the reasons in question are not reasons for the law but only reasons for the wrongdoer. But it seems unlikely.

All of this leaves open the possibility, however, that the same reasons are personal in respect of conformity, in the sense that only the wrongdoer himself can ultimately do the relevant repairing. There clearly are some reasons that work like that. If I accept an invitation to dinner at your house, that I did so is a reason for me to show up at the appointed time, and in accordance with the classical view it doubles as a reason for my aunt or my driving instructor or a passing stranger to drop me off at your address at the appointed time. Yet it does not double as a reason for my aunt or my driving instructor or a passing stranger to turn up for dinner at your house in place of me. Clearly, they would need an accepted invitation of their own before doing that. In turning up for dinner, they would clearly not be conforming with the reason given by *my* accepted invitation.

Equally clearly, however, not all reasons work like this. If I have a reason to collect my teenage stepdaughter from school after an evening drama rehearsal, quite possibly other people can go in my place and the reason will still be fully conformed to. It just depends what the reason is. If the reason is that it will be too late for my stepdaughter to use the bus alone with confidence, then a range of adults whom she knows can substitute for me. But if the reason for me to collect her is that she is worried about her father's level of commitment to her theatrical activities, then woe betide me if I am not the one who is waiting for her afterwards. No substitute adult can provide conformity with *this* reason.

Now imagine, to up the stakes a little, that these are not merely two reasons I have to collect my stepdaughter after the rehearsal, but two reasons, each of which suffices on its own to put me under a duty in respect of the collecting. In that case, I have two duties. One of them is a duty to collect my stepdaughter myself (that is the duty that exists for the reason that she is worried about my commitment). The other is a duty to see to it that she is collected (that is the duty that exists for the reason that she will find the bus journey intimidating). I can perform the latter duty by performing the former, but not *vice versa*. We could call the latter a 'delegable' duty. Some but not all of my duties are delegable. Which of my duties are delegable depends on the reasons for their existence. Those reasons give the duty its content. But notice: whatever their content—be they delegable or not—the duties remain mine, as do the reasons for them. The fact that someone else's action can substitute for mine in my performance of my duty, and in my conformity to the reason for it, doesn't mean that the duty or the reason stops being mine to perform, or mine to conform to as the case may be. It only affects what *counts* as my performing it, or what counts as my conforming to it, as the case may be. Even when I get someone else to collect her, as my stranded stepdaughter might well point out, the buck still stops with me. For the duty remained mine, whoever was roped in as my delegate performer.

Even once we have noted the distinction between what is personal in respect of attention and what is personal in respect of conformity, in other words, we have still have an ambiguity about 'conformity' to clear up. All reasons are in one sense personal in respect of conformity, just by their very nature as reasons. Reasons, as Joseph Raz once put it, are not just facts but 'relations between facts and persons'.[23] The ultimate question is always whether I did all that I had reason to do, whether you did all that you had reason to do, whether the law did all that it had reason to do, and so on. It is merely that reasons differ widely in respect of what *counts* as one's doing all that one had reason to do. Often the actions of others are capable of counting towards one's conforming to a reason. Often, by the same token, the actions of others qualify as possible (and sometimes even as necessary) ingredients of one's performing a duty.

All this is just as well for private law for, as we noted already, private law not only attends to the reasons that apply to wrongdoers in getting wrongdoers themselves to perform their reparative duties but it also, under some circumstances, substitutes the actions of others for the actions of wrongdoers in the very performance of those duties. The wrongdoer's reparative duties, or some of them, are regarded by the law as delegable. When they are so regarded, is the law losing sight of the fact that these duties are the personal duties of the wrongdoer? Not at all. The expression 'personal duties' here (like 'agent-relative duties' as the expression is used by Perry) is a pleonasm. It simply means 'duties'. Even when my bank remits funds from my account to the successful plaintiff's account under a court order, it is my own duty of repair that is being discharged. By appointment of the court, the bank is acting as an agent for me in that discharge. It has its own duties, of course, but it does not (yet) have its own duty of repair. So far it has done no relevant wrong of its own; it has no action of its own to rectify or remedy.[24] Its duty is to remit my funds as

---

[23] Raz, *Practical Reason and Norms* (Hutchinson 1975), 19. *Pace* Raz, the reason is not exactly the relation. It is the fact, as it relates to the person.

[24] I say 'so far' because, of course, the bank may err and send the money from the wrong account or to the wrong account. Then it is apt to incur reparative duties of its own.

the court directs, an action that, albeit bypassing me, helps to discharge *my* duty of repair. If the remitted funds do not cover the damages, notice, I still owe the rest. The reparative buck, if you like, still stops with me.

There are interesting issues about the delegability of private law's *primary* duties. In contracts, both delegable and non-delegable duties are common. The difference between delegable and non-delegable duties is central, for example, to distinguishing between an ordinary contract for the supply of services and a contract of employment.[25] In torts, a general principle of non-delegability is complicated by some indeterminacy in the rules of vicarious liability. They are sometimes treated as rules regulating what the employer or principal should have done through the employee or agent, as opposed to rules requiring the employer or principal to act as insurer regarding the employee's or agent's torts.[26] But none of this should detain us here. Our present concern is with the delegability of private law's *secondary* duties, in particular its reparative duties. And this is a quite separate matter.

To see why, return to my stepdaughter's drama rehearsal. Let us suppose that I have only the non-delegable duty in respect of her collection, the one that exists for the sole reason that she is worried about her dad's level of commitment to her theatrical activities. Apart from that worry, she would be happy to use the bus. If (unlike my stepdaughter) you find it hard to accept that I could have a duty to collect her for this paltry reason alone, just add this further fact to the mix. The quarrel that my stepdaughter and I had about her getting home from last week's rehearsal culminated in my promising that she would be collected this week, and the point that she emphasized in our quarrel—that she is worried about my level of commitment to her theatrical activities—compels an interpretation of the promise according to which, this week, I am going to collect her in person. Now suppose that, on the way to collect her as I am duty-bound to do, I suffer a flat tyre. Changing the tyre will take long enough that I urgently need to make an alternative arrangement for her to be collected. Otherwise (never having any power in her phone by the end of

---

the day) she will be at a loss as to what to do next. So I call her friend's mother, who is already on her way to the school, and ask if she will help out by collecting my stepdaughter too. I am not culpable in respect of my failure to turn up in person, let's agree. I have a robust excuse. My stepdaughter will accept this and will not pick a fight. In fact she will be sympathetic. There will be no rift between us merely because I did not collect her in person, and so there will be no question of reconciliation on that score. There may, however, be other scores to settle between us. The question will still arise of whether I have so far done anything, and if so whether there are nevertheless things that it is still open to me to do, to conform to the reason why I was duty-bound to collect her personally in the first place.

Surely I have already done *something* towards that conformity. Just by setting out (trying to collect her) I have reassured my step-daughter that I was serious when I conceded her point, last week, that I should show more commitment to her theatrical activities. My trying constitutes, in this case, partial conformity with the reason for my duty (which is *ex hypothesi* a duty to succeed) even though it didn't work out and I did not end up actually doing my duty. By phoning her friend's mother, moreover, I quite possibly added to the same reassurance: I didn't regard my commitment to collect my stepdaughter in person as something totally flimsy, to be abandoned at the first sign of trouble. But even this, my stepdaughter may reasonably say, was the very least I could do in the circumstances. There remains a gap between doing only this much and doing what *ex hypothesi* I had reason to do, viz. collect her in person. Under the continuity thesis, then, the question arises of whether there is more that I am still in a position to do, after my failure to do my original duty, towards conforming with that reason.

And surely there is more that I am in a position to do, as my stepdaughter will doubtless point out if I don't do any of it. I could still get her friend's mother to drop her off where I am stuck right now, changing the tyre by the roadside, so that my stepdaughter and I can talk about how the play is coming along as I take her the rest of the way home. And I could probably get my friend Ben, who is a playwright, to join me at the actual performance next week and to chat to my stepdaughter afterwards, so that she can see that I am really proud of her theatrical endeavours. And I could still take her on Saturday to see a West End version of the same play, and make sure we talk about it afterwards. Probably, I have a duty to do one or more of these things (although perhaps not all) so as to make up, so far as it can still be done, for my breach of duty in not showing up to collect her in person.[27] Notice that whatever duty I have now will be a new duty (a secondary duty, as lawyers put it) even though it will exist for the same reason(s) that went unconformed to when I failed in my original duty (my primary duty). And notice, more to the point, that the secondary duty is partly delegable in a way in which the primary duty *ex hypothesi* was not. The primary duty, *ex hypothesi*, required me to collect her in person. The secondary duty, whatever its exact content may be, is open to the participation of others in its performance: that of my stepdaughter's friend's mother, that of my playwright friend Ben, even that of a large West End cast.

What the secondary duty has as its content, so far as the continuity thesis is concerned, depends only on what would provide the best conformity still available with the reason or reasons that went unconformed to when I breached the primary duty. There is no reason to think that, just because the primary duty was non-delegable, the secondary duty will be non-delegable too (nor that if the primary duty was delegable, the secondary will be delegable too). Nor is there a reason to think that the secondary duty is fixed forever at the moment of breach. For it too may be breached and then there may be yet further duties that spring up according to the continuity thesis. One might be tempted to call them

---

[27] A duty with disjunctive content (performed by either φing or γing) is sometimes known as an imperfect duty, although that terminology is better avoided. The imperfection of a duty has come to be associated with a number of cross-cutting properties that are not always differentiated. See George Rainbolt, 'Perfect and Imperfect Obligations', *Philosophical Studies* 98 (2000), 233. A particular risk is that any duty with latitude as to how it is performed will, under the heading 'imperfect', be treated as if it had disjunctive content. All duties have latitude as to how they are performed (even the delivery driver whose actions are closely monitored can make his delivery by unloading box 1 before box 2 or box 2 before box 1, by parking 5 cms further forward or 5 cms further back, etc.). But not all duties have disjunctive content (the driver has no duty to unload either box 1 before box 2 or box 2 before box 1, or to park either 5 cms further forward or 5cms further back, etc.).

'tertiary', 'quaternary', etc., but it is better to think of each as a secondary duty relative to the previous duty, non-performance of which brought it into existence. That is also how the law tends to see it: at each stage there is a further breach of duty (first my failure to take adequate precautions against damaging your tail light, then my failure to pay for the damage, then my failure to abide by a court order requiring me to pay for the damage, etc.), each calling for a new, more desperate, remedy. Thus even if a non-delegable duty to repair arises at the start, there is no reason to assume that further down the line the duties to repair remain non-delegable. It will all depend on how, in the later-prevailing circumstances, the wrongdoer can best conform (or we might now add 'be conformed') to the reasons that he failed to conform to when he breached the primary duty. Eventually, we may have to conclude that the best that can be got out of a wrongdoer, by way of conformity with his original reasons, is whatever we can get by ordering a payment by his bank or his employer, now appointed by the law to act on his behalf. Or (in the case of my stepdaughter's drama rehearsal) whatever my wife can achieve by ordering a facsimile of the First Folio of *The Comedy of Errors* on the internet in my name. If we were to reach this stage I would need some remarkable excuses to avoid being seriously culpable. My wife would have a major bone to pick with me, even if (as my wife hopes) my stepdaughter never finds out that the book came from her. Fortunately, before we get to that stage, I still have several possible ways of acquitting myself a good deal better by the light of the continuity thesis.

6. From the personal to the interpersonal

Some people think that the interpersonal duties of private law stand to be contrasted with duties of some more purely personal kind. That was one reading of what Arthur Ripstein said in the passages that were quoted in Chapter 2. No doubt there are duties that are in *some* sense more purely personal than those found in private law. We could even make that claim trivially true by defining a purely personal duty as one that has no legal recognition. Nevertheless, in the sense in which the duties of private law are inter*personal*, all duties, whether found in private law or not, are personal duties: all are owed *by* someone in particular. Interpersonal duties, in the relevant sense, are just those that are, as well as being owed by someone in particular, owed *to* someone in particular. And whether a duty is owed to someone in particular depends on the reason(s) why it exists.

In the example we just explored, the primary duty I owe to my stepdaughter, to collect her in person from her evening drama rehearsal, is strictly relational, as we explained strict relationality in Chapter 1. It exists because she is my (step) daughter or because of my promise to her or both. But it is perfectly easy to dispose of the strict relationality, while maintaining the interpersonality (or 'loose relationality' as I called it in Chapter 1). If I find a younger pupil stranded without a phone or a bus pass when I arrive at the school to collect my stepdaughter, I may well (depending on whether the school is still open, her friends are waiting with her, etc.) have a duty to help her contact her parents, and perhaps a duty to get her home if her parents are still absent and uncontactable after we have all been waiting for some time. But never mind whether I have the duty or not, and what exactly its content might be. The point is that if I do have the duty, it is a duty owed to somebody in particular. It is owed to the stranded youngster if, say, the threat to her safety or peace of mind is the reason why I have it. It is owed to her parents if the duty exists to save them from worry about the whereabouts of their daughter. (Imagine that the girl herself is blithely happy to spend the night at a friend's house, where only an older sibling is going to be at home and no questions are going to be asked about the guest.)

Of course, these reasons may all figure side by side in the rationale for my duty, whatever that duty may be. When the case for the existence of my duty is overdetermined, when either the predicament of the youngster or the predicament of her parents would be enough by itself to place me under the same duty, then that duty is owed to the daughter and to the parents alike. In a different idiom, albeit one that the parties themselves might avoid so as to avoid raising the temperature between them, there are multiple rightholders. 'He just left me there' and 'he just left her there' are both possible grievances, each coming from a different rightholder, and each reflecting one strand, one nexus, of my duty's interpersonality. But still not reflecting any strict relationality: my duty does not, I am assuming, arise from or depend on my daughter being friends with the stranded girl or attending the same school as her, or my being on good terms with the parents, etc. We might not expect these particular rights and duties to be upheld by the law of torts, which resists 'positive duties to act' in the absence of any strict relationality. But that resistance calls for separate explanation. The explanation is not that the duties that I owe in the case of the stranded girl do not display the private law kind of interpersonality.

That much concerns the primary duties of private law. You may wonder whether the secondary duties are perhaps interpersonal in some stronger way, perhaps even qualifying as strictly relational. We already know, from Chapter 1, that the simple answer to that is no. Inasmuch as the fact that one person wronged another is the reason why that one person now owes a new duty to the other, the new duty is not strictly relational. It is not based on the *value* of their relationship. What is owed now is owed thanks to a connection between them which, so far as its relevant features go, is wholly regrettable. The connection is that the plaintiff crossed the defendant's path and came to grief at his hand. But you may be starting to wonder whether things are really so simple. Is it really true, according to the view that I have advocated in this chapter, that 'the fact that one person wronged another is the reason why that one person now owes a new duty to the other'? Surely the continuity thesis says, rather, that the reasons that went unconformed to *in* one person's wronging another (i.e. in failing to perform her primary duty) are the reasons why that one person now owes a new duty to the other? In which case, surely the question of whether the secondary duty is strictly relational resolves into the question (to which the answer varies from case to case: see Chapter 1) of whether the primary duty in turn was strictly relational?

The two formulations differ only in emphasis. The fact that I have a duty is always one reason to perform it. It is a mandatory, categorical reason. It is also the only reason to perform my duty which is such that *necessarily* I fail to conform to it when I fail to perform my duty. Not surprisingly, it is often the first reason to be cited in explaining why I now have a secondary duty, a duty of repair. How should it be cited? Here are two ways: first, we could cite the fact that I had the primary duty, the one that went unperformed; secondly, we could cite the fact that I didn't perform the primary duty (or in other words that I committed a wrong). These are not two different facts, any more than the fact that I travelled on the bus, sitting down, is a different fact from the fact that I was sitting down while I travelled on the bus. So they are not two different possible reasons for my having a secondary duty.[28]

They are one and the same reason. There is nothing strictly relational going on so far. Things get tricky only because this 'first reason to be cited' does not end the story of why I have the secondary duty I have. According to the continuity thesis, the further reasons *why* I had my primary duty are also still in play. At least some of them went at least partly unconformed to when I failed to perform my primary duty. Just as they shaped my primary duty, so they now shape my fallback secondary duty. Only when we know why I had my primary duty, in other words, can we work out what would count as the next best thing to do, now that it is too late to perform my primary duty. Maybe those further reasons include the fact that I promised, or the fact that these were not just anybody's theatrical interests but my stepdaughter's, or such like. Then surely these too are among the reasons why I have the secondary duty I have, which is therefore strictly relational too? Perhaps. But it scarcely matters. It only goes to show that the line between strictly relational duties and interpersonal duties that are not strictly relational is not a very sharp one. There are many indeterminate cases. So what? My objective in drawing the distinction, back in Chapter 1, was to establish that some but not all of the duties recognized by private law are strictly relational, even though all are in a looser sense relational, or interpersonal. And that was my objective mainly because I wanted to steer clear of, and be seen to steer clear of, two extremes (I called them 'hyper-relationalism' and 'hypo-relationalism'). These extremes

---

[28] Compare Emmanuel Voyiakis, *Private Law and the Value of Choice* (Hart Publishing 2017), ch 1, where, on my reading, an attempt is made to drive a wedge here.

have for too long dominated, between them, theoretical reflection on private law.

7. Wrongs and losses

Return to the case of the stranded girl. I owe a duty to her (or to her parents) for the simple reason that, at the time when my duty exists, she is (or they are) especially vulnerable to, or dependent on, my actions. That is also, at base, the rationale of many duties in private law. Leaving aside those that are strictly relational, many primary duties in private law exist for the simple reason that, at the moment when the duty exists, the person to whom it is owed is especially vulnerable to, or especially dependent on, the action of the person who (therefore) has the duty. It need not be a life or death vulnerability or dependency. It may be just some small aspect of the rightholder's life that is at stake: her taking up of a new job, her peaceful enjoyment of her home, her participation in some beloved pastime, her completion of a complex transaction, her contribution to the parenting of her children, her rapport with her friends, or her identification with her hometown. She may stand to lose in any number of different ways, from what the duty-bearer does or doesn't do, and that standing to lose is what explains, at base, why the duty-bearer bears his duty.

This formulation helps us to see how private law's preoccupation with wrongs (unperformed duties) relates to its preoccupation with losses. In some cases the loss is a constituent of the wrong: one commits the tort or contract only when the loss to the rightholder actually materializes. But even when that is not so, the avoidance of losses is typically central to the rationale for the duty as private law sees it. Whether the loss materialized may not have mattered in determining whether one breached the duty, but it still matters in determining to what extent, in breaching the duty, one conformed to the reasons why one had the duty. So even when a tort or breach of contract is 'actionable per se' (which means that it still counts as a tort or breach of contract, even in the absence of any loss), loss at the hands of the tortfeasor or contract-breacher remains what the law is oriented to protecting the rightholder against.

In thinking about duties of repair, in private law or otherwise, many have wondered: What it is, exactly, that is supposed to be repaired? Is it the wrong or is it the loss? Those who join Margaret Walker in gravitating away from 'corrective justice' and towards 'restorative justice' sometimes do so because they associate 'corrective justice' with the repair of losses that people suffered at the hands of wrongdoers. They want to assert the importance, instead, of repairing the wrongs themselves.[29] But if there are differences between 'corrective justice' and 'restorative justice', this is surely not one of them. Repairing (compensating, redressing) a person's losses, whether in money or in kind, just is how you repair (mitigate, ameliorate) a wrong against that person, where your duty, the one that you did not perform, existed to protect that same person against those same losses.

That is the continuity thesis in action. Could it be that believers in 'restorative justice' are simply interested in a different kind of wrong, one that is not loss-based in the same way? To judge by the examples of the 'clamour for amends' that we had in mind at the start of this chapter, and that predominate in the related literature, the answer is no. They are mainly examples in which people have suffered grievous losses at the hands of wrongdoers—a loss of family or friends in a genocidal atrocity, a loss of way of life or livelihood through colonization or enslavement, a loss of trust or motivation in the wake of severe betrayal, a loss of sleep owing to nightmares in which one relives torture or rape, or even, in extreme cases, a loss of any sense of self. And the main question thrown up by these examples and emphasized by most believers in restorative justice is just as you would expect: How are wrongdoers to be involved in the stemming, so far as possible, of losses still to unfold and in the reversal, so far as possible, of those already borne?

The frustration of believers in 'restorative justice' comes largely, it seems to me, of those little words 'so far as possible'. They tend to think that the courts, and policy-makers, and probably many others besides, have shown a lack of imagination in what kinds of

---

[29] Walker, *Moral Repair* (n 5) 210. For an equivalent gravitation in the literature specifically about tort law, see John Goldberg and Ben Zipursky, 'Torts as Wrongs', *Texas Law Review* 88 (2010), 917 at 926.

reparative measures they regard as possible, and (concomitantly) in what kinds of losses they regard as candidates for repair, and (concomitantly) in how the wrongs associated with such losses are to be understood. The law of torts and breach of contract are, not unreasonably, taken to epitomize this lack of imagination. They are good with 'material' compensation for 'material' losses and the duties that exist to prevent such losses, and pretty hopeless in coping with the rest.[30] If this is all that 'corrective justice' offers, say the critics, then what we need is a different kind of justice— let's call it 'restorative'.

Now, of course, this is not really all that corrective justice offers. It is merely all that private law offers, or offers with any confidence or conviction, under the heading of corrective justice. The problem, then, is not with corrective justice but with its legal implementation. That is where we should be applying our pressure. As soon as we begin to ask of private law that it adopts a more ambitious programme of corrective justice covering a wider range of losses, however, we realize that failure of imagination is not the only obstacle. There are also numerous problems of efficacy and feasibility, and numerous conflicts with other important ideals. The law should no more insist on the perfection of reparation than Larry David should do so in his squabble with Ben Heineman. And many of the considerations that support the case for self-restraint by Larry support a fortiori the case for self-restraint by the law. For the law is lumbered by its nature (or by moral restrictions borne of its nature) with the kinds of intrusive, clumsy, escalatory, overkilling, and generally dangerous techniques for getting things done that make Larry's approach seem almost light touch. That helps to explain some of the limits on the legal availability of specific performance as a remedy for breach of contract. But it also helps to explain much of the law's reluctance to attempt the repair of losses that are not 'material' and cannot eventually be turned over to banks, insurance companies, bailiffs, and the like.

Here the frustration for 'restorative justice' enthusiasts lies with our inevitably limited institutional techniques for securing

---

[30] Walker, *Moral Repair* (n 5) 210; Radzik, *Making Amends* (n 5) 49.

conformity with reparative duties. Yet the words 'so far as possible' also capture another, and in some ways more profound, source of frustration for 'restorative justice' enthusiasts, one that has nothing specifically to do with institutional failure. Theirs is to some extent, it seems to me, the perennial human longing to somehow repair the irreparable. It is a longing that is also portrayed, as Radzik pointed out, in *Sex, Lies, and Videotape*. We are not talking, at this point, about a longing to repair what will go unrepaired merely because of clumsiness, resource shortage, failure of imagination, independent moral restrictions, or the like. Now we are talking about a longing to repair what is irreparable in virtue of the general truth that is said to have been formulated in the fifth century BC by the poet Agathon: 'For this alone even God cannot achieve/To make undone what has been done.'[31] You may say that this chapter has challenged the generality of that truth. But it has not. This chapter has concerned itself with such repair (mitigation, amelioration) of wrongdoing as is possible by the repair (compensation, redress) of loss. The wrong, although now mitigated, was of course still done. There is always at least that much left behind.

And yet there is a familiar residual hankering somehow to annul it. 'Out, damned spot! out, I say!' insists Lady Macbeth, scrubbing in vain at a bloodstain that is, in truth, not on her hand but on her conscience.[32] She is deluded about the whereabouts of the stain. But is her struggle with the indelible residue of her actions wholly deranged? Or can we make some rational sense of her efforts to expunge wrongdoing even beyond the point at which the continuity thesis runs out of fallback solutions? If it were *sheer* irrationality, *utter* madness, would Lady Macbeth's now compulsive hand-washing have much to contribute to the themes of the play? Utter madness in the wake of her wrong would be a harsh fate, to be sure, but wouldn't it be even worse, at any rate *humanly* even worse, for her to retain enough sanity to grasp the true complexion of what she has done, and to be driven to a much narrower affliction, to a waking nightmare of extreme reaction,

---

[31] Cited by Aristotle, *Nichomachean Ethics* 1139^{b}9.
[32] Shakespeare, *Macbeth*, Act V, Scene 1.

by that cold and clear truth she still sees? Lady Macbeth is not concerned with reparation or apology. Yet her yearning to undo what cannot be undone is a yearning she shares with many who *are* concerned with repair and apology. Here the questions of the next chapter are beginning to take shape.

4

Say It with Flowers

If I'm considered accountable for my distance
I don't know if I should apologize
or think of compensation, reparations.

Michael Morse[1]

1. The irreparable remains

'We can become better people in the future, but can we ever make
up for the past?' That, recall, was Linda Radzik's question, the one
that was raised for her by Soderbergh's film *Sex, Lies and Videotape*.
In Chapter 3 I offered a partial answer, one that incidentally prob-
lematized the question. For I implicitly challenged Radzik's distinction (which she herself later challenges in a different way)
between making up for the past and improving the future. I did so
by wielding something called 'the continuity thesis'. According to
the continuity thesis, what I should do by way of repair is whatever
would bring me closest, given how things now are, to doing what
I should have done in the first place. When I do that, there is a sense
in which I am making up for the past. But there is also a sense in
which I am creating a better future. For it is a future in which I will
have come closer to doing what I ought to have done when I had
the chance, hence a future in which I will have left less undone. That
is not necessarily an improvement in *me*, but it is necessarily an improvement in my life. You may say that, as it stands, that is a very
localized, unambitious, even vainglorious, kind of progress to seek.
But as rational beings, alas, it is the only kind of progress we know
how to make. We can intentionally make the world a better place

[1] 'Void and Compensation (Poem as Aporia Between Lighthouses)', *The
Literary Review* 54 (2011), 5. Many thanks to Michael Morse for giving me permission to use these words as an epigraph, even though they were omitted from the
later version of the same poem in his collection *Void and Compensation* (Canarium
Books 2015).

only by conforming more closely to more of the reasons that apply to us. We may disagree about what reasons there are and what importance to attach to them. In this book, I am placing particular emphasis on the following reasons for and against action: that the lives of (specific) other people will be especially affected by what we do; and that we have special relationships with (specific) other people. These are the reasons that justify private law's famous 'interpersonal' duties, when they are justified. I do not claim, and private law does not claim, that they are the only reasons we ever have. Whatever reasons we have, however, our contribution to the world—the story of our lives—lies in the extent of our conformity with them. The continuity thesis merely takes that fact seriously.

The thesis rests on the idea that the reasons that I did not conform to still call for conformity even once the time for perfect conformity with them is over. Now they call for the nearest-to-perfect conformity that is still available. And when they were reasons that originally put me under a duty, a duty that I breached, they are not simply to be returned to the *mêlée* of other reasons that now apply to me. They now place me under a duty of repair. It is not an absolute duty. We should not be monomaniacs about it, in the manner of Larry David in *Curb Your Enthusiasm*. Like all duties, however, including the original breached duty that it now replaces, the duty of repair does regulate the range of arguments that are available to justify or excuse its breach. One cannot simply brush it aside with the convenient thought that, since the original breach, one has lots of new reasons to attend to. Like all duties, it has a tighter hold than that, for it is a categorical requirement. It applies irrespective of changes in the duty-holder's prevailing personal goals (that is what 'categorical' means) and to the exclusion of at least some countervailing reasons (that is what 'requirement' adds). The continuity thesis, in short, yields a nice interpretation of William Faulkner's aphorism: 'The past is never dead. It is not even past.'[2] And it lends the lie to the seductive blank-sheet futurism of Antonio's incitement to murder in *The Tempest*: '[w]hat's past is prologue; what to come/In yours and my discharge.'[3]

---

[2] Faulkner, *Requiem for a Nun* (Random House 1951), 85.
[3] Shakespeare, *The Tempest*, Act II, Scene 1.

Even as the continuity thesis holds out the hope that we can make up for the past, however, it ultimately snatches that hope away. For by the lights of the continuity thesis, the amends we make can only ever be incomplete. By hypothesis, when the continuity thesis applies, the time for perfect conformity is over. One did not do one's duty. All one can do now is perform another duty, a secondary or fallback duty, fulfilment of which serves the same reasons but allows for only imperfect conformity with them. Once I do not show up on time to give my lecture at Rutgers, showing up on time is no longer an option; we have to settle for something close, but something less. Once Larry rear-ends Heineman's car, it is too late for him not to have rear-ended it; what he does now can at best be second-best. There is always, in other words, what we might call a 'rational remainder', a residue of unconformed-to reason, a remnant of the past that remains stubbornly inaccessible to reparative resolution by the lights of the continuity thesis. If nothing else, there is the bare fact of my unperformed duty, the fragment that contract lawyers call the 'performance interest'.[4] It remains even when all losses (be they 'material' or otherwise) have been covered, and the question arises: What is to become of this rational remainder, what does it mean for us, given that *ex hypothesi* here is nothing left to be done in the way of eliminating it by conformity?

Some say: ignore it, let it go, put it behind you, move on. 'What's gone and what's past help/Should be past grief,' soothes Paulina in *The Winter's Tale*. But here Paulina is being indulgent, fleetingly affected by an uncharacteristic pity for the repentant King Leontes. Leontes recognizes her remark for the pandering therapeutic hogwash that it is, and will have none of it:

Thou didst speak but well,
When most the truth; which I receive much better
Than to be pitied of thee. Pr'ythee, bring me
To the dead bodies of my queen and son:
One grave shall be for both; upon them shall

---

[4] See Brian Coote, 'Contract Damages, *Ruxley*, and the Performance Interest', *Cambridge Law Journal* 56 (1997), 537. Better still the 'bare performance interest': see Mindy Chen-Wishart, *Contract Law* (4th edn, Oxford University Press 2012), 479.

The causes of their death appear, unto
Our shame perpetual. Once a day I'll visit
The chapel where they lie; and tears shed there
Shall be my recreation: so long as nature
Will bear up with this exercise, so long
I daily vow to use it. Come, and lead me
To these sorrows.[5]

'Unto our shame perpetual,' says he. 'To these sorrows' is where
he wants to be led. And not only to get the full measure of those
sorrows. To express them too: 'tears shed there shall be my recreation,' he vows. So there are, for Leontes, things to be done by
wrongdoers even after the point of no repair, even when the continuity thesis offers up no further salvation. Nor are those things
limited to token gestures. They are capable of being gruelling,
life-consuming. Leontes is entirely serious about that. Sixteen
years later, encountering in Cleomenes another would-be therapist, Leontes resists the proposal that in his 'saint-like sorrow' he
has now 'paid down/More penitence, than done trespass'. No, he
replies, he must 'still think of/The wrong I did myself'. Indeed, he
now has Paulina employed to keep the wrong he did on his mind
and in his heart, by periodically berating him for what he did.
She does so with passion, still stoking her own fury as she faith-
fully fortifies Leontes' woes. Hoping in vain that she might now
economize on her reproaches, Leontes tells her that his wrongdoing remains 'as bitter/Upon thy tongue, as in my thought.
Now, good now,/Say so but seldom.'[6] This call for lenity has to
be put to Paulina as a humble entreaty because, under Leontes'
own scheme for perpetuating his shame, Paulina is now fully in
charge of his fate. Witness:

> PAULINA: Will you swear/Never to marry but by my free leave?
> . . .
> LEONTES: My true Paulina,/We shall not marry till thou bidd'st us.
> PAULINA: That/Shall be when your first queen's again in breath.

And so the emotional flagellation continues unabated.

---

[5] Shakespeare, *The Winter's Tale*, Act III, Scene 2.
[6] ibid Act V, Scene 1.

The comic ingredient here is not unlike that of Larry David's single-minded insistence on the repair of Heineman's car. We may well think that Leontes and Paulina have gone overboard with their pact to keep the king's wrongdoing at the forefront of his thoughts and feelings, and that Cleomenes is right that some kind of attempt at a new life, or at least a new pattern of thought and feeling, must eventually be allowed. We may be tempted to agree with Cleomenes that by now Paulina 'might have spoken a thousand things that would/Have done the time more benefit.' And yet it would surely be a mistake to conclude that Leontes and Paulina are entirely beyond reason in perpetuating their own shared purgatory. Even Cleomenes avoids this mistake. His thought is not that there are no reasons to experience retrospective negative emotions such as shame, grief, and anger. Nor does he suggest that it is irrational to express such emotions by marking and visiting graves, weeping, wailing, reproaching, berating, and so on. Cleomenes' modest proposal is only that sixteen years of this, unabated, to the exclusion of so many other possible concerns, is disproportionate. It is not that the king should not have been penitent to begin with. It is that the king has now 'paid down *more* penitence than done trespass'. And to judge by his humble entreaty to Paulina, Leontes is starting to think the same. He is starting to think that the bitterness that is always in his thoughts, partly because so often on Paulina's tongue, is now verging on the ridiculous.

2. Reasonable emotions

So here are some theses that Shakespeare treats, not implausibly, as common ground between his characters:

(a) Emotions can be excessive, insufficient, confused, or misdirected, and they can be the wrong emotions for the occasion. In short, emotions can be reasonable or unreasonable. It follows that they answer to reasons. Can they also be controlled by reasoning? That is not so clear.

(b) The reasons that some emotions answer to include reasons that were not fully conformed to at some prior time. Or perhaps they include, rather, the further reason that those reasons were not fully conformed to. Either way, the reasons that are left behind still hold sway over our emotional lives.

(c) There is some rationally intelligible connection between having an emotion and expressing it in action. In some sense emotions call for their own expression. But is there always a reason to express a reasonable emotion? That is not so clear. What is clear is that there can be reasons not to do so: there can, for instance, be better uses for one's time and energy.

I believe that these three theses are all sound. It would require too much digression to defend them in full. But allow me to explore each of them enough to bring out what is relevant to our investigations. The aim of those investigations is to make rational sense of the instincts we all sometimes have, and the attempts we all sometimes make, to repair the irreparable.

(a) The common idea that emotion belongs to the non-rational part of the soul—indeed that emotion is to be contrasted with reason—reflects the common experience that emotions are not easily kept in check. Can one decide to stop being angry or afraid, and thereby stop being angry or afraid? Not directly. Perhaps indirectly. Perhaps by a programme of deep breaths, contrived happy thoughts, diverting conversation, yoga routines, therapy sessions, etc. Emotions have their own momentum and need to be managed in cunning, roundabout ways to contain their potential excesses, misdirections, and other errors. But there we see precisely why emotions cannot be relegated to the non-rational part of the soul. If they can be excessive, misdirected, or otherwise erroneous, then they answer to reasons. One's anger can be out of proportion to the reasons for it. One can be afraid of things that one has no reason to be afraid of. One can fail to be ashamed when one has reason to be ashamed ('shameless'). Or one can react with *Schadenfreude* when the appropriate emotion would be concern or distress (because, for example, the *Schaden* befell one's friend). That emotions cannot be directly brought into line by the will does not establish, then, that they do not answer to reasons. It establishes exactly the opposite. For it entails that there is a line for emotions to be brought into, that they have a proper measure, albeit one that, alas, they are prone to miss. Emotions can run high, as the stock expression has it, only relative to some benchmark at which they run correctly.

Compare beliefs. One cannot start or stop believing some proposition at will. The best that one can achieve by deciding to achieve it is the suspension of one's disbelief. Then one accepts (treats as if one believed) some proposition that one does not believe. Notoriously, beliefs are sometimes hard to shake off. Think of beliefs that one grew up with, that chime with one's way of life or self-image, that help one to find order in chaos or simplicity in complexity, etc. Such beliefs can be sticky. Yet it would be a wild leap from the acknowledgement of cases like this to the conclusion that beliefs do not answer to reasons, and hence that they cannot qualify as reasonable or unreasonable. The main lesson of these cases is precisely the opposite. It is that beliefs can, on occasions, be unreasonable. Beliefs can fail to respond adequately to the reasons, even to the reasons that the believer is aware of, for and against holding them. On the other hand, to the extent that beliefs do respond adequately to the reasons for and against holding them, they do so, as it were, of their own accord. There is no role for any intervening decision to believe.[7]

The will is not involved. One comes upon new evidence and, barring malfunctions, one's beliefs adapt. The fact that this happens without the mediation of the will should not lead one to imagine that it also takes place without reasoning. Weighing up the evidence, and more generally coping with various reasons to believe that point in different directions, often calls for close, patient, complex deliberation. We instruct juries, for example, to deliberate slowly and with great care before coming to any conclusions. My point is only that once they come to their conclusions, there is no further step to take, no decision to make, before they arrive at their beliefs.[8]

---

[7] The classic treatment of why this is so is Bernard Williams, 'Deciding to Believe' in Williams, *Problems of the Self* (Cambridge University Press 1973), 136. Williams' first argument at 148 is misguided; his second at 149, however, hits the nail on the head.

[8] The case of the jury has additional complications because juries are instructed to disregard various valid reasons for belief (e.g. what they have heard about the defendant's actions from reliable sources other than evidence admitted in the trial). That means that sometimes jurors do not arrive at beliefs but instead at conclusions that they are bound to accept for the purpose of the trial. They may

All of this is true, *mutatis mutandis*, of emotions too. When the
going is good, one's emotions respond of their own accord to the
reasons for them. One is angry when one has something to be
angry about, and afraid when one has something to be afraid of,
and regretful when one has something to regret, and so on. If one
discovers that one misinterpreted the situation, taking it to give
one cause for anger or fear or regret that it did not give one cause
for (or taking it to give one cause for more anger or fear or regret
than it gave one cause for) then, barring malfunctions, one's anger
or fear or regret (as the case may be) simply recedes of its own
accord. The problem is that here, as with beliefs, the possibilities
for malfunction are legion. The going is not always good. Like a
stubborn belief, one's anger or fear or regret may be hard to shake
off. In particular, a strong emotion may interfere with one's deliberation about the reasons for it and thereby impede its own abate-
ment. Noticing that the original thing that one was angry about
never happened (or was less grave than one took it to be), one may
well hunt around for another thing that would warrant one's still
being just as angry, even perhaps to the point of stirring up something to be angry about. This is a variant of the same malfunction
that is known, in connection with beliefs, as 'confirmation bias'.
One is hoping to bring the world into line with one's emotion,
given that one's emotion has so far staunchly refused to fall into
line with the world.

When the going is good, emotion, like belief, falls into line
with the world. This is sometimes known as the 'direction of fit'
of beliefs and emotions, and it is sometimes contrasted with the
'direction of fit' of actions and intentions.[9] Your beliefs and emotions are supposed to fall into line with the world, the story goes,

believe, on inadmissible evidence, that the defendant is guilty but accept that, on
the admissible evidence, he is not guilty. In that case, an intervening decision (a
suspension of disbelief) is called for. Beliefs respond to deliberation but not everything that responds to deliberation is a belief. The belief/acceptance distinction is
nicely developed, and its importance nicely revealed, by L Jonathan Cohen, *An
Essay on Belief and Acceptance* (Clarendon Press 1992), in which special attention is
given to the position of the jury at 117–26.

[9] The contrast is traceable to Elizabeth Anscombe, *Intention* (Basil Blackwell
1957), 56. The terminology is traceable to Mark Platts, *Ways of Meaning* (Routledge
& Kegan Paul 1979), 256–7.

whereas the world is supposed to fall into line with your actions and intentions. Although temptingly tidy, this way of carving up rationality is mistaken. It errs in both directions. On the one hand, when your beliefs or emotions change, that is already a change in the world. It is no different, as changes go, from a change that you bring about, by your actions, in the beliefs or emotions of other people. It had better be a change for the better, in other words to a world in which more reasons are conformed to. On the other hand, when the going is good, actions and intentions, like beliefs and emotions, are responsive to the world. All reasons are facts. The ultimate question with actions and intentions, as with beliefs and emotions, is whether one's response was appropriate to the situation that one was truly in. So there is no distinction in respect of 'direction of fit'. Yet there clearly is *some* distinction in the neighbourhood. How to draw it? Here is a suggestion.

An emotion or belief, unlike an action or intention, may be appropriate even though it is valueless. More precisely, the fact that one conformed to a reason for belief or a reason for emotion does not entail that one brought any value into the world beyond the value of adding to the stock of reasons that were conformed to. Whereas the fact that one conformed to a reason for action does entail that one brought additional value into the world. That it is approximately spherical is the only reasonable belief for modern people to have about the shape of our planet Earth, even if there is nothing (beyond the mere fact of conformity with more reasons to believe) to be gained from believing it. Awe, similarly, is the only reasonable emotion to experience on first seeing planet Earth from its moon, even if (apart from the fact that by experiencing it one conformed to reasons for awe) the awe did nobody any good at all. By contrast, if there is nothing to be gained from *investigating* the shape of the Earth or from *travelling* to the moon, then one has no reason to do it and it cannot be a reasonable thing to do (or to intend to do). True enough, by hypothesis one does have at least the following minimal reasons to investigate the shape of the Earth and to travel to its moon: doing so will enable one to conform better to reasons for belief and reasons for emotion. If one never saw Earth from its moon, one's life was lacking in at least one respect. One never experienced the appropriate awe of seeing that sight for the first time. Is there any further value in experiencing that appropriate awe? Perhaps. It may help one to overcome one's depression, to become a less narcissistic person, to work hard for environmental causes, or to enthuse children about physics. But there need not be any such further value. For even without it, awe is the appropriate emotion, the one that befits one's first breathtaking glimpse of planet Earth from its moon. That is how the awe qualifies as reasonable, and continues to do so even if, alas, it mainly motivates one to do wholly unreasonable things (such as abandoning one's friends and family in the search for ever more awesome experiences, or plotting a terrorist attack on Earth in the name of restoring human humility).

This explains how there can be unreasonable actions borne of reasonable beliefs and emotions. It also shows that there is an important role for the will in helping one to avoid getting carried away to unreasonable actions by reasonable beliefs or emotions. That they have got carried away like that is the charge that Cleomenes lays against Paulina and Leontes when he objects that Paulina 'might have spoken a thousand things that would / Have done the time more benefit.' Paulina may reply that her regular reinforcements of Leontes' remorse do have a benefit, namely that Leontes is experiencing the measure of remorse that befits his wrongs. Leontes is thereby conforming to reasons better than he otherwise would. Even if Cleomenes accepts this, however, it does not fully answer his challenge. For he is concerned that there is no longer much *further* benefit, beyond emotional appropriateness, in Leontes being kept in that emotional space. Paulina could have been so much more therapeutic, so much more constructive, so much more positive!

That, however, is a tendentious charge. It is the charge of a rather practical person who already tends to prioritize action over feeling (dare we say 'sense over sensibility'?[10]) when the two are competing for space in a single life. Yes, we may agree with Cleomenes' verdict in the case of Leontes, whose virtually all-consuming remorse has been prolonged by Paulina for

---

[10] That would be daring because Jane Austen's novel adeptly problematizes the distinction drawn in its title. See e.g. Inger Sigrun Brodey, 'Adventures of a Female Werther: Jane Austen's Revision of Sensibility', *Philosophy and Literature* 23 (1999), 110.

sixteen years. But should we generalize the prioritization of the
practical as Cleomenes invites us to do by his insinuation of a
'benefit' metric?[11] Or should we rather learn the lesson of the
bereft lover in Kirsty MacColl's song 'Over You', who discovers
belatedly that practicality (meaning: emphasis on doing what
is to be done) is not the whole of rationality (meaning: responsiveness to reasons): 'I've made a point of never thinking back
on the past at all/I figured out that wishes have never changed
the world before/So my time was sewn up tight/For years
I thought I had it right/But you changed my ideas overnight.'[12]
MacColl concedes, notice, that part of the value of keeping
oneself busy may be to protect oneself from the experience of
harsh emotions. What she adds is this: the fact that those harsh
emotions have insufficient value to make up for their harshness
is not enough to warrant always keeping them at bay. For quite
irrespective of their value, they may still be the right emotions
to be feeling.

(b) You may be tempted to conclude, from what I have said,
that insofar as we aim only to have reasonable emotions, we need
not concern ourselves with reasons for action. But that conclusion is wrong in various ways. Here is the most basic way. Often
action, or the lack of it, is the *object* of appropriate emotion. A few
months ago, I was excited to be planning a trip to Brazil. I was
disappointed that, because of the dates that worked for the rest
of the family, my stepson would not be joining us on the trip.
I was nervous about managing the logistics, with two younger
children in tow, and also a little panicky about the brand new
lectures I had promised to give during my stay. While we were
there, I was buoyed by the culture of lively political protest and
activism in Sao Paolo, but dispirited by the official concealment
of poverty, as it seemed to me, in Rio de Janeiro. Yet in both cities

---

[11] For an affirmative answer more extreme than anything Cleomenes has in
mind, and antithetical to the line I am taking here, see Rüdiger Bittner, 'Is it
Reasonable to Regret Things One Did?', *Journal of Philosophy* 89 (1992), 262.

[12] Kirsty MacColl, 'Over You', originally the b-side of 'See that Girl' (Polydor
Records 1981), rereleased on the MacColl anthology *All I Ever Wanted* (Union
Square Music 2013).

I was overwhelmed by the *joie de vivre* and the warm welcome. Back home, I am therefore full of *saudade*[13] when I think of the many new friends and acquaintances I made, now so far away. Yet I am also full of gratitude towards our hosts for inviting us and for looking after us so well.

On this list, there is a wide range of emotions—some positive, some negative. The negative ones have as their object some action which, in my thoughts, is not entirely as it should be. There is my leaving my stepson out of a once-in-a-lifetime adventure, the possibility of my messing up the lecture slides or losing the passports, the municipal authorities screening off the favelas, and my perhaps never going back to Brazil. There need be no suggestion that any of these actions is or was or would be wrongful, or culpable, or unjustified. For each negative emotion on the list to be supported by a reason, there need only be a reason for someone to do, or to have done, something other than what, in my thoughts, that someone does or did. A reason for me to return to see my friends in Brazil? Then a reason for *saudade* at the possibility that I might never do so. A reason not to conceal Brazil's social problems from visitors? Then a reason to be dispirited at how Rio's image is managed. A reason for my stepson to come along? Then a reason to be disappointed that he had to be left out of the trip. A reason not to lose the passports? Then a reason to be nervous at the possibility that I might do so. And so on. To generalize: A deficit in conformity with a reason for action? Then already, without further ado, a reason for some negative emotion. And if it is a trifling reason for action, or a trifling deficit in conformity? Then only a trifling reason to feel bad, by itself warranting perhaps only a flicker of negativity.

The negative emotions on my Brazil list did not strictly need to have actions as their objects to qualify as appropriate. But some negative emotions do. They are essentially concerned with things done. Guilt and indignation are examples. Obviously, I do not mean that nobody ever feels guilt or indignation at things that simply happen. The experience of 'survivor guilt' among those who escaped a natural disaster in which others

---

[13] See Tiffany Watt Smith, *The Book of Human Emotions* (Profile Books 2015), 230–1.

perished is well documented. What I mean is that guilt without an action of the guilty party (or at least of a collectivity of which she is a member) is misplaced. For one's survivor guilt to be appropriate, then, its true object had better be, not the mere fact that one survived, but the paucity of what one did to merit such good fortune, or something like that. Otherwise, survivor guilt is akin to a phobia. It is pathological. One feels guilty even though one has nothing to feel guilty about. Here at last we have a suitable case for a therapist. Or so it seems to me. You may not have exactly the same views about what qualifies as a reason for guilt. Maybe you think that, in these assessments, I have confused guilt with remorse. Still, whether it is guilt or remorse that we are talking about, you will recognize the wider idea of what is often called a 'moral emotion', a distinct emotion part-constituted by the thought that some action was not as it should have been. It may be an action of one's own, as with guilt and remorse, or an action of another, as with indignation and outrage. Either way, there is somewhere a deficit in conformity with a reason for action.

The label 'moral emotion' is far from ideal. As in many other stock uses, 'moral' carries distracting overtones. It may lead to a premature emphasis on culpability, for example, and from there to a warped picture of negative emotions as akin to self-executing punishments, appropriate only if deserved. Arguably guilt befits only culpable actions. Arguably remorse befits only actions that are both wrongful and culpable. But these are special features of particular emotions. Bernard Williams urges us to resist the idea that, in the absence of such special features, there are no apt negative feelings that are essentially concerned with our actions. One might always regret an action or some aspect of it, of course, but one might equally regret an earthquake or a lightning strike. Should a blameless agent react to the costs of her own actions as she would react to the costs of earthquakes or lightning strikes, namely as if they were simply unfortunate things that happened while she was nearby? Is such vanilla regret all that is called for? Williams says not. Just as guilt and remorse strike him as too specific, so regret strikes him as too generic. He insists on the existence of a distinct emotion, 'agent-regret', which befits the situation of one whose own

actions, innocently or otherwise, leave some regrettable remainder behind:

> The lorry driver who, through no fault of his own, runs over a child,
> will feel differently from any spectator, even a spectator next to him
> in the cab, except perhaps to the extent that the spectator takes on the
> thought that he himself might have prevented it, an agent's thought. . . .
> We feel sorry for the driver, but that sentiment co-exists with, indeed
> presupposes, that there is something special about his relation to this
> happening, something which cannot merely be eliminated by the con-
> sideration that it was not his fault.[14]

Notice, adds Williams, that this agent-regret 'does not necessarily
involve the wish that, all things taken together, one had acted
otherwise.' It extends to cases in which one 'is sorry that things
turned out they did' or 'wish[es] that one had not had to act as
one did', and yet one still stands by one's decision. So not only is
agent-regret an apt emotion for those with valid excuses for what
they did (like the lorry driver who can point to his skilful emergency stop),[15] but equally for those with ample justifications for
what they did (like Sophie, who is forced to choose between her
two children at the beginning of *Sophie's Choice*).[16]

Williams' proposal tends to meet resistance from two directions. There are those who think that the distinct emotion of
agent-regret exists, but that it must be irrational inasmuch as it
survives the realization that one was not at fault. It is then a path-
ology akin to survivor guilt. It is not that Sophie slides into acute
depression because she is (appropriately) tormented by what she
did. Rather, she is (inappropriately) tormented by what she did
because (after the traumas of the death camp, including the loss of
her daughter) she is acutely depressed. On the other hand, there
are those who think that the distinct emotion of agent-regret
would be appropriate enough in a case like Sophie's, if only it existed. But there is no such distinct emotion.

---

[14] Williams, 'Moral Luck', in Williams, *Moral Luck* (Cambridge University
Press 1981), 20 at 28.

[15] For a subtle literary exploration (in psychological-thriller form) of agent-
regret in 'valid excuse' cases, I commend Owen Sheers, *I Saw a Man* (Faber &
Faber 2015).

[16] Discussed in ch 1, s 3.

As you will have worked out by now, I have no sympathy with the first line of resistance. But I have some with the second.

Consider Williams' case for regarding agent-regret as a distinct emotion. Here is the gist of it: 'The differences between agent-regret and regret felt by a spectator come out not just in thoughts and images that enter into the sentiment, but in differences of expression.' These, it seems to me, are inadequate criteria for the individuation of emotions. The second ('differences of expression') puts the cart before the horse. We need to be sure that a distinct emotion exists before we can work out whether we are witnessing the expression of it. Meanwhile the first ('differences ... in thoughts and images') invites the following counterproposal: that what Williams regards as the distinct emotion of agent-regret is instead a combination of two separate, but interacting, experiences. One is ordinary, vanilla regret. The other is the thought of one's own responsibility for what is regretted. I regret the injury to the child who ran out in front of my lorry, and on top of that I hold myself to have been responsible for it.[17] Then, naturally enough, I also regret the fact of my responsibility. My pained thoughts include not just 'if only the lad hadn't run out' but also 'if only I had gone for a different route this morning' (or a smaller truck, earlier start, etc.).

Agent-regret is, on this view, a kind of compound regret. The extra thought of my own responsibility does not transform my emotion into a different one. It makes for more of the same emotion, but now with two objects: the fact of the injury and the fact of my own responsibility for it. The additional dose of regret is appropriate, of course, if and only if I am indeed responsible. But that is not such a tall order. That I am responsible in this sense—the same sense that we came across in Chapter 2—does not entail that I am at fault, culpable, blameworthy. It entails only that, if there are justifications or excuses to be offered, they are mine to offer. If there is a rational explanation to be given, it falls to me to give it. This basic responsibility condition is met whenever I do

[17] This formulation is supposed to anticipate and mitigate the worry, noted by Williams, 'Moral Luck' (n 14), 28–9, that I might view my own actions 'externally', perhaps regretting my responsibility for what happened, but only in the sense of regretting that I may be held responsible by others and end up having to pay. This is not 'holding oneself ... responsible', and that is why the regret in question is not agent-regret as I understand it.

not conform to a reason, say a reason for me to stop short when a child appears in the road in front my lorry. It is now for me to explain (even if only to myself) why I did not stop my lorry in time.

These considerations are clearly not conclusive against the Williams portrayal of agent-regret as a distinct emotion. But they do open the way to the thought that, quite apart from agent-regret, there might also be such things as agent-embarrassment, agent-pity, agent-disappointment, and so forth, all calling for a similar compound analysis. Williams himself hints at the same. Recall that, according to Williams, '[w]e feel sorry for the driver' and that this 'sentiment ... presupposes' that the driver is in a special position vis-à-vis the child's fate. Is this not agent-pity, of which the correct analysis is not that it is an emotion distinct from pity but that it is pity compounded? The driver, we might think, is doubly pitiable: there is the pitiable situation of his having an injured child under the front of his lorry, a situation not to be envied even if he were a mere passenger, and then there is the pitiable extra feature that, as the driver of the lorry, he is basically responsible for the child's being there.

In spite of the possibility that we are really talking about a range of different emotions that can be compounded by thoughts of responsibility, allow me to retain Williams' label 'agent-regret' to encompass all those in the range that are self-directed. That is not an entirely stipulative proposal. It seems to me plausible to think that agent-embarrassment and agent-shame, for instance, are part-constituted by agent-regret as I have just reanalysed it.

(c) You may have the impression, from my examples of deadly decisions, that I am thinking of agent-regret as an apt response only to the irreparable. Not so. I am thinking of it, rather, as an apt response to what has so far gone unrepaired, of which the irreparable is but the purest case. In a case in which repair is still possible, one's agent-regret can serve as a valuable impetus towards repair, an extra motivation to do what one should anyway do, in keeping with the continuity thesis. How does one's agent-regret provide that extra motivational service? When one repairs in accordance with the continuity thesis, one mops up some of the residue of unconformed-to reasons for action that were left behind by one's previous action. One thereby reduces the cumulative force of reasons to feel agent-regret. And one thereby (all being well) assuages the agent-regret itself. By that process, as Samuel Johnson put it, the pain of agent-regret 'necessarily direct[s] us to [its] proper cure'.[18]

In this explanation, you will notice, I already presuppose that the extra reason to repair that our agent-regret gives us (namely that repairing will assuage our agent-regret) does not figure in the rational case for experiencing agent-regret. The rational case for experiencing agent-regret is that the agent-regret befits the situation one finds oneself in. The fact that the agent-regret gives one an extra reason to do what one should do anyway is but a valuable side-effect of experiencing it. In calling it a 'side-effect', I do not mean to cast doubt on the possibility of one's deliberately manipulating oneself to acquire (or to maintain) an emotion, as Leontes recruits Paulina to help him do. If one were not prone to spontaneous agent-regret, but knew oneself to be highly averse to pain, one might manipulate oneself to become more agent-regretful (say, by hiring a Paulina-equivalent). One might do that precisely in order to give oneself an extra reason (a pain-relief reason) to do what one knows one should do anyway (namely repair the damage) but might otherwise be too weak-willed or forgetful to do. The pain will spur one on if nothing else does! Doesn't one here have a (deviant) reason to feel agent-regret— namely a reason to feel it for its value in getting one to do what one should be doing anyway? Couldn't one similarly have a (deviant) reason to hold Christian beliefs, namely to pass the tests of faith that the Inquisition will set for one? I think not. These are reasons for action: reasons to make oneself feel agent-regret, reasons to make oneself believe in the Holy Trinity. They are not reasons for the emotion or the belief itself. Do not imagine that we never have any reasons to make ourselves respond less than rationally, e.g. with exaggerated or attenuated emotions, or with unwarranted beliefs. Of course we do. These are sometimes called 'the wrong kind of reasons'[19] but that is a misleading name. They

---

[18] Johnson, 'The Proper Means of Regulating Sorrow' *The Rambler*, issue 47 (28 August 1750).

[19] The nomenclature goes back to Justin D'Arms and Daniel Jacobson, 'Sentiment and Value', *Ethics* 110 (2000), 722, at 734. For a good survey see Jacobson, 'Wrong Kind of Reasons Problem' in Hugh LaFollette (ed), *The International Encyclopedia of Ethics* (Wiley 2013), 5553. I am not saying that there is

are not the wrong kind of reasons for what they are reasons for, viz. for the actions one undertakes with a view to acquiring new emotions or beliefs. They are the right kind of reasons for that. But they are also not the wrong kind of reasons for the beliefs or emotions in question, because they are not reasons for those beliefs or emotions at all. They point to value in having those beliefs and emotions, but the value of having a belief or emotion is not a reason for having it.

The ordinary rational case for experiencing agent-regret, to repeat, is its appropriateness to the situation in which there are reasons that one failed completely to conform to. The problem, as we already know, is that there is no *total* cure for agent-regret in this dimension of appropriateness. Even if repair in accordance with the continuity thesis is assiduously and promptly carried out, there must always linger some residual ground for agent-regret, some unrepaired and irreparable remainder. Then, as Williams puts it, 'only the desire to make reparation remains, with the painful consciousness that nothing can be done about it.'[20] Notice that this desire—I would rather call it a wish or a longing—is not irrational. By hypothesis one still has a reason to repair. That is the unconformed-to reason in virtue of which one's agent-regret is appropriate. The problem is only that one has no derivative reason to *try* to repair, no reason to *take any steps towards* repair, because by hypothesis all such steps are doomed to fail. They would be futile gestures.

Yet we may think, with Leontes, that there are nevertheless some things still to be done, and that even if they are gestures, they might well be more than token gestures. One's agent-regret still calls for expression, be it by tears, by confession, by holding a lonely vigil at the graveside, by denying oneself a remarriage, etc. Expressing an appropriate negative emotion is the only way forward, we may think, when there is nothing left to do by way of making the emotion less appropriate. We may think so. But are we right? Notice that the question is not whether there might sometimes be what is sometimes called a 'cathartic' reason to express

no 'wrong kind of reasons' problem anywhere. In ch 2, s 2, I already allowed that, occasionally, we have deviant reasons to intend.

[20] Williams, 'Moral Luck' (n 14), 29.

an emotion. Some people find that 'blowing off steam' can help to contain their fury, that 'letting it out' can help to alleviate their grief, that there can be a 'talking cure' for their morbid anxiety ('the more [Anna O] chattered on, the better it went'[21]), and so on. Whether catharsis works is a contingent matter, subject to empirical testing. It does not offer the kind of invariant connection between the experience of emotion and the expression of emotion that we are looking for. And there is also another consideration, brought out by the example of Anna O's 'talking cure'. Although we arguably have a reason to alleviate any negative emotion (even when appropriate, after all, they are still painful), that reason to alleviate applies a fortiori to exaggerated negative emotions, and with the greatest force of all to negative emotions like Anna O's for which there are no reasons at all. If there are no reasons at all to experience an emotion, however, then the reasons for experiencing it cannot double as reasons to express it. Our interest is in the thesis that they do so double: that a reason to feel a certain way is, or entails, a reason to express how one feels. So our interest is not an interest in possible reasons to express, and thereby to curtail, irrational emotions. We are interested, on the contrary, in appropriate emotions and in the supposed appropriateness of their expression that is owed to the very fact that they are appropriate emotions.

John Skorupski suggests that there is a 'bridge principle' in play here. As he formulates the principle, 'there is a reason for x to do what the affective responses that there is a reason for x to feel would characteristically dispose x to do.'[22] Formulated in this way, the principle gives the expressive reason even to those who do not actually have the emotion. They have a reason to act as if they do have the emotion. We will come back to that kind of masquerade. For now, let's think about a less radical version of the 'bridge principle' in which x actually feels as he should feel and is disposed to express how he feels. Does he indeed have a reason to do the expressing? One can see the appeal of the proposal that he does.

[21] Jacques Lacan, *The Four Fundamental Concepts of Psycho-Analysis* (W W Norton & Co 1994), 157, discussing Josef Breuer's experimental treatment of patient Anna O, a treatment that lay at the foundation of Freud's theory of psychoanalysis.

[22] Skorupski, *The Domain of Reasons* (Oxford University Press 2010), 24.

Emotions clearly do apply some kind of pressure for action; there is some sense in which they agitate or campaign for their own manifestation. And quite apart from their intention-free physiological symptoms (welling up of tears, reddening of cheeks, butterflies in the stomach, etc.), many emotions do have specific intentional actions in which they are characteristically expressed. Anger disposes one to rant, fear disposes one to flee, shame disposes one to hang one's head, and so on. Sometimes these actions are futile or self-defeating. Were it not for their expressiveness, there would be nothing to be said in favour of them. Fleeing from a bear is a tempting but terrible idea. Ranting at teenagers is often counterproductive. But does not the sheer expressiveness of the act lend it a kind of rationality all the same? In a way it does. It does not entail that there is any reason in favour of doing it. Yet it does make the expressive action, in a way, rationally intelligible.

Suppose that I am hiking along the clifftop and spot a solitary swimmer struggling hopelessly in the heavy seas below. So here I am, alone in a remote location with no equipment and no phone signal. I can't swim to save my own life, never mind another's. Attempting a rescue would be futile, and worse. I am beside myself with frustration. I shout, flail around ineffectually, wring my hands, dance from foot to foot, move towards the cliff-edge then move back, run around like a crazy thing. What is all this in aid of? Maybe I am simply being indecisive because I have not yet fully adapted to the hopelessness of my situation. But maybe, on the contrary, it is precisely the hopelessness that has got to me. I am pathetically straining against my predicament as a rational being, absurdly trying to find a way of saving the swimmer without trying to save him. In that very absurdity, in my straining against my predicament, I exhibit very starkly my rationality. There are reasons galore for me to save the swimmer. I am all too aware of them. I am highly sensitive to them. I have the emotions to prove it. The wish that things were otherwise, and the motivation to make them otherwise, is built into the emotions. The emotions motivate me to act by, so to speak, foregrounding salient reasons for action. And yet right now there is nothing for them to motivate me to do by way of conformity with the very reasons for action that they foreground. So I flounder. My floundering is unreasonable action on the strength of reasonable emotion. It is unjustified but probably (unless it distracts me from other pressing concerns) excused. Imagine the contrasting case in which I did not react at all. Imagine that, recognizing at once the futility of any attempt I might make to rescue the swimmer, I had not even given him a second glance. Imagine that I had just hiked past. That would, I think, have been justified. It would not have needed an excuse. All the same, it would not have reflected well on me. It would have revealed me as a person so practically-minded that my 'heart ran a couple [of] degrees colder' than a regular human one.[23] And not, notice, because our human hearts are irrational. No, precisely because they are rational: because in them we feel the force of reasons that apply to us even when it is impossible for us to do anything to conform to those reasons, and hence even when it would be irrational for us to attempt conformity.

3. Making apology intelligible

Our modest 'bridge principle' is false and so, therefore, is Skorupski's more radical one. Even though one's reasonable emotions may powerfully drive one to do it, there is no standing reason to express what one reasonably feels, let alone what one merely has reason to feel without feeling it.

So why apologize? The revival of this question, raised but unanswered in Chapter 3, may strike you as coming out of the blue. Yet we have been building up to it. What I will call a 'model apology' is an expression of agent-regret for what one did to someone, where that someone is the addressee and recipient of one's apology. A model apology expresses the apologizer's heart-felt wish that things had been otherwise with what she did, al-though it does not necessarily express a wish that, all in all, she had done otherwise.[24] It also expresses her acceptance of her basic

---

[23] Philipp Meyer, *American Rust* (Simon and Schuster 2009), 283–4: '[H]is daughter was practical. Her heart ran a couple degrees colder.'

[24] Compare Nick Smith, *I Was Wrong: The Meanings of Apologies* (Cambridge University Press 2008), ch 2. Smith's model apology involves 'accepting blame' (33). That means accepting that all in all one should have done otherwise, such that one 'would [not] commit the offense again in similar circumstances' (69).

responsibility, although not necessarily her belief in it. What she regrets, in a model apology, includes the part she played in what she regrets. I call it a 'model apology' because other apologies are modelled on it. There are the vicarious apologies that are made on behalf of someone else, or received on behalf of someone else. There are the insincere apologies that are issued with the intention of inducing their recipient to believe that the apologizer is regretful when she isn't, or that she accepts responsibility when she doesn't. Some of these are evasive apologies, which may express regret, but subtly shift responsibility to the addressee: 'I am sorry that you were offended' instead of 'I am sorry that I offended you.' Perhaps most interesting for our purposes are 'formal' apologies, as we might call them. Stock apologetic phrases such as 'I regret what I did' and 'I am sorry for what I did' are not always used to report or express the speaker's emotions and—more to the point—they are not always understood to do so. Sometimes, they are understood on both sides as performative utterances by which the utterer accepts responsibility, without any element of emotional report or emotional expression. Such an apology is sometimes disparaged as meaningless or empty. But it should not be tarred automatically with the same brush as an insincere apology.[25] When the conditions are such that the formal apology will not be understood by anyone to be a report or expression of an emotion, but only a performance, there is no insincerity involved. A formal apology may sometimes be more worth giving and more worth having, indeed, than a model apology. Its

Whilst in Smith's main supporting example (Richard Nixon's resignation speech) the speaker *is* blameworthy, he is so glaringly so that nobody who accepted responsibility could sincerely deny it. That Nixon's apology seems empty, verging on a pseudo-apology, comes mainly of his evasiveness about his responsibility, of which the refusal of blame is but a symptom. It is true, of course, that today's clamour for amends coincides with a passion for blaming. Hardly surprising, then, that many people get grumpy when the apologies they receive do not express contrition as well as agent-regret. That, however, is not because people want a model apology (although maybe they also want that). Rather, it is because they want an apology that also serves as a confession of guilt and, ideally, a self-abasing request for forgiveness—several birds with one stone.

[25]   Gijs van Dijck's excellent review of psychological literature on the effects of apologies (see van Dijck, 'The Ordered Apology', *Oxford Journal of Legal Studies* 37 (2017), 562) is slightly marred by its labelling of formal apologies as insincere.

deliberateness may be a plus. It may bespeak a greater investment in obtaining it, or a greater investment in making it, or both. Nevertheless, a formal apology, like an insincere apology, is modelled on a model apology. 'I regret what I did' is a stock phrase in which to formulate a formal apology precisely because apology is the characteristic action of the agent-regretter.

Is there any reason to express one's agent-regret by apologizing? Clearly there often is. Sometimes the expression of one's agent-regret is cathartic. One gets it off one's chest. Sometimes it is recuperative for the person to whom one apologizes. It helps him to get over what was done to him. And sometimes, as we agreed in Chapter 3, it is reconciliatory. It helps to avoid the destructive escalation of a conflict between the giver and the receiver of the apology, or to bring an already destructive conflict to an end, possibly restoring cordial, or even friendly, relations. Sometimes, it does all of these things together, either in mixture or in compound. Sometimes (to take a compound case) an apology is cathartic because reconciliatory and reconciliatory because recuperative. Obviously, there can be various other reasons in the mix or in the compound. For example: meeting social expectations, pleasing one's parents, avoiding a sour look, gaining a feeling of superiority, negotiating a better settlement. Many of these are also possible reasons for one to apologize even though one is not remotely agent-regretful. They are reasons to act as if one were agent-regretful, often the more convincingly the better. Where one cannot muster any agent-regret, one may still be able to contribute to someone else's recuperation or avoid a nasty escalation by doing a good impression of someone suitably agent-regretful. Sometimes, indeed, one works up to a model apology from an insincere, or otherwise shaky, start. Edith Nesbit has her fictional children kiss and make up like this:

So Dicky said, 'Don't be disagreeable yourself, H. O. Let her alone and say you're sorry, or I'll jolly well make you!'

So H. O. said he was sorry. Then Alice kissed him and said she was sorry too; and after that H. O. gave her a hug, and said, 'Now I'm *really and truly* sorry.' So it was all right.[26]

---

[26] E Nesbit, *The Story of the Treasure Seekers* (T Fisher Unwin 1899), 139.

The older brother Dicky, surely a restorative justice facilitator in the making, calculated right. An end to the petty bickering would best be served by a model apology. That apology is best attained by one of the little ones making the first move. Under pressure from Dicky, H. O. duly utters a reluctant and probably insincere apology, and then his sister, appreciating her sibling's effort, responds with a more sincere and affectionate (but still perhaps somewhat calculated and humouring) counter-apology. This self-denying gesture fills the little lad with genuine agent-regret for the mean things he said to his sister—and he is moved spontaneously to express it, 'really and truly'. Now they have patched up their differences, made things 'all right'.

None of this is unfamiliar. Yet it is mysterious. How does it work? How does apology make things right? That is the question that we originally put to Margaret Walker and Linda Radzik in Chapter 3. The first puzzle facing those who offer reconciliation or recuperation as a rationale for apologetic action is the question of why apologetic action is reconciliatory or recuperative. What makes issuing an apology, rather than doing six somersaults or singing a sea shanty in Serbo-Croat, the natural way to achieve reconciliation or recuperation? Is it only an arbitrary social convention, such that we might expect a remote Amazonian tribe to have gone for something quite different, maybe leaving a pair of old shoes cooking on the fire? Or would the discovery of that Amazonian convention simply put us in need of clever anthropologists who can explain to us why this shoe-roasting ritual has come to be regarded as a way of apologizing? In which case we can forget the puzzle of the shoes, because we are back to the deeper and less parochial puzzle that we started with: why apologize? Is there some case for apology—apology in particular—that is independent of, and hence capable of explaining, such reconciliatory or recuperative effect as it has?

It is no answer, at this stage, to plead the continuity thesis. It is true that apology can sometimes serve as a mechanism of repair in accordance with the continuity thesis. If one of the reasons not to have done what one did was that one damaged one's valuable relationship, and if by making an apology one can move towards some kind of reconciliation (thereby curtailing the damage to the relationship), then apology is a straightforwardly reparative measure in accordance with the continuity thesis. Similarly, if one of the reasons not to have done what one did was that one left someone else feeling insecure or suspicious, and if by making an apology one can help with that person's recuperation—the restoration of their psychological equilibrium—then once again apology becomes a straightforwardly reparative measure in accordance with the continuity thesis. Here, to use a different lingo, restorative justice is simply corrective justice as it applies to certain special kinds of losses (losses of relationship, losses of psychological equilibrium). But noticing such applications of the continuity thesis does not move us forward with our present line of inquiry. It merely takes us back to the question of how apology works such strange magic when it does. What is it about apologizing—apologizing in particular—that lends it such reconciliatory and recuperative power as it has?

If you followed the analysis in the previous section of my predicament as a would-be rescuer floundering uselessly on the clifftop, you can anticipate the gist of my answer. A model apology is a rationally intelligible reaction to things left undone, to reasons left unconformed to, even when any attempt at repair would be futile. That it is an expression of agent-regret gives it a rational salience, a meaningfulness, that can sometimes be carried over into reparative uses, that enables it to be used derivatively as a device for repairing damaged relationships or repairing psychological disturbance or the like. For even if it is too late for me to repair anything, even if it is now too late for me to conform to any of the reasons for action, it does not follow that it is too late for me to be sensitive to those reasons, to give them suitable attention or recognition in how I think and feel. Part of feeling their force is being disposed to act, even if only in futile expression of how one feels. Although Jane Austen surely comes out top in Anglophone literature for her finely-tuned portrayals of apology in all of its variety,[27] for a representation of the most basic human

---

[27] My personal favourite, a treasure trove of moral and psychological insight, is Willoughby's apology in Austen, *Sense and Sensibility* (Thomas Egerton 1811), vol iii, ch 8 (ch 44 overall). Offering his apology, the already-forgiven Willoughby asks to be forgiven 'again ... on more reasonable grounds' in the light of his apology.

impetus to express agent-regret through apology it is hard to beat this example from Nick Hornby:

> Over the last couple of years, the photos of me when I was a kid . . . well, they've started to give me a little pang or something—not unhappiness, exactly, but some kind of quiet, deep regret . . . I keep wanting to apologize to the little guy: 'I'm sorry, I've let you down. I was the person who was supposed to look after you, but I blew it: I made wrong decisions at bad times, and I turned you into me.'[28]

By erecting extra logical obstacles between the narrator and the repair that he dreams of, Hornby wittily plays up the oddity at the root of all apology. A model apology is an act displaying one's sensitivity to reasons for action (namely, reasons to repair) even if the reasons are not reasons for that particular action (even if the apology will repair nothing). When an apology does repair something—e.g. by making its addressee feel better, or putting a relationship back on an even keel—we have that strange truth about model apology to thank.

We might be tempted to generalize: where it is too late for any measure of conformity with a reason, sensitivity to that reason in one's reactions is the next best thing. We should, however, hesitate to embrace that reformulation. It might be taken to mean that we are still working through the implications of the continuity thesis. But by hypothesis we are not. The continuity thesis explains repair as mitigation. Reparative action is partial conformity with a reason for action that one failed perfectly to conform to in the first place. But in this discussion we have moved away from even partial conformity. The most that is available now, by hypothesis, is sensitivity to a reason that one did not conform to. We can still *respect* the reason, if you like, even in our nonconformity with it, by holding ourselves to it and feeling the right way about it. In Chapter 5 we will have more to say about respect. For now, the point is only that a model apology, like other expressions of appropriate emotion, can be understood as an act of respect for a reason even when that reason is not, strictly speaking, a reason to apologize. We should avoid the 'next best thing' formulation if it will be understood to mean that apologizing is just the symbolic action

---

[28] Hornby, *High Fidelity* (Victor Gollancz 1995), 157.

that the continuity thesis recommends when all else is lost. No: the continuity thesis only recommends apology when apology can be used to repair. Otherwise, the rationality of apology, such as it is, lies beyond the application of the continuity thesis.

There is a second cause for caution with the 'next best thing' formulation (or perhaps it is another facet of the same cause). The continuity thesis is concerned with conformity with reasons. Normally, from the point of view of the continuity thesis, it does not matter in what spirit one repairs so long as one repairs. Normally, spontaneity in making repairs matters only because delay will add more losses, or make the existing losses harder to repair, or such like. There are, of course, exceptions. In some cases, the reasons one did not conform to in the first place were reasons to exhibit certain emotions or more generally to display certain sensitivities to reasons. In those cases, the success of one's repair, even according to the continuity thesis, may well depend on one's ability to muster the necessary spirit in doing so, one's ability to put one's heart into it, to show that one cares, etc. (Suppose that what one is trying to repair is one's failure to issue a model apology when a model apology was called for.[29]) Still, these are special cases. In the normal run of cases, it is what one does that the continuity thesis attends to, never mind the spirit in which one does it. With apologies, things are quite different. The spirit in which an apology is issued is often of the essence. A model apology is often what is craved by those who are on the receiving end. They would like the apology to express the agent-regret of the apologizer, that the apologizer is 'really and truly sorry'. 'I wanted to see the good in him,' says one victim of a dangerous driver, 'but he never said sorry.'[30] With continuity-thesis repair, conformity matters more than sensitivity on the part of the conformer. With apology, by contrast, sensitivity matters more than conformity. But why not attach importance to both? Many people who have been wronged by others do attach importance to both. Ideally, they would like the wrongdoer's reparative measures to double as, or accompany, apologetic gestures.

[29] Which is part of the story in 'United's Apologies: A Timeline', New York Times (14 April 2017). The apologetic timeline did not end there.
[30] 'Experience: a car crashed into me in the bath', The Guardian (1 April 2017).

As soon as we see that possibility we realize that apology is not to be sidelined as reparation's poor relation, something to be sought only *faute de mieux*. That apology may still be in order even in respect of the irreparable does not show that apology is a mere consolation prize, of no interest to those for whom continuity-thesis repairs are still available. If the 'next best thing' formulation suggests otherwise, it is best avoided.

4. Putting your money where your mouth is

Reparative measures can double as apologetic gestures. Meaning travels across the divide in both directions. Sometimes, as we have seen, an apology serves, derivatively, to repair. Someone was left unsettled and an apology helps to restore his peace of mind. A friendship was destabilized and an apology puts it back on an even keel. To uncover the private law implications, however, let's begin with the converse situation, in which a reparative measure, such as a payment of money, is capable of carrying, derivatively, an apologetic meaning.

Remember Larry's insistence on upholding the continuity thesis in *Curb Your Enthusiasm*? Predictably, he is soon hoist on his own petard. At a beach party held to announce her engagement, acquaintance Marla borrows Larry's jacket without asking, and stains it with chocolate. Larry makes a fuss (in a characteristic-ally passive-aggressive way) and Marla later sends him a cheque. Back at the beach on the occasion of her wedding some weeks later, Marla notices that Larry is still wearing the chocolate-stained jacket. Interrupting her own wedding vows (she is indeed a worthy adversary) she publicly lambasts Larry for not replacing the jacket, and does so in much the same terms in which, earlier in the episode, Larry challenged Ben Heineman for leaving his car unrepaired.[31] Predictably, Larry attempts with Marla much the same defensive line that Heineman attempted with Larry, and of which Larry previously took such a dim view:

LARRY: It's my money, I can kinda do whatever I want to with it, no?

[31] See ch 3, s 4.

MARLA: No, that was my money that I gave to you to replace the soiled jacket.

. . .

LARRY: I don't need to buy a jacket just because you say.

MARLA: Did you read the memo of the check I sent you, Larry? It said: 'Replace fleece jacket.'[32]

Although the tables are nicely turned on him, Larry is not being straightforwardly inconsistent. (When is he ever straightforward?) On receiving Marla's cheque earlier in the episode, he seemingly did not pay any attention to the memo. He misinterpreted the cheque as apologetic rather than reparative:

LARRY: Boy, you don't see that very often.

CHERYL: What's that?

LARRY: Well, somebody does something wrong and they make up for it with something like this. This is quite a gesture ... You do something wrong, you say it. That's what she did. That's what that check is about.[33]

Of course, Larry's misinterpretation of the cheque as an apology did not deter him from cashing it. He does so on the thin pretext that otherwise Marla's payment records will be inaccurate. His mistakes are nothing if not convenient. He also conveniently overlooks the point that the apologetic meaning of the payment, as he interprets it, may co-exist with its ordinary reparative role, and so does not exclude the application of his beloved continuity thesis. So—apology or no apology—by his own doctrine he should still clearly have replaced the jacket.

Be that as it may, however, Larry's misinterpretation of the payment helps us to see what the law is sometimes trying to do with awards of damages. Whether or not they count as apologies, some damages payments ordered by courts are closely modelled on apologies. They are supposed to 'make it all right' in much the way that an apology 'makes it all right', when it does.

I am thinking here of what are known as 'general damages' awards. Or at any rate certain types of general damages awards, namely those that comprise arbitrary sums of money awarded by

[32] 'The Korean Bookie', *Curb Your Enthusiasm* (dir. Bryan Gordon, HBO, 27 November 2005), at 25.07.

[33] ibid 13.43.

the courts in respect of losses that defy quantification in money terms. Examples include damages for bereavement or 'loss of society', for pain and suffering, for 'loss of amenity', for disappointment, and (this one we noticed before under the heading of the 'performance interest') for bare 'loss of a right'. Nominal damages belong on the same list. The continuity thesis applies to these awards, when it does, only in the derivative way already mentioned. Take the relatively rare case of damages for disappointment.[34] What the defendant did to the plaintiff—say, failing to provide the fabulous funeral service for his mother that the marketing literature portrayed, or failing to take photographs at his wedding of a suitably professional quality—was wrong partly because it disappointed the plaintiff. The payment of general damages is supposed to stem the disappointment. It cheers the plaintiff up, but not by giving him the money to hold another funeral or another wedding. Those were unrepeatable occasions. (If they were repeatable, the cost of repeating them would fall under 'special damages'.) Rather, it cheers him up by giving him a feeling of relief, consolation, or satisfaction.

But where does the plaintiff get that feeling, given that apart from the feeling, nothing is being repaired? It is akin to a placebo effect. A placebo is in a sense a medicine; it is unusual only in being a medicine with no medicinal value independently of the thought, on the part of the patient, that it has such value. An award of general damages (of the kind under discussion) is likewise in a sense reparative; it is unusual only in being reparation with no reparative value independently of the thought, on the part of the recipient, that it has such value. And this thought, it follows, need not be straightforwardly mistaken. The payment, or the award of it, can indeed have reparative value thanks to the thought that it does. It can make people feel better about themselves, about their lives, or about each other. It can be used to prevent a further wasteful escalation of conflict, and to stem feelings of resentment and bitterness on the part of those who

---

[34] 'Relatively rare' because, as the continuity thesis leads one to expect, such damages are awarded only where the avoidance of disappointment to the plaintiff was one of the reasons why, according to the law, one had a duty not to act as one did: *Farley v Skinner* [2002] 2 AC 732.

are compensated, bringing 'closure' to all involved. In a way, of course, this is all parasitic on the force of the continuity thesis. The continuity thesis makes the ordinary vanilla case for repair, and the placebo-like effect of general damages comes of the consequent association of damages awards with repair. But in a more fundamental way the placebo-like effect of general damages has its basis outside the continuity thesis. The payment, even if not strictly an apology, has a meaning akin to that of an apology. It is the acknowledgement of a rational remainder, of the leftover reasons that can no longer be fully conformed to. It thereby bespeaks respect for value that was irretrievably lost in the wrongdoing. Someone died in the accident. There were long nights of lost sleep or long days of slow recovery, nights or days that can never be brought back. A one-off event, or precious memories of it, have been spoilt forever. The plaintiff's power to refuse to sell to the defendant was usurped by the defendant's going ahead and using the plaintiff's property anyway, in a way that is now irreversible.[35] As the placebo analogy showed, a recipient who regards damages pegged to such losses as reparative need not be straightforwardly mistaken.[36] But nor, we should add, need he be irrational. Like Larry, he may be interpreting the payment apologetically. He may take it to be an expression of respect for reasons that it is now too late for the defendant to conform to. And that may indeed be just what it is.

It may be, but is it usually? Remember the apology given by Network Rail for an accident that occurred before Network Rail existed? I was sceptical about that back in Chapter 3. I was not sceptical about the relief, consolation, or satisfaction that it gave

---

[35] Or which the court will not reverse by granting an injunction, say because of the wastefulness of having a perfectly good house demolished, as in *Wrotham Park Estate Co Ltd v Parkside Homes Ltd* [1974] 1 WLR 798. In general, my remarks about irreparable losses extend to cases in which a possible continuity-thesis repair is ruled out for independent reasons.

[36] But it is not surprising that the legal classification of them as reparative is contentious, as is the classification of placebos as medicines. For a good survey of the debate see Andrew Burrows, 'Are "Damages on the Wrotham Park Basis" Compensatory, Restitutionary, or Neither?' in Djakhongir Saidov and Ralph Cunnington (eds), *Current Themes in the Law of Contract Damages* (Hart Publishing 2008).

to the victims and relatives who demanded it. I was sceptical about the rationality of their demand. Should we not be similarly sceptical, on similar grounds, about many awards of general damages inasmuch as they are modelled on apologies? Probably we should. We should regard some such awards as humouring their recipients, as giving them relief, consolation, or satisfaction of the type that they want even though it is an inappropriate type of relief, consolation, or satisfaction for them to want. The gesture is empty; more fool the plaintiff for finding meaning in it. But we should not be too quick to dismiss gestures modelled on model apologies as empty merely because they are not model apologies. I am sceptical about the Network Rail apology, but not because I am sceptical about formal apologies in general. The main reason why I am sceptical about the Network Rail apology, as I said, is that Network Rail did not exist at the time of the accident that was being litigated. It was in the position of an insurer for its predecessor. Like any insurer, Network Rail was in a position to express regret and accept basic responsibility *on behalf of* the person insured (in this case, Railtrack plc). But it is a totally different idea, a crazy idea, for it to have accepted its *own* basic responsibility for the accident. Should we want a motor insurer to say, falsely: sorry that we, Remote Insurance Ltd, drove into the back of your car and hurt your children? Surely not. We should want an apology only from the insured driver herself (even if she is not the one who delivers it).

So I am making a special objection to a special feature of the Network Rail case. It does not extend to the case where an insurer pays general damages on behalf of its insured, which may reasonably be interpreted as apologetic gesture on behalf of the insured. Nor does it extend to formal apologies of the kind that might be issued by an insured person through a lawyer or other representative, and which might constitute genuine acceptances of responsibility by that person even though not particularly heartfelt (e.g. because offered only under pressure as part of a negotiated settlement). As we know, these apologies take their meaning, their rational intelligibility, from model apologies. Yet in some cases they can be even more worth having than model apologies. Whereas model apologies may come naturally and easily to those who make them—personally, I issue far too many of them—formal apologies (when sincere) typically demand the swallowing of pride, the overcoming of embarrassment, the sublimation of resentment. It is not as if they inhabit an emotion-free zone, even when issued through an intermediary. If they do, we understandably doubt their sincerity. For rational beings, or at any rate human rational beings, experience reasons in how they feel as well as in how they think and act.

Not all feel agent-regret as sharply as I do and not all (therefore) are moved to express it as often as I do. One can go too far with that business; witness the extreme case of Leontes under the ever-watchful eye of Paulina. But all bar the extremely psychopathic have their feelings touched by what they do and fail to do, and formal apologies, given where they come in the catalogue of error and recrimination, tend to be rife with them. Aaron Lazare tends to emphasize the suffering of the apologizer, the reciprocation of humiliation, as central to the insistence upon apology: 'What makes an apology work is the exchange of shame and power between the offender and the offended.'[37] So the more agonizing the process for the apologizer, all else being equal, the more powerful the apology. The logic of apology partakes, then, of the logic of punishment. I would not want to deny that there can be cases like that. People have lots of ways of punishing each other. Even litigation that has no punitive pay-off so far as the law is concerned can have a punitive use in the hands of the plaintiff; he may just want the defendant to have sleepless nights worrying about the case. But its punitive potential is not what I have in mind when I emphasize the emotional (and other) work that may go into a formal apology. I am thinking not of the apologizer's suffering so much as the apologizer's seriousness. When it comes to acknowledging and affirming the force of reasons that one did not conform to, and thereby accepting basic responsibility, saying it deliberately and with solemnity may be as good as, sometimes even better than, saying it spontaneously and with feeling. And when it comes to solemnity, the law is in its element. Rather than getting in the way of a meaningful apology, then, the law sometimes helps to make a meaningful apology possible, or a possible apology meaningful.

---

[37] Lazare, 'Go Ahead, Say You're Sorry', *Psychology Today* 23 (1995), 40.

5. Say it with money; say it with flowers

The blend of apology with money compensation that we find in an award of general damages has built-in instabilities. On the one hand, there is squeamishness about the idea that certain losses can be priced. So there should be. Would you have accepted a money payment to send your children to their deaths, or even to increase the risk to their lives?[38] If you would have done, you are not fit to be a parent. But if you would not have done, how can you regard a money payment as helping to make things all right when your children die in an accident? Not a money payment to cover the incidental costs, I mean, but to pay for the actual loss of the children? If money would not have worked back then, how does it work now? On the other hand, once such losses are habitually priced by the law, even squeamishly, there are built-in inflationary pressures. Injured children may have lost future earnings from which they would otherwise have been able to support themselves in adulthood, and they may need expensive long-term care. The special damages awarded in respect of these and similar losses do not arise when the same children are killed outright. When they are killed outright they have no future in which to support themselves and no further costs of care. There may be funeral expenses and such like, of course. But beyond that, general damages may be all that the bereaved parents can expect from the law. In a system like that used in many US states, where juries assess damages, you can expect the general damages to be inflated (or augmented with punitive damages) to make them more substantial. But in the more restrained climate of judicial damages assessment, such as is favoured in the UK and much of the (British) Commonwealth, the fact that general damages are only supposed to be gestural, awarded on the model of an apology, has tended to keep them relatively low.

---

[38] Notice that the money here is paid to the parents for increasing a risk of death, not merely not spent by the parents on decreasing a risk of death. The two are relevantly different. The first requires parents to confront the question of how much their children's lives are worth in cash. The second is consistent with their never confronting that question. On why this matters, see Joseph Raz, *The Morality of Freedom* (Clarendon Press 1986), 345–57.

So it becomes, as the Association of Personal Injury Lawyers puts it in the UK, 'cheaper to kill than to maim'.[39] The perverse incentives which this disparity introduces are the principal concern of some critics.[40] The criminal law exists, in part, to neutralize these perverse incentives. But whatever it can do to neutralize the perverse incentives, the criminal law cannot be expected to neutralize, and indeed may tend to aggravate, the social meaning of a relatively low damages award. 'Look how little my child's life was worth!' becomes the refrain in both settings: in the criminal law because the sentence is not entirely, or even mainly, pegged to anybody's loss; in private law because the plaintiff's loss is pathetically represented in the quantification of general damages. The problem begins with the placebo effect. Once we are lured into thinking that the award of general damages is somehow reparative apart from our thinking it so—as we must be lured in order to think it so—we come to regard general damages as having an independent metric of the kind that is provided, where special damages are concerned, by the continuity thesis. We are drawn into the illusion that the irreparable is reparable, and from there into the illusion that there is an independently quantifiable sum of money to cover what we have lost, just like the cost of replacing our stained jackets or the cost of repairing our dented cars. Our loss is greater when our children die, so we demand, as it were, larger placebos.

These remarks can be generalized beyond the terrifying case of a parental bereavement. The blend of apology with money has many pitfalls even in respect of mere stained jackets and dented cars. It can insult people who regard what was lost as non-monetizable. It can also insult people who regard what was lost as worth a lot more than the arbitrary sum offered. It is hardly surprising that outside the context of litigation, when we work out what to do about the irreparable aspects of our everyday wrongs, we often prefer not to say it with money at all, but to say it with

[39] See the Association's 2016 'Agenda for Change' poster at https://www.apil.org.uk/files/campaigns/apil-agenda-for-change-2016-v2.pdf. Note that the Association is a campaign group 'fighting for the rights of injured people': https://www.apil.org.uk/what-is-apil.

[40] Geoffrey Sant, 'Driven to kill: why drivers in China intentionally kill the pedestrians they hit' *Slate* (4 September 2015).

flowers. Even with flowers, of course, the question soon arises of how big the bouquet has to be to qualify as suitably apologetic, given what the recipient has lost. The bouquet is a conventional mode of apology, displaying sensitivity to those reasons that can no longer be conformed to, respecting what the recipient of the flowers has irretrievably lost at the flower-sender's hand. But does this big bunch of carnations show enough sensitivity? And does it show it enough? For six weeks of anxiety over the mislaid passport, should it not it be rare orchids? Notice that we do not stop running into questions of corrective justice just because the continuity thesis runs out. 'All I can do is apologize' says the builder who didn't show up. The retort from the aggrieved householder who waited in all morning: 'Yes, but how fulsomely can you apologize?' We come back at last to the case of Leontes, not apologizing exactly, but still repenting after sixteen long years since his wrong. Has he really 'paid down more penitence than done trespass', as Cleomenes protests? How would we even begin to work that out?

5

The Way Things Used To Be

They say that this is the greatest grief: to stand ... outside
the right and the beautiful that one knows, [driven away]
by necessity.

Pindar[1]

1. Holding on and letting go

Samuel Johnson writes:

The other passions are diseases indeed, but they necessarily direct us to
their proper cure ... But for sorrow there is no remedy provided by nature; it is often occasioned by accidents irreparable, and dwells upon objects that have lost or changed their existence; it requires what it cannot
hope, that the laws of the universe should be repealed; that the dead
should return, or the past should be recalled.[2]

In Chapter 4, we discussed the possibility that nature—meaning
our nature as rational agents—directs us to a cure for what Bernard
Williams called agent-regret. Apology, I argued, is in a way a rational response even when unjustified; it is rationally intelligible
that one would wish to express one's rationally felt regret, as the
agent of another's misfortune, even if there is no reason to do so.
And when there *is* a reason to do so, I suggested, that is because
apology already has this independent rational intelligibility, independent, I mean, of any reason one has to apologize. That is the
route by which, as Johnson says,

regret for negligence or errour ... may animate us to future care or
activity ...; the pain which arises from these causes has very salutary

---

[1] Pindar, *Pythian Ode* IV, 287–9. I borrow the translation from Hannah Arendt,
'What Is Freedom?' in Arendt, *Between Past and Future* (The Viking Press 1961),
142 at 158.

[2] Johnson, 'The Proper Means of Regulating Sorrow' *The Rambler*, issue 47
(28 August 1750).

effects, and is every hour extenuating itself by the reparation of those miscarriages that produce it.[3]

In this chapter we turn our attention, with Johnson, to the sufferer of the misfortune, the one whose life was disrupted or interrupted, the patient as opposed to the agent. It is the sorrow of this person, sometimes rising to grief or desolation, for whom there is, according to Johnson, 'no remedy provided by nature'. There is nothing which stands to such feelings of loss, he thinks, as apology stands to agent-regret. As Johnson puts it:

Into such anguish many have sunk upon some sudden diminution of their fortune, an unexpected blast of their reputation, or the loss of children or of friends. They have suffered all sensibility of pleasure to be destroyed by a single blow, have given up for ever the hopes of substituting any other object in the room of that which they lament, resigned their lives to gloom and despondency, and worn themselves out in unavailing misery.[4]

I am not totally sure that Johnson is right about the 'unavailing' bit. One may weep, wail, reminisce, remonstrate, or otherwise 'let it all out'. Does doing so not parallel, in respect of its rationality, the self-abasement of the authentic apologizer? Or do such merely cathartic actions, even when justified, fail to tick the box of serving some *further* good that counts, for Johnson, as the hallmark of a suitably constructive emotion like agent-regret?

I do not intend to solve or even tackle this question here. Instead, I intend to tackle a prior question that lurks within it. The question is, roughly: why should we care about the loss of what we lose? You may think that this is a daft question. It is an analytic truth that loss is bad, an absence of something worth having. We should care about it just as we should care about any absence. But that response misunderstands my question. To care about something lost is not merely to care about an absence, in the way that an eleven-year-old may feel hard done by in not having a pet cat or a smartphone like her friends. No, a loss is an absence that was once a presence. To care about a loss in the sense that will concern us here is not just to care about an absence but to care about the absence of what was once a presence. For the eleven-year-old, it is missing the *vanished* cat or the *mislaid* phone. It is wanting things to go back to how they used to be.

In 'Requiem for a Friend', Rilke writes: 'We need in love to practice only this: letting each other go. For holding on comes easily; we do not need to learn it.'[5] That much we already know, and not only in love. Even revolutionaries are conservatives about the revolution. Even in triumph, they feel sadness that their job is over and that their lives must assume a new post-revolutionary shape. In understanding the 'Continuity IRA', we may need to give more attention to the first part of the group's name than to the second. In the same way, in Lauren Child's *Charlie and Lola* stories, Lola wants to take out the same library book every time.[6] No other book can replace it in her affections. Until one does— and then, she concludes, no other book can replace *that* one. That is holding on, refusing to let go. It is part of human nature, we sometimes say, as if that were explanation enough.

But it is not explanation enough. We also need to know how holding on fits into human nature. Is it part of our nature as rational beings? Holding on comes more easily than letting go, as Rilke says, even when (as with Lola's book) all else is equal. But should it? Is there any rational support for the local conservatism implicit in the sentiment 'I don't want to lose you' or 'let's pick up where we left off' or 'I just want my old life back'?

The question is of great importance for private law. Possibly its importance would most easily be explored in connection with the law of property, where 'holding on' carries (you might think) its most literal connotation. It's my car. I get to keep it. If you take it, I get it back. But as the last step in this line of thought already brings out, the question carries over interestingly into the rest of private law. Even where there is no car to hand back, and more generally nothing that can be the subject of *in specie* return, there are still hopes of somehow putting things back the way they were by some proxy device. The law of torts and the law of contract,

[5] Rainer Maria Rilke, 'Für Eine Freundin' in Rilke, *Requiem* (Insel Verlag 1909): 'Wir haben, wo wir lieben, ja nur dies:/einander lassen; denn dass wir uns halten,/das fällt uns leicht und ist nicht erst zu lernen.' Translation by Stephen Mitchell, from Mitchell, *Ahead of All Parting: The Selected Poetry and Prose of Rainer Maria Rilke* (Random House 1996).

[6] Child, *But Excuse Me That is My Book* (Puffin Books 2006).

in particular, both use money payments ('reparative damages') as their proxy device, and use *restitutio in integrum* as the regulative ideal for their assessment.[7] It is the ideal of 'making the plaintiff whole', making it as if, for her, the defendant's tort or breach of contract had never been committed. Such restoration of the *status quo* for the plaintiff is the imagined perfection according to which awards of reparative damages, even in their acknowledged imperfection, are to be judged.

Sometimes the law of torts and the law of contract are presented as parting company on the question of which is the relevant *status quo* for the purpose of this imaginative exercise. Damages for breach of contract default to the so-called 'expectation' measure which is supposed to bring the plaintiff as close as possible to the situation that she bargained for, to the way things would have been right now in another possible world in which the contract had been performed. This world we might call the *status quo aliter*. Tort damages are said to focus, by contrast, on restoring the *status quo ante*, the way things used to be before the tort was committed. But this way of understanding the tort measure seems to me to be mainly a conceit of contract lawyers.[8] It seems to me that the law of torts and the law of contract alike invite us to think about another possible world right now in which the wrong (the tort or breach of contract as the case may be) has not been committed. And both branches of the law have us imagine, for the purpose of assessing damages, how things would have worked out for the plaintiff in that alternative world. What we care about in tort cases and in breach of contract cases alike, it seems to me, is the *status quo aliter*. Awards of reparative damages in both areas of law

---

[7] On regulative ideals, the best work known to me is Dorothy Emmet's unjustly neglected *The Role of the Unrealisable* (MacMillan 1994).

[8] There are certain breach of contract cases in which successful plaintiffs are awarded reimbursement of sums expended in reliance on the projected performance of the contract *instead of* loss of profit arising from its non-performance. This 'reliance measure' has sometimes been labelled as 'the tort measure' even though, as Fuller and Perdue explain, it is hard to think of a tort-law situation, except for torts committed in pre-contractual negotiations, where the contrast between the two contractual measures even makes sense: LL Fuller and William R Perdue, 'The Reliance Interest in Contract Damages: 2', *Yale Law Journal* 46 (1937), 373 at 409.

are equally oriented, as Lord Blackburn's famous dictum puts it, towards putting the plaintiff 'in the same position as he *would have been in* if he had not sustained the wrong for which he is now getting his ... reparation.'[9]

At the same time, however, both the law of torts and the law of contract invite us to imagine the relevant *status quo aliter* on the footing that the plaintiff's life would in other respects have carried on much as before. In a contract case, this usually means 'much as before, but improved by the performance of the contract', whereas in a tort case it more often means 'much as before, and in particular *un*improved by the non-commission of the tort'. That 'no-improvement' assumption explains the impression that what we care about, in the tort case, is the *status quo ante*. But it is a false impression. We care about the way things were before, in the tort case and the contract case alike, only because we care about the way things were already *heading* for the plaintiff when the wrong came along.[10] In their approach to the assessment of damages, the law of torts and the law of contract therefore share the same built-in conservative feature. They aim to put the plaintiff's life back on its previous track, or at any rate to enable the plaintiff to put her life back on the previous track (*aliter*), even though not necessarily at its previous (*ante*) position on that track. For the purpose of damages assessment, the plaintiff is accordingly treated as if she were a holder on. She may in fact be a letter-go, but that fact is generally kept below the juridical radar. She gets her damages on a holder-on basis all the same, and then she can use the money to let go to her heart's content. That is how the doctrine of *restitutio in integrum* is interpreted and applied in the courts.

Some testing critiques of private law, and of the remedial model that it institutionalizes, rest on the thought that this element of conservatism is indefensible. It is not just that *restitutio in integrum* is overplayed to the exclusion of conflicting considerations.

---

[9] *Livingstone v Rawyards Coal Company* (1880) 5 App Cas 25, at 39 (Lord Blackburn) (emphasis added).

[10] Cases in which other independent problems for the complainant were already looming at the time of the wrong, as in *Jobling v Associated Dairies* [1982] AC 794 and *Golden Strait Corporation v Nippon Yusen Kubishka Kaisha* [2007] UKHL 12, are particularly problematic for the law of damages.

Worse: there is not even a prima facie case for *restitutio in integrum*. The mere fact that we had something before does not point to any reason why we should have had it, and so does not point to any reason why we should get it back when it is snatched from us. Or as Jules Coleman puts the point:

> [If] you have no right to your wealth under the relevant principle of distributive justice ... how can you have a right to have it restored ...? ... [W]hat sort of justice is it that permits ... injustice?[11]

Notice that, unlike some objections to the law of torts, this one does not favour the replacement of the law of torts with alternative compensation schemes of the kind associated with automobile accidents in New Zealand. It is not a complaint about the supposed doing of corrective justice inter partes in particular. It is equally applicable to any compensation scheme that has *restitutio in integrum* as its regulative ideal. It applies equally, for example, to ordinary private first-party insurance policies (e.g. for travel cancellation, damage to the home or its contents, etc.). Such policies promise, typically, to cover the insured person's losses. They hold themselves out to be judged on how perfectly they do so ('new for old!' 'low excess!' 'few exclusions!' etc.). Why? You may say, applying an economistic thought pattern that I hope you do not apply when you try to sustain your personal relationships, that *restitutio in integrum* is simply what people want. That's why the market provides it, or something based on it. I reply that this is no answer to the question that interests us here. The question that interests us here is whether those who want *restitutio in integrum* have reason to want it. Certainly, they exhibit the conservatism of human nature. But is it the conservatism of human rational nature? Is their wish to have what they used to have supported by reasons?

The problem is not even restricted to the domain of compensation. Here is a question of the same type that arises in contemporary social policy. In my country, we have a shortage of housing. Some people have bigger places than they need. One readily imagines a perfect distribution in which the single people

---

[11] Coleman, *Risks and Wrongs* (Cambridge University Press 1993) 304–5.

live in one-bedroom flats, the large families live in larger houses, etc. So our government recently came up with the following bright idea, now forever to be known as the 'bedroom tax'. Where housing costs are publicly subsidized through the welfare benefits system, the government decided to reduce pro rata the public subsidy of accommodation that is too big for its occupants according to the above conception of a perfect distribution. The effect is that people deemed to be over-accommodated, who have no way to make up the shortfall, have to leave to make way for people who are under-accommodated. There are many problems with the scheme. The imagined perfect distribution turns out to be not as perfect as it looks, because of many people's complex accommodation needs (dialysis machines, wheelchair lifts or ramps, children living with them only part time, etc.). And there is a disproportionate shortage of small homes for single people to move to. And so on.

But here is one objection that directly implicates our topic. A distinction should be drawn, many say, between getting people out of houses they are already living in, on the one hand, and finding houses for those who are homeless or who are trying to move, on the other. The *status quo* should carry some weight in the redistribution. Thus, say, the subsidy changes should not be retrospective (i.e. should not affect the housing subsidy of those already housed and subsidized) or should be phased in only very slowly for such people. People should be given an opportunity to hold on, to continue on the same track, to keep the lives they already have. They should not be treated as if they did not already have those lives, as if their home were just an empty space up for distribution from scratch. There may be differences of opinion about the weight, if any, to be attached to this concern. But one can hardly deny that, for whatever it's worth, it's a pertinent concern about the bedroom tax. And that is already enough to show that a shift from thinking about corrective justice to thinking about distributive justice does not absolve us from considering the rationality of our wish to keep what we have. Whether there is a case for holding on rather than letting go is a question that matters for distributive justice too.

2. Reasons for holding on

Elizabeth Spelman expresses a common disquiet about *restitutio in integrum*, and more generally about trying to get things back to how they used to be. She says: '[R]epair is presumptuous in its insistence that a given point in the history of something ... is more important than any other point.'[12] Her formulation certainly helps to bring out the broad sweep of the challenge. It is no longer a mere Coleman-style challenge to the restoration of an unjust *status quo*. It is a challenge to the restoration of anything, including a piece of furniture or a work of art. But notice that it is not just any old anything that concerns us here. It is a life, or an aspect of a life. And, *pace* Spelman, it is not really a 'point' that is being privileged. It is a narrative, an arc that has already passed through many points. The puzzle is to understand what reason I have to want the narrative of my life to continue, or to have continued, on the same arc as before. We are not seeking a decisive reason, one that overrides all objections. Any reason will do, so long as it is a reason that fixes, not on my life having some independently specified ingredients but on my life continuing to have whatever ingredients it already has. Possibly, when we reach the reckoning, we should only want to hold onto our lives when the going is good. But obviously it will not be enough for our purposes to find a reason to want the going to be good. It must be a reason to want to continue with the good going that is already going—to prefer it, even when all else is equal, over various other good goings, and possibly even over some better goings that we could have instead of the good going we have.[13] Here are some suggestions.

(a) Consider first the costs of change. As one's life changes in one way, one may be constrained to change it in others. Suppose one suddenly has a dependent relative or a collapsed business.

[12] Spelman, *Repair: The Impulse to Restore in a Fragile World* (Beacon Press 2002) 72 and 125. Spelman is reporting or imagining this critique, rather than advancing it.
[13] In other words, we are looking for what Hart christened a 'content-independent' reason for holding onto one's life. See HLA Hart, 'Commands and Authoritative Legal Reasons' in Hart, *Essays on Bentham* (Clarendon Press 1982), at 254 ff.

One may need to move house or move job or move the children to a new school, even perhaps move to a new country. One may need to find a new doctor, sort out new insurance, get a new bus pass, have a new boiler installed, learn a new language, meet new neighbours, even get a new passport. Even when the new will (once established) eat up no more money, time, or effort than the old would have done, the transition itself eats up money, time, and effort. That in turn can bring anxiety, irritation, and other negative feelings. To avoid the costs of transition is already a reason to want to stick with the life one has, all else being equal.

This helps us up to a point. It explains some of our resistance to change and accounts for some items we might include on our tally of losses when change is forced upon us. But notice that our focus, when we put these items on the tally, is not on what was lost. It does not matter what was lost. We may think it was worth keeping or we may not. All that matters is how much *extra* we stand to lose now in changing it. For example, one may wish nothing more than to be free of an abusive partner, and rightly so. One may long since have lost the love that once tied one to the abuser, and rightly so. Yet one stays because of the challenge of extricating oneself. How will one cope with temporary homelessness? What will the children eat while one is sorting out emergency funds? How will one get them and their treasured belongings out of the house? How will one afford the necessary legal help to put an end to the relationship? How will one manage the inevitable stalking and manipulation, the reactions of the children, and the need to keep up their contact with their other parent, and so on? What does the future hold? So one holds onto the relationship. But this holding on is not the kind that interests us here. One does not hold onto the relationship *as such*. One cares only to be out of it, if only one could cope with getting out. The problem is only with that process of extrication.

The example reveals that some emotional costs of change— including fears for the future—should be set aside for the purpose of our inquiry. They are not reasons for holding on as such. But surely other emotional costs should be included? What about the pain of losing what was lost, absent in this example but present in so many others? What about the abused spouses who yearn to go back, who grieve for their old life and their old love, even after they have managed to extricate themselves and start a new life? Do they not hold on 'as such'? Yes, they do. We should think of their transitional grief as relevant to our inquiry. That, however, is because it is part of what we are seeking to make rationally intelligible. It is part of our *explanandum*. It is not part of our explanation. We are interested not in the avoidance of transitional grief as a reason not to lose what one has, but rather in losing what one has as a reason to feel transitional grief. How can the fact of a loss, as opposed to the mere fact of an absence, be rendered intelligible as a reason to feel as one does?

(b) You may say this: one brings value into one's life by adopting goals for oneself, personal goals, which are in turn structured by relationships with other people, objects one identifies with, activities and excellences that differentiate them, and so on. They may be goals of the kind we discussed in Chapter 2, in which only an outcome or pay-off of one's endeavour will qualify as success. But they need not be. They may be goals dominated by endeavour, such that, although the endeavour is still necessarily towards something beyond itself, it is the endeavour itself that one glories in as the possessor of the goal.

It is an interesting question, to which I will have cause to return in a moment, whether adopting something as one's goal really makes its pursuit more valuable. But an answer to that question on its own would not help us. For the answer, whatever it is, holds equally with old goals (those that we already have or have had) and to new goals (goals that we have yet to have). So the answer by itself could not help us to understand why we should care more about what is integral to our pursuit of old goals, than to our pursuit of new ones, and hence why we should continue to hanker after the old life that was constituted by the old goals. When our pursuit of old goals is disrupted, we may be uncertain about what new goals we might end up with and how successful our pursuit of them might be. But as we already saw, the cost of that uncertainty—e.g. the associated anxiety and trepidation—is just another transaction cost. It gives us no reason to regard pursuit of our future goals as contributing to the value in our lives any less than did pursuit of the goals we have just been called upon to surrender or rethink.[14] What any of them contribute to

[14] The point is explored at great length, and in several variations, by Derek Parfit in Parfit, *Reasons and Persons* (Clarendon Press 1986), pt II.

our lives will depend on which goals they are and whether we succeed in them, not on whether we acquired them before or after the point from which we now view them.

(c) Nevertheless, thinking about the question of success in our personal goals can perhaps take us a little further. Sometimes, a disruption to your life can make it the case that now you can never succeed in one or more of the goals that you were pursuing before the disruption. Pursuit of the goal brought value into your life, but, since the pursuit aimed at some success beyond itself, failure in it damaged your life. Sometimes, depending on the centrality of the goal, its connection with your other goals, you will even say that your life was reduced to ashes by the failure. Let's say your marriage ends. The goal you had, to which you committed yourself by marriage, was a lifelong relationship of mutual loving and honouring and having and holding and cherishing (etc.) with your former spouse. The divorce entails failure in that goal, even if (while the marriage was still in good shape) you routinely succeeded in the subsidiary goals of mutual loving, honouring, having, holding, cherishing, etc. So you look back and regard those successes as a blessing, as something to remember warmly, while at the same time as regarding them as tarnished. Why tarnished? Because the successes were, in a way, steps on the path to failure. They no longer hold the meaning that they had for you when success in the larger goal of sustaining them for the rest of one's joint lives was still, so far as anyone knew, possible. So from where you stand now the relationship-successes of those good years, while they lasted, are almost like salt in the wounds of the eventual break-up. They add to the sense of your life having been destroyed. It is not only that you did not get a chance to live the rest of your life the way you set out to do at, or indeed before, your marriage; even the successes of the part of your life that you did live that way have been retrospectively rendered as failures when considered as the parts they were supposed to play in that larger whole. You may even be tempted to say that, given how things turned out, you wasted all those years.

Assuming that those who have worthwhile goals have reason to succeed in their goals—which takes us back to the topic of Chapter 2—one has reason to fear and to regret failure-inducing disruption of one's life. What one longs for under this heading is not exactly the life that one has lost or is in the course of losing, but the success in it that is to be or has been snatched from one. There is here a rational intelligibility, in at least some cases, to holding on rather than letting go. But notice that the cases to which this point is restricted are cases in which the disruption does indeed bring about failure in the pursuit of a goal. It does not apply in cases in which one has already succeeded in some overarching goal and a new goal is called for. It also does not apply in cases in which failure is anyway on the cards, and in which persisting with the goal is therefore futile. In such cases, so far as the considerations just adduced are concerned, one should welcome any disruption which facilitates making a break.

(d) There is, however, a more far-reaching point to be made about our relationship with our personal goals. When certain goals are ours, we cannot regard them as just possible goals among others. We may know full well in the abstract that, apart from our having adopted them as ours, they would just be possible goals among countless others that are no less valuable. In the grand scheme of things, as we might admit in a reflective moment, they are nothing special. But adopting them as ours means coming to stand in a special relationship of commitment to them. Whatever we may say when we stand back to reflect, in our everyday engagements with them, we cannot but treat the goals we have made our own as if they were more valuable, all else being equal, than any of the alternative possible goals that we did not make our own. Otherwise we are, as Bernard Williams once explained, left with no possible goal in life other than that of indiscriminately serving all the possible goals that we might have adopted, in proportion only to the value they have independently of our commitment to them.[15] We cannot then rationally prefer our goals to any other, all else being equal. And in that case, we cannot really have any goals at all, even the advertised goal of indiscriminately serving all possible goals in proportion only to the goal-independent value of doing so.

These remarks may be overgeneralized. Arguably, they do not apply to subsidiary goals that we adopt only as instruments

---

[15] Williams, 'A Critique of Utilitarianism' in JJC Smart and Bernard Williams, *Utilitarianism: For and Against* (Cambridge University Press 1973) 116–17.

to serve other larger goals that we have. Marking some student essays is one of my personal goals for today. It is on my 'to do' list. It is there as an instrument of a goal that I clearly do treat as if it were more valuable than other things I might be doing with my life, namely the goal of providing help and advice to my students. But do I necessarily treat the subsidiary goal of marking the essays today as if it were more valuable, all else being equal, than the various other valuable things that I could have done with that couple of hours? Maybe not. It depends on what is meant by 'treat as if'. There is a sense in which I treat doing the marking as if it were more valuable than its rivals just in case the marking is what I do. But this is surely the wrong sense of 'treat as if'. In the relevant sense, 'treat as if' surely implicates my attitudes as well as my actions. It is partly about how I *regard* the value of my goals, to repeat another word I used in the last paragraph. How do I regard the subsidiary goal of marking those essays? Not with much enthusiasm. There are many other uses of my time that strike me as more valuable. That is why I had to write 'essay marking' on my 'to do' list. I need cognitive and motivational reinforcement. Is this consistent with the kind of commitment that I am supposed to have towards my goals? Can one, for example, be weak-willed in respect of the pursuit of a goal and yet have the right kind of commitment to it for it still to pass the Williams test? Presumably, yes: *akratic* action is action in spite of what one takes to be the superior value of the path not taken, and so does not point to any undervaluation of that path. But perhaps the attitude I must have to be committed to my goals goes beyond cognition. Perhaps. The issue need not be resolved here. For there is no doubt, in the essay-marking case, that I am committed in the relevant way to the larger goal of providing help and advice to my students. This is not a case in which I am left goalless if I lack commitment to getting the essays marked today. On the contrary, it is a case in which, if my lack of enthusiasm for essay-marking gets the better of me, I chide myself for failure by the lights of my larger goal, a chiding which surely manifests my commitment if anything does.

Why would it be so terrible to be goalless? We are not only rational beings but finite ones. We have to exist within a lifetime, and have a life, and live it as valuably as a life can be lived.[16] There is no life without goals, even if only the classic drifter's or slacker's goal of living as goallessly as one possibly can. That makes having goals—I mean goals to do valuable things—themselves valuable. There is the value of the thing done, and then there is the value of having the doing of something valuable as a goal. If it is valuable to have goals, then commitment to it cannot but be valuable too, for one can have no goals without commitment to at least some of them (even if not all the subsidiary ones). And once we have this commitment, we cannot treat the life we are living on the same footing as some other possible life, as just another life for whatever it is worth independently of our commitments. This one is ours and we cannot live it without giving it a certain rational priority. Since an unlooked-for disruption of one's life, an unlooked-for deflection from one's goals, does not disrupt one's inevitable commitment to those goals—if the commitment is so easily disrupted, in what sense is it a commitment?—one cannot but wish that one had not been deflected from them. Until, of course, one finds others that one adopts to replace them, or until one comes to think that they were not valuable enough to merit one's commitment. This last proviso attaches because, from the inside, one does not think of the extra value as lying, content-independently, in the fact of commitment to the goal. To be committed, one must think of the extra value as lying in the goal itself, meaning in its content. So losing one's relative overvaluation of the goal means losing the goal too.

In a sense, then, being a finite rational being means living an illusion. It is a rationally necessary illusion. By our rational nature we must all imagine our goals to have, or at least treat them as having, more value than other goals we could have had. In reality, they have that value because of the value of our having goals. For each of us, however, from the inside, the value seems to be in the particular goal we have. From day to day I cannot but treat and regard my interest in culinary experimentation as superior to my stepson's interest in nutritional optimality; similarly, I cannot but treat and regard my interest in high-octane conversation as better than his penchant for broody silence. My taste is good, I say to myself, and worth supporting. His is less good, I say to myself, and to that extent less worth supporting. But at least his taste is good enough for me to be glad that he has it rather than some other teenage tastes, and it is worth supporting, to some extent, under *that* heading. So I have reason to help him pursue his goals, with which these tastes go hand-in-hand: buying him more boring turkey fillets to grill, making his bedroom suitable for retreat from family life, etc. For me that is because his goals are (i) at least minimally acceptable and (ii) his goals. For him it is because, in his committed way of looking at them, they are the best or the right goals to have. We are both living our own illusions, such that each has a more detached assessment of the other's goals than he has of his own. We humour each other, on a daily basis, accordingly.

This example shows that the conservatism of the first-person point of view, in which the existing goal counts for so much more than any number of possible alternatives, can be carried over somewhat into the third-person point of view. I agree that it is important for my stepson to have goals and I agree that this means he has reason to hold onto them. This means that I have reason to support him in his attempts to hold onto them. Things are made more complicated by the fact that different people may have different reasons, with different force, to support others in pursuing, and therefore holding onto, their goals. Some may make it their goal to help support particular others, or others in general, in support of their goals. Some have duties to provide such support irrespective of their own goals. The complications mount. However, all contribute to the rationality of holding on, which is not only the rationality of the holder-on, but also, often, the rationality of others who give that person their support.

(e) This brings us to one final point, a point about our human relationship with value in general. As finite rational beings our common goal—our *ergon*—is not to pursue, serve, promote, realize, or maximize all value pro rata, with the relevant *ratae* assessed independently of our personal goals. For that, as Williams explained, would amount to our having no personal goals, which means having no lives, which means losing the chance (and the added value) of *living* valuably. Our *ergon*, then, is to live valuably: to bring value into the world by selective engagement with it, by lacing it into our personal goals, which means changing the *ratae*. Yet those who claim that as finite rational beings we answer to all value alike, even that which we do not make part of our lives by lacing it into our personal goals, are surely not mistaken. They are right to think that, if we are to bring value into our lives through our goals we must be valuers, and they are right to think that success as a valuer means having sensitivity or responsiveness to all value alike, to value conceived apart from our own selective engagement with it. Their only mistake is to think that the relevant sensitivity or responsiveness to all value alike must lie in the pursuit of all value alike. Not so: in evaluating one's success as a valuer there is also the question, which was already alive in our Chapter 4 discussion, of what attitude one takes to value that one does not personally pursue. It is one thing not to serve some particular value, by declining to give some or all of one's life over to its pursuit; it is another thing not to *respect* that same value when one's life brings one into contact with it, whether through one's pursuit of it or otherwise. This already entails an asymmetry, in our rational sensitivity to value, between value that is realizable, that could be brought into the world, and value that is realized, that is already present in the world. It is not open to us, as rational beings, to treat the latter as if it were just another example of the former; to obliterate it, for example, as if that were (transaction costs apart) just the same as failing to have brought it into the world in the first place.

Many writings in moral philosophy have struggled with the correct way to make this contrast more precise while maintaining its generality, i.e. its application across the whole range of values. Many debates that are ostensibly about the doctrine of double effect, the relative priority of imperfect and perfect duties, the basic principles of moral arithmetic, rights as trumps, and so forth, are better interpreted as (or better interpreted as mixed up with) debates about how to draw the contrast between not respecting value and failing to bring it into the world. One common difficulty with such debates is that their protagonists are looking for more determinate borderlines than the subject can be expected to afford. But another difficulty is that such debates are often conducted in the expectation that the distinctions being drawn will play out in the same way, irrespective of which value is at stake. With the distinction that interests us here, this is clearly not so. One does not respect the value of friendship if one offers to swap an old friend for a new one. But doing the same thing with books is consistent with respecting their value as books. On the other hand, respecting the value of books, even damaged ones, is inconsistent with their deliberate destruction, whereas sometimes the best way to respect the value of friendship is to bring a damaged friendship deliberately to an end. Such distinctions can only be drawn at the level of particular values. Yet for all values there is a difference between failing to do whatever it takes to respect them in their instantiations and failing to bring the same instantiations into being in the first place. Our reasons to support and care for friendships already made and books already written and food already prepared and children already existing are more stringent,[17] all else being equal, than our reasons to make new friends or write new books or prepare new food or bear new children (or to assist others in doing so). Whether all else is equal can, of course, depend on many factors. It can be affected in various ways by people's goals. But even those goals themselves are subject to the same consideration: all else being equal, we each have more stringent reasons to respect the valuable goals that people already have—which may include helping them to achieve those goals—than we have to help them acquire those same goals to begin with, given the wide range of other valuable goals they might acquire.

This is not because as yet uncreated value is somehow less valuable than already created value. I already rejected that idea in (b) above. My point here does not rest on any ranking of values or types of value. It is not, for example, a distinction between things that have a kind of value called 'dignity' and things that don't have it. In a sense—on the view I am presenting—everything has its dignity, a way it should be treated in virtue of its value. That is true of children and friends but equally of chisels and food. Chisels should be used for chiselling, not for levering the lids off

---

[17] I choose this vague expression to leave open whether there is an extra 'reason of respect' or whether what we are talking about is simply an effect on the force or hold of the existing reason given by the value. I also leave open whether the relevant stringency is only (or even) a matter of how much weight attaches to the reason in conflict with others.

paint tins or planting out seedlings.[18] Food should be eaten and enjoyed, not left to rot. This last example helps to make clear that the distinction I am drawing does not map onto the act/omission distinction beloved of lawyers. *Both* eating food one has (or having others eat it) *and* omitting to eat it (or omitting to have it eaten)—the first respectful of the food, the second disrespectful— are to be contrasted with not obtaining or preparing that food in the first place. However, the main point of my including the example here is different. The point is to make clear that one respects the value of anything by treating it as instantiating that value once it instantiates that value. It does not follow that there is the same reason to add further instantiations of the same value, even though if there were such instantiations they too should be treated in a way that respects the value they instantiate. So what we are ranking here are not values but ways of relating to value—not values but *valuers*.[19] For any value, our responsiveness or sensitivity to that value, the responsiveness or sensitivity that constitutes our quality as valuers, lies in the way in which we treat the value's instantiations, and not in our creating or helping to create further instantiations that would have the same value (even though, if we do create further instantiations, our responsiveness to their value lies in the way in which we treat those instantiations too, including during their creation.)

3. No life without a past

Samuel Scheffler writes that there is 'something approaching a conceptual connection between valuing something and wanting

[18] I have written at greater length elsewhere (I jest not) about the morality of chiselling and the dignity of chisels. See Gardner, 'Fifteen Themes from Law as a Leap of Faith', *Jurisprudence* 6 (2015), 601. An important point I make there is that the respect that is due to things of value is not limited to things of intrinsic value. Instrumental value also calls for respect. In this way the foundations of the position I present in this chapter are at odds with those in G A Cohen, 'Rescuing Conservatism: A Defense of Existing Value' in R Jay Wallace, Rahul Kumar, and Samuel Freeman (eds), *Reasons and Recognition: Essays on the Philosophy of T.M. Scanlon* (Oxford University Press 2011). A more pressing disagreement with Cohen will emerge in s 4 in this chapter.

[19] For an attempt to connect such a ranking to the *value* of valuers, see Joseph Raz, *Value, Respect, and Attachment* (Cambridge University Press 2001) ch 4.

it to be sustained or preserved.'[20] I agree. Indeed, as you now know, I see not just one connection but two. The first is the connection that Scheffler notes when he says that 'we want the people and things we care about to flourish,'[21] where this has the implication that we wish them to continue, and to continue as part of our lives.[22] This wish to hold on, borne of the way in which we relate to our goals, was what I tried to make rationally intelligible in (c) and (d) above. But my subsequent remarks in (e) have drawn attention to a more impersonal conservative pressure on us as rational beings, one that supports our 'sustain[ing] and preserv[ing]' people and things *quite apart from* their place in our personal goals, and hence in our lives.

It belongs to what Scheffler calls 'the implicit framework'[23] of our lives as beings capable of having goals, i.e. as finite rational beings. As our goals take shape, as we engage selectively with value, the terms of our engagement are set by value that is already instantiated, and by the people and things that already instantiate it. One cannot fall in love with a future person. One cannot play a yet-to-be invented game or watch a film that hasn't been made. One cannot learn a language that is still to emerge. And one plays one's part in the coming into being and inventing and making and emerging of such new things only through one's engagement, albeit selectively, with people and pursuits that are already in existence. To have personal goals, to be able to engage selectively with value, is to inhabit a world in which value is instantiated,

---

[20] Scheffler, *Death and the Afterlife* (Oxford University Press 2013) 22.

[21] ibid.

[22] What transpires after our deaths is, as Scheffler says, still capable of counting as part of our lives. He aptly (if teasingly) calls this 'the afterlife'. To repeat, many but not all possible goals are such that only bringing about or contributing to a certain outcome will qualify as success in them. In some cases, it will still qualify as success if the outcome will be realized only *post mortem*, e.g. in one's children's having long and happy lives or in one's work finally being acknowledged. Those who have these goals fail, and their lives are pro tanto failures, if (after their deaths) their children lived on only briefly or miserably, or their work still went unacknowledged. For a meditation on how 'the afterlife' as conceived in traditional religious doctrines could be thought of in these same (broadly Schefflerian) terms, one could do worse than watch Powell and Pressburger's *A Matter of Life and Death* (Eagle-Lion Films 1946).

[23] Scheffler, *Death and the Afterlife* (n 20) 59.

made concrete, and thereby made available for engagement. Even trying to save future generations from climate change or totalitarianism or Ebola works that way; it is a possible goal (and yes, I mean 'possible' in 'something approaching a conceptual' sense) only for those who can also relate properly, as valuers, to value that is already instantiated in their world.

Think of Orwell's *Nineteen Eighty-Four*. Think of the role of love, nature, writing, song—even tatty antiques—as fragments of instantiated value that are fleetingly recovered from a world that was largely obliterated to make way for the extreme monotony of human existence under Big Brother. Think of the connection that Orwell repeatedly makes between the recovery of such fragments and the longing, on Winston Smith's part, for 'life [to be] worth living again'.[24] And think, indeed, of the doubts that Orwell raises about Winston's capacity to live such a life. What the story ultimately turns on is, after all, his and Julia's shared failure (true, under torture) to sustain their respect for the value that they briefly rekindled from another world:

'I betrayed you,' she said baldly.
'I betrayed you,' he said.[25]

In some readings of the book, the various fragments of recovered value are associated with a longing for personal autonomy, for a life shaped by choice, a life which Big Brother's regime stamps out, both generally and (by way of illustration) in the particular case of Winston and Julia. But that, it seems to me, is too adolescent a reading of *Nineteen Eighty-Four*, and one that makes it a much more boringly superficial book than it is. The reading places too much emphasis on the coercion and manipulation themes, and too little on the theme of betrayal. It thereby underestimates the threat that totalitarianism, according to Orwell, poses to 'the spirit of Man'.[26] Not all of our valuable goals are ours by choice; nor should they be. What Winston longs for is not a *choice* of valuable goals—he dare not yet long for that, even if he can conceive

---

[24] George Orwell, *Nineteen Eighty-Four* (Secker & Warburg 1949), 202.

[25] ibid 336.

[26] ibid 309. Winston, his interrogator tells him, is 'the last man', if 'man' is understood to have this 'spirit': 'Your kind is extinct. We are the inheritors'.

of it—but the mere possibility of having valuable goals, be they chosen or not. The possibility of Winston's having valuable goals depends—we gradually grasp—on his recognition of the traces of value he finds secreted around him, in a chestnut tree, a coral paperweight, the scent of real coffee, even a 'drivelling song'.[27] It is all value which (as the *dénouement* of the book is surely intended to teach us in a notably brutal way)[28] cannot be participated in, cannot be engaged with, unless first it is respected. As a lover one respects the value of one's relationship by, inter alia, not betraying one's lover to the enemy. As a valuer, one respects value in general, in the various different ways in which it calls to be respected. And one does so, irrespective of how it stands to one's goals.

4. From holding on to going back

My remarks about *Nineteen Eighty-Four* bring us back, by a circuitous route, to our earlier topic: the case for recovering or restoring what has been taken away. Not before time, you may say. Most of the last two sections were concerned with the rationality of holding on to a life that one still has. But that was surely a digression. We were supposed to be getting to grips with the regulative ideal of *restitutio in integrum*. Where that ideal is in play, it is *ex hypothesi* not true that one still has those parts of one's life that the ideal would have us restore to their original trajectory. The whole point is that those parts of one's life have been taken away. That is why it makes sense to ask about their restoration. A list of reasons for one to have held onto them may admittedly double as a list of reasons for one to grieve over their loss now that they

---

[27] ibid 161, 247.

[28] The same lesson is perhaps even more brutally taught in William Styron's *Sophie's Choice* (Random House 1979), aspects of which we discussed in Chapter 1. In both books, the reader is easily drawn into thinking that the betrayals count less as betrayals because coerced. But all that the coercion does in each case is justify or excuse the betrayal. It does not eliminate it. And in each book that is the crucial point. Without that the books are mere tales of psychological damage inflicted by thugs; with it they are tales of failure by lover and parent respectively, which, even though deliberately wrought by the evil schemes of others, makes the psychological damage fully rationally intelligible and in that sense manifestations of a specifically human predicament.

are gone, to rue the day that one let them go, to feel bitter at the fortunes of those who took them away, and so on. But how does it double as a list of reasons for putting things back as they were? Things have changed, and surely you need to get used to it. Although 'to the heart of a man [it is] treason,' as Robert Frost says, has not the time come

To yield with a grace to reason
And bow and accept the end
Of a love or a season?[29]

We could read Orwell as making the same point, applied not only to a person but also to a population. Winston's coral paper-weight belongs to a world of 'childhood memory', now 'mostly unintelligible',[30] tempting him into a futile, ultimately disastrous, search for restoration. Orwell's warning: once that world is gone, it's gone: 'If you want a picture of the future, imagine a boot stamping on a human face—forever.'[31]

So did I really digress when I talked about holding on instead of going back? This misunderstands the indirect way in which my points about the rational intelligibility of holding on were designed to feed into a defence of the *restitutio in integrum* ideal. In defending the holder-on from charges of irrational sentimentality, I was hoping to explain, in the first place, the typical shape of what lawyers call 'primary duties' (or 'primary obligations') in the law of torts. These are the duties, non-performance of which constitutes the defendant's tort and first breaches the plaintiff's right. In these duties, there already lurks the asymmetry that interests us, the asymmetry between a life already in progress and other lives that might be lived instead. Our primary duties in the law of tort are mainly duties not to do certain things that set others back (or tend to set others back) in the lives they already have. Just occasionally they are 'positive' duties to protect others from having those same lives set back. But either way it is the life one already has before one, with its current trajectory, that is protected by the performance (and by the existence) of the

---

[29] Frost, *A Boy's Will* (David Nutt 1913), 'Reluctance'.
[30] Orwell, *Nineteen Eighty-Four* (n 24) 3–4.
[31] ibid 307.

duty. It is the house that the potential plaintiff already lives in or is already trying to buy, the car she already drives or has already set her heart on, the work she already does or is already training to do, the relationships she has already formed or is already in the course of forming, the state of health she already enjoys or is already on the way to, the peace and quiet she has already found or was already seeking. The law of torts gives the potential plaintiff rights which, if they go unviolated, will help to keep her life on its existing track in these and various other respects, never mind whether that is the best track or the right track for her life to be on—never mind whether she should have had a smaller house, or a bigger car, or better health, or more peace, etc. Neil MacCormick aptly calls these 'security' rights, and I will adopt his terminology.[32]

The considerations I adduced in the previous section are relevant, in the way I have just explained, to the defence of security rights. Indeed, it seems to me that they are needed—some or all of them—to make the 'security' aspect of security rights defensible, even rationally intelligible. Other considerations bearing on the defence of such rights piggyback on these ones. So, for example, Arthur Ripstein says that 'certain security interests are protected [by the law], based on a conception of their importance to leading an autonomous life.'[33] Possibly so. But to make an autonomy-based case for security rights in general, as some might read Ripstein to be doing, is akin to focusing on the regime's stifling of personal autonomy in *Nineteen Eighty-Four*. It misses deeper and less sectarian concerns. One can be an autonomous person only if one can have personal goals; but the reverse is not true. Not all valuable goals are chosen or even confronted as objects of choice. Across human history, I would guess, most goals of most people were inherited, drifted into, accepted as already *fait accompli*, borne of necessity, etc. Yet those whose goals came to them in these ways were no less people with personal goals. They also had valuable things to hold onto. They had children, siblings, lovers, friends,

<hr>

[32] MacCormick, 'The Obligation of Reparation', *Proceedings of the Aristotelian Society* 78 (1978), 175 at 177.

[33] Ripstein, *Equality, Responsibility, and the Law* (Cambridge University Press 1999) 55.

homes, jobs, pieces of land, religions, games, pets, diaries, keep-
sakes, stories, etc. They had hopes for the winter and the harvest,
and fears about illness and war and displacement. They too were
closely engaged with value. Should one think that autonomous
people (in general) are *more* engaged with value (in general), and
hence have more cause to hold on to it? It seems no less plausible
to suppose the opposite, or to suppose—most plausibly—no general link at all. Those with personal autonomy may become more
invested in their goals thanks to the fact that they chose them (e.g.
more invested in how their children fare, since they chose to have
children), but they may also become less invested in their goals
(e.g. inclined to think of everything as just another ephemeral en-
tertainment to be dropped as readily as it was picked up). We see
the second consequence of personal autonomy instantiated in contemporary culture at least as often as the first. No *special* link, then,
between security rights and autonomy.

Be that as it may, once one has the beginnings of a case for security rights, and recognizes that the primary duties of tort law
are duties to respect such rights, it is tempting to jump straight to
the conclusion that the same is true of tort law's secondary duties.
If the primary rights protect security then so do the secondary.
It looks like a simple application of what, in Chapter 3, I called
the 'continuity thesis'.[34] The continuity thesis, you will recall, is
a thesis about the continuity of primary and secondary duties in
private law, and more generally about the continuity, as Robert
Musil nicely conveys it, between 'what one does' and 'what one
does next'.[35] When I fail to do what I have a reason to do, says the
continuity thesis, the reason for me to have done it survives the
failure, and calls for such fallback conformity on my part as may
still be possible. I forgot, say, to phone you on your birthday to
reassure you that I was thinking of you on the occasion of your
birthday. The same reason—that I would thereby reassure you
that I am thinking of you on the occasion of your birthday—then

---

[34] Indeed, these were the examples that originally prompted me to spell the
continuity thesis out in Gardner, 'What is Tort Law For? Part 1: The Place of
Corrective Justice', *Law and Philosophy* 30 (2011), 1.
[35] Musil, *Der Mann ohne Eigenschaften, vol 2* (Rowohlt Verlag 1933) ch 9: 'Nie
ist das, was man tut, entscheidend, sondern immer erst das, was man danach tut.'

becomes a reason to, say, send a text message overnight and/or phone you early the following day. That is to say, it becomes a reason to do whatever is the next-best way, still available to me, to reassure you that I was thinking of you on the occasion of your birthday. And if I fail to *that*, I look for the next-best alternative, and so on. By a couple of days after your birthday, my call or message may do the opposite of reassuring you that I was thinking of you on the occasion of your birthday—the occasion is now too long gone—and so it no longer yields any measure of conformity to the original reason. At that point there may indeed be nothing left to do by way of conformity with the original reason. (Although it does not follow that there is nothing left to do, full stop. There may be some of our Chapter 4 measures to be taken. Perhaps one could still say something relevant with flowers.)

One might regard the early-next-day phone call in this example as a kind of remedy for the failure to make the original call, perhaps even (in the legal idiom) as the performance of a secondary duty that arises for the same reason that one failed to conform to when one breached the primary duty. And one may then conclude that this is how it also goes with tort law and more generally with reparative duties structured by the *restitutio in integrum* ideal. No doubt your security is a reason for me not to, for example, injure your left eye. No doubt your left eye is something you use quite a lot in various aspects of your life. You play tennis, you are a keen online gamer, you do botanical drawings, you like to cook or read or knit, you often drive at night to visit your sick mother, or you like to take flattering selfies and get noticed on Tinder.[36] Any of those pursuits might well be made more difficult or less rewarding or less successful with a damaged eye. So if I do injure your eye with, say, a small retaining screw that flies off my badly-maintained power tool as I use it, your security—the same security that was my reason not to injure your eye in the first place—is now a reason for me to ameliorate what I did, to put

---

[36] I mention the last example to guard against overmoralistic interpretations of the value in our goals. Having fun is good too, although it is a more complicated puzzle whether the value extends entirely to immoral ways of having fun, e.g. having fun torturing people. On the perils of overmoralization, see Susan Wolf, 'Moral Saints', *Journal of Philosophy* 79 (1982), 419.

you back, so far as it can still be done, in the position you would
have been in had I never injured you. You need minor surgery?
You have to miss a few days' work to recover from it? You need a
good-quality concealer for that little scar? You missed the contest
you'd already paid to enter so that you'll have to enter the next
one instead? Just put it on my tab. Whatever it takes to get you
back on the internet or on the court or on the road pronto, to let
you pick up where you left off, as if it had never happened.

But now suppose that, although decent sight in your left eye
can quickly be restored by minor surgery, it will never again be
quite the same as before, and in particular will never be quite
good enough to allow you to resume your career as an airline
pilot, or to allow you to carry on as a volunteer firefighter, or to
win more archery tournaments. It is too late for you to hold on
to those aspects of your life. Letting go is the only option, for you
and so (as repairer) for me. So why would your future lost income
as an airline pilot, or the costs of your retraining for another volunteer role or a different sport, go on my tab? Surely the basis for
these debts, whether they are branded as *restitutio in integrum* or
not, must have more to do with your starting afresh than with
your continuing where you left off?

Not so. The key to what is going on here is a point made in
passing in our brief discussion of transaction costs back in section
2. As one's life changes in one way, we noted, one may be constrained to change it in others. Our goals are in various ways
nested and interconnected. Earning your salary as an airline pilot
allowed you to take time off to be a volunteer firefighter. Being
a volunteer firefighter allowed you to be a contributor to local
life, in spite of your extended absences on long-haul routes. Both
allowed you to be a certain kind of parent, bringing a spirit of
adventure and wonder to the children' lives that might be missing
if you were more of a homebound person. The steady airline
work allowed you to cover the rent and utilities and childcare
and insurance (more holding-on!), and still to be able to afford
proper holidays with your family to make up for your anti-social
work schedule. Through your global travels you were able to ex-
pand your cultural horizons in architecture and music, your twin
passions, which the children lapped up through your regular
communiqués from exotic locations. The firefighter work was

partly about team camaraderie of a kind that you could not find in the world of airline crew rosters and rapid airport turnarounds, and also partly about developing extra team-leadership skills that would later allow you to get accredited as a pilot supervisor and to cut back on the flying hours. And so on. The point is that there are still plenty of other things for you to hold onto in your existing life, either constituents of what you used to do that can be preserved in new roles or relationships, or extrinsic benefits of what you used to do that can be preserved if only the benefits can be found from another source—some of them, no doubt, on my tab. The law of torts assumes that this is how life is for most people, and accordingly does not ask plaintiffs to account for the whole of their lives, for all of the numerous interdependencies among their goals, in assessing their damages.

5. Some unexplained points

Various considerations, some of which will loom large in our final chapter, militate in favour of the making of this bold assumption by the law. Most immediately it is made to avoid the courts being required to make vast and complex adjudications on exactly what goals people have, the relative importance in their lives of their various goals, their relative prospects of success in those goals, the value of those goals independent of the fact that they were adopted as goals, how that value, and the goal of pursuing it, is properly to be respected, and so on. The law's unwillingness to embark on such determinations may sometimes seem excessively cautious. It certainly strikes some law-users as alienating, as stripping human or moral meaning out of the law of torts. This leads them to seek meaning elsewhere, for example in less formal dispute resolution models such as 'restorative justice' processes, through which the way in which the wrong impacted on them personally can be brought home to those who wronged them. I am sympathetic to this quest, as my discussion of apology in Chapter 4 may already have suggested.

I say that the law of torts tends to shy away from mapping and assessing our goals, and more generally scrutinizing the value in our lives to work out to what extent it is worth holding onto. But of course, the court sometimes cannot avoid noticing that there is very little there for an injured plaintiff to hold onto. On the one hand, there are cases of catastrophic injury which may leave a plaintiff incapable of having a future life structured by interlocking goals, or indeed by any significant personal goals at all. On the other hand, there are cases of plaintiffs, often younger children, who before they were injured didn't (yet) have a life structured by interlocking goals, or by any significant personal goals at all. Such cases raise difficulties for the ideal of *restitutio in integrum*. They may sometimes call for arguments based on the goals of others, on whom the plaintiff is dependent, or on the transaction costs of adding extra changes to the changes that have already taken place even though, without those transaction costs, it might be better to start again from scratch. It would be foolish to attempt to catalogue all the various considerations that might bear from time to time on the calculation of damages in tort law, let alone to try to catalogue the types of cases to which each might apply. It would also be a mistake to suppose that even the whole list of such considerations, if it could be marshalled, would determine what exactly the associated legal rules should say. Most legal rules are (at least in part) coordination rules, the content of which is left underdetermined by their rationale. The task I set myself in the previous section was merely to show how one and the same rationale could be the rationale of primary and secondary duties alike, at least in the law of torts. I showed this by showing how reasons for holding on to value in one's life could double as reasons for getting that value back, despite the obvious difference that, if one is interested in getting it back, then evidently one did not manage to hold onto it. I left it open precisely how, and indeed to what extent, the rules of the law of torts should reflect this concern to get the value back.

In saying 'of the law of torts' I am acknowledging that I went mysteriously silent about the law of contract. This is not because what I said in defence of the ideal of *restitutio in integrum* does not apply, *mutatis mutandis*, to the law of contract. It is because the *mutanda* that need to be *mutata* are extremely complex. Keeping them in play would have created many distractions in what I wrote. In particular, the 'injuries' that are at stake in breach of contract cases typically include (as we noted) the non-receipt of benefits contracted for, and the interdependencies with other goals of the plaintiff typically include some that are owed to ways in which the plaintiff altered his or her position on the basis that the contract would be performed and its benefits obtained. The rights asserted in such cases are still security rights, it seems to me, but even in respect of the primary duty there are extra logical puzzles about these security rights. Do contracts give us such security as they do because there is a duty to perform them, or is it that there is a duty to perform them because they give us some independently specifiable security? Is the contribution to our personal autonomy that comes of our being able to make binding contracts a consequence of the security of performance that is associated with their bindingness, or is it the other way round?[37] This is not the place to tackle these puzzles. In this book I am trying to tackle puzzles that arise throughout what some contemporary lawyers call 'the law of obligations', rather than problems that are specific to one branch of it. But, however we answer these additional questions about contracts, it seems to me, the security that is served in the performance of a contract will turn out to be the same one that is served in a fallback way by the reparative damages for breach of contract one obtains when the same security went unserved in the contract's non-performance. In that respect, to reprise a theme of Chapter 3, breaches of contract are just like torts.

6. Justice in security

MacCormick thinks that at least some of the security rights recognized by tort law, namely rights to 'security of persons from harm', may 'be treated as uncontroversial',[38] from which he concludes that no defence of them is needed. That is the wrong conclusion. Uncontroversial ideas need not less but more critical

---

[37] For recent discussions in the context of promising rather than contracting, see David Owens, 'The Problem with Promising' in Hanoch Sheinman (ed), *Promises and Agreements: Philosophical Essays* (Oxford University Press 2011), and Joseph Raz, 'Is There a Reason to Keep a Promise?' in Gregory Klass, George Letsas, and Prince Saprai (eds), *Philosophical Foundations of Contract Law* (Oxford University Press 2014).

[38] MacCormick, 'The Obligation of Reparation' (n 32) 180.

scrutiny, since they generally get such an easy ride. MacCormick himself pays a philosophical price for giving rights to 'security of persons from harm' such an easy ride. He contrasts them with 'more controversial' rights to 'security of possessions', our view of which is 'properly conditional on our view as to the justice or otherwise of the distribution of assets within a society.' He fails to notice that the distribution of 'assets' *is* a distribution of security. It is a distribution of the ability to hold on, e.g. to hold on to things that one is no longer making any use of. Once we notice that, we should see that there is always a live question about how security *itself* should be distributed, and we should see that this question arises just as much for 'security of persons' as it does for 'security of possessions'. Indeed, all valuable security, including security of possessions, *is* 'security of persons'—it is all about how much ability we each enjoy to hold on to aspects of our existing lives—and one cannot avoid the question of whether that ability is justly allocated among persons.

My point is not that security is the only 'currency of justice', to use G A Cohen's apt expression.[39] On the contrary, any valuable thing that is capable of being bestowed or withdrawn—love, reputation, praise, freedom, medical care, working hours, reparation, pocket money, bedtimes, you name it—can be justly or unjustly bestowed or withdrawn. My point is merely that for every other thing that can be justly or unjustly bestowed or withdrawn there is a further question of what would count, in turn, as *security in* that thing being justly or unjustly bestowed or withdrawn. Just as the distribution of speech is not identical to the distribution of freedom of speech, so the distribution of homes is not identical to the distribution of security in homes (since some people are owner-occupiers, some renters, some squatters, some living in flood zones, some living in war zones, etc.). Cohen himself seems to get this surprisingly wrong. In his defence of conserving some 'existing value', otherwise not too far distant from mine, Cohen writes as if the case for holding on to existing value runs up against our concern with justice only when people start wanting to hold on to injustices.[40] But right from the start there

---

[39] Cohen, 'On the Currency of Egalitarian Justice', *Ethics* 99 (1989), 906.
[40] Cohen, 'Rescuing Conservatism' (n 18), at 204.

is the broader question of the justice of their getting to hold on more effectively than others to *anything*, even when the thing to be held onto is not an injustice.

A couple want to switch, say, from (pretty securely) renting their home from a local authority to (even more securely) owning the freehold themselves. It's not unjust, let's stipulate for argument's sake, that they want to hold onto the home they already have; it's not a grand place, they rented it fair and square, they have made something of it, and so on. But that is not the issue. Nobody is suggesting that it should stop being their home. The question is whether it is just that they now acquire the extra security that they seek in respect of their home. Should they be able to acquire the freehold under a 'right to buy' scheme, which comes, let us suppose, at the price of eroding public housing stock and which will therefore leave other people with huge reductions in housing security later on, even if it brings about no reductions in actual housing (the stock of rentable houses will still be there and habitable and rentable, let's imagine, only now not rentable very securely at all because from amateur landlords looking for a low-expenditure, high-income investment, not from a public authority interested in making sure that people are housed). I already said, of course, that we might feel differently about lives already being lived and lives yet to take shape. But what I said on that front was about not *disrespecting* the lives already being lived, and here nobody (by hypothesis) is attempting to do that; the would-be freeholders are not faced with a threat of eviction or anything like that. So that does not affect the example. And, in any event, the question about the example that concerns us is not whether the would-be freeholders have justice on their side; the question is whether a question of justice arises in relation to the allocation of housing security *as well as* in relation to the allocation of houses. The example, it seems to me, confirms that it does.

The law of obligations (as I will now call it myself) could be thought of as a scheme for allocating security, indeed for allocating security rights in a certain distinctive pre-packaged form.[41] Obviously, it allocates what Guido Calabresi and Douglas

---

[41] I explore the points in the next two paragraphs at much greater length in J Gardner, 'What is Tort Law For? Part 2. The Place of Distributive Justice' in John Oberdiek (ed), *Philosophical Foundations of Tort Law* (Oxford University Press 2014).

Melamed call its 'initial entitlements':[42] what will qualify as a tort or breach of contract against whom, or (in other words) who owes which primary duties to whom. In the same fell swoop, however, it allocates a distinctive 'mode of protecting these entitlements',[43] namely reparative damages available as of right for breach, a secondary duty to provide *restitutio in integrum* in the event of non-performance of the primary duty. Some security rights are property rights, but these ones are not.[44] These security rights are only 'liability' rights, as Calabresi and Melamed like to put it. But still, in the same way as property rights, they cannot but be allocated selectively by the law; and still, as with property rights, the question therefore cannot but arise of the justice of the allocation.

Here are some of the classic security-distributive questions that have shaped the modern law of obligations. Should there be greater tort law protection for consumers injured by defective products, meaning more tort law duties on producers and distributors (*Donoghue v Stevenson*[45])? Or greater protection for customers against resort to small print exclusions in standard form contracts, meaning harder-to-limit contract law duties on service providers (*Thornton v Shoe Lane Parking*[46])? Should there be more tort law protection for trespassers who encounter dangers on private land, meaning more tort law duties on occupiers of such land (*British Railways Board v Herrington*[47])? And what about narrowing the range of cases in which employers can disclaim the tortious acts of their employees while the latter are at work, meaning better tort law remedies for third parties who would otherwise be restricted to recovering damages from impecunious defendants (*Rose v Plenty*[48])? These examples, only a tiny sample, show that the law of obligations cannot be assigned to the role of doing 'corrective justice' as opposed to 'distributive justice'; for what the law of obligations must do above all is justice *in the*

---

[42] Calabresi and Melamed, 'Property Rules, Liability Rules, and Inalienability: One View of the Cathedral', *Harvard Law Review* 85 (1972), 1089 at 1097.

[43] ibid 1089.

[44] Although of course they may be used to help *protect* property rights.

[45] [1932] AC 562.   [46] [1971] 2 QB 163.   [47] [1972] AC 877.

[48] [1976] 1 WLR 141.

distribution of the very corrective justice that it dispenses, where that corrective justice is in turn a specialized juridical scheme for allowing some people, often at the expense of others, to hold on more tightly, with the support of the law, to what they already have, or recently had, in their lives.

Since security is conservative—it is all about holding on—it is natural to associate it with *social* conservatives who want to see the old social order retained. And indeed, the rhetoric of 'security' often serves the purposes of such people, who manipulate other people's reasonable worries about change and loss in their own lives to yield an obnoxiously repressive and privilege-entrenching social ideology. But being socially conservative is a big jump from the conservatism to which I have given some modest support in this chapter. One need not be a social conservative to see the role that holding on plays in the lives of human beings. One need not be a social conservative to be a believer in housing security, income security, and job security. Social security, you will probably recall from the days when we still had it, was a post-war Labour government initiative. This too suggests that any scheme for social progress, however radical, needs to make progress *with* security, not against it. Curiously, capital-C Conservatives in today's politics tend to resist this progressive emphasis on security as it enables ordinary folk to resist the destabilizing effects of capital mobility, which nowadays do more than anything else to keep the powerful powerful. The same Conservatives often want to make it harder to sue in tort, as recent developments in both the UK and the US have shown. Could there be a connection? Could Conservative governments have noticed that inflicting insecurity on the ordinary population is a terrific way of wielding, and thereby entrenching, privilege elsewhere, and that having effective security rights, at least today, helps to strengthen the pockets of resistance? There is no reason to think that tort law, or more generally the law of obligations, has to be a socially conservative force just because of the way in which it allows people to hold on to what they have. The main historic problem with tort law, it seems to me, lies not in its concern with security rights as such but in its view about whose security rights deserve the most protection and who should get access to it. The main struggle is not to abandon its concern with security rights but to make sure that the security rights are justly distributed and that access to them is not restricted to the already security-advantaged.

So now, at long last, we can see a possible way of responding to Coleman's troubling question about the conservative aspect of the law of obligations:

> [If] you have no right to your wealth under the relevant principle of distributive justice ... how can you have a right to have it restored ...?

This question has two misleading aspects. First, it assumes that the only 'relevant principle of distributive justice' concerns the distribution of wealth. More immediately salient is the question of the distribution of security. In many kinds of society, being wealthy can also give you extra security, because extra security can be bought. And that extra security can also help you to become and to stay wealthy. But in societies where the rule of law holds, there is also the possibility of protecting security in ways that are relatively independent of wealth, by the conferring and upholding of legal security rights. My suggestion here is not that the rights given to people in the law of obligations help them to get such security rights. Rather, it is that they *constitute* such security rights. The law of obligations distributes a certain kind of security right. And this brings us to the second way in which Coleman's question is misleading. He talks as if there is a distributive state of affairs that exists independently of the law of obligations, and which the law of obligations helps to maintain (by, inter alia, returning us to it when it is disrupted). Maybe so. But there is also the distributive state of affairs that is not independent of the law of obligations but that resides, rather, in the distribution of the relevant legal obligations themselves, which is also a distribution of rights. The first question of distributive justice facing the law of obligations is not how to distribute wealth but how to distribute the legal obligations that give the law of obligations its name. What these legal obligations are primed to offer (to return to our first point) is not wealth but security. This security could, if the obligations are well distributed, be relatively independent of wealth, and indeed be a mode of social power capable of rivalling wealth.

6

That Was Then and This Is Now

If a scale exists, the balance does not tip.
If there is justice, here it is.

To die as much as necessary, without going too far.
To grow back as much as needed, from the remnant that
survives.

Wisława Szymborska [1]

1. Private law as a scheme of freedom

In Chapter 5, I tried to disentangle our timeless human concern
to preserve the lives we already have, which shapes so much of
private law, from our characteristically modern concern to live
our lives autonomously, by choosing how we live. Holding on,
I pointed out, is not a distinctively liberal preoccupation. Orwell's
Nineteen Eighty-Four is only incidentally a portrayal of the threat
that totalitarianism poses to personal autonomy. The threat is
more far-reaching than that. It is a threat to the very possibility of
having valuable goals, chosen or otherwise. And having valuable
goals, as Orwell repeatedly reminds us, is essential to having any
kind of life. For people like Winston and Julia, who struggle even
to have a life, choosing a life for oneself may seem a fantastical,
maybe decadent, luxury. Witness, if further examples be needed,
the concerns of Scots smallholders of the mid-nineteenth century, holding on by their fingernails:

'We have no use for opportunities here,' said my father. 'The boy is required to work on the croft and earn money for his family through his

---

[1] Szymborska, *Sounds, Feelings, Thoughts: Seventy Poems by Wisława Szymborska*
(trans Krynski and Maguire, Princeton University Press 1981), 'Autotomy', p 137.
(Quoted by kind permission of Princeton University Press; permission conveyed
through Copyright Clearance Center, Inc.).

labour.' ... [H]ad I been asked I would have agreed with my father that I am now required to work for the family.[2]

Although there is no freedom without security, to boil it down, that is because there is no life without security. The need to hold on has nothing especially to do with living freely.

Earlier chapters made similar points. In Chapter 2, thinking about the dissonant relationship between endeavour and achievement in *Death of a Salesman*, I cautioned against a reading that would associate that theme of the play too narrowly with the ideology of twentieth-century America that is Miller's immediate critical target. The ideological context merely amplifies the dissonance, I suggested. It does so by juxtaposing a late modern delusion, the American Dream, with the timeless and unavoidable reality that it contrives to conceal. The point was supposed to carry over into our thinking about the law. The problem of authoritatively assigning outcomes to agents, the problem that occupied us towards the end of Chapter 2, is heightened or at least made more conspicuous under late modern conditions. Those conditions increase the potential for conflicts among people as well as increasing the potential for rival interpretations of such conflicts. At the same time, they increase the importance of placing constraints on the law—I mentioned the ideal of the rule of law and the harm principle as two such constraints—in the cause of protecting people's autonomy. These constraints are not private law specific, but nor is private law exempt from them. They are necessitated not by special features of private law but by an emerging set of social conditions to which private law, like the rest of the law, has to adapt. These are conditions in which people's autonomy plays a greater role, not just instrumentally but also constitutively, in the success of their lives. It is anachronistic to read this heightened importance of autonomy back into the whole history of private law, and in particular to think that an emphasis on personal autonomy is necessary to justify or make intelligible private law's most durable features. By 'its most durable features', I mean those discussed in this book: its preoccupation with duties owed to others and their breach; the emphasis it places on how those breaches affect those others, in particular in

---

[2] Graeme Macrae Burnet, *His Bloody Project* (Saraband 2015) 46.

disrupting the flow of their lives; and the primacy it gives to reparative remedies, which are those designed to minimize the disruption and thereby mitigate the breach.

You may think these points too obvious to be worth making. After all, Roman law in the classical period had a law of contracts and a law of torts (delicts) a long time before our late modern preoccupation with choosing our own goals, and hence our own lives, took root. Yet in making these points, and more generally in developing the arguments of this book, I have conspicuously parted company with a body of contemporary thought in which private law is presented as creating, for better or worse, a peculiarly liberal scheme of interaction and regulation. Without any invocation of 'equal freedom', or lacking an 'autonomy-based' approach, or failing to enlist 'liberty interests', or neglecting the 'value of choice', or more generally sidelining a panoply of distinctively liberal values, we cannot make sense of what is going on in the law of torts and contracts, never mind in property law. Or so it is said. Thus, for Arthur Ripstein:

The 'cumbrous and expensive machinery of the state' serves as guarantor of this equal freedom provided that it both articulates the appropriate standards of conduct and, should those standards be violated, it makes it as if the wrong had never happened.[3]

And according to Emmanuel Voyiakis:

The reason why others may require one to make repair in [private law] situations is not that one made a certain choice, but that one had a choice that one had reason to value e.g. the opportunity to shape one's voluntary commitments to others, to choose how and where to drive, to control one's use and enjoyment of one's own land, and so on.[4]

For Hanoch Dagan, meanwhile:

[T]he core irreducible mission of private law is to provide all of us with a diverse inventory of credible institutions of just interpersonal relationships intrinsically valuable for our self-authorship.[5]

---

[3] Ripstein, 'As If It Had Never Happened', *William and Mary Law Review* 48 (2007), 1957 at 1969; the words quoted by Ripstein (slightly reordered in the process) are from Oliver Wendell Holmes, *The Common Law* (Little, Brown & Co 1881), 96.

[4] Voyiakis, *Private Law and the Value of Choice* (Hart Publishing 2017), 96.

[5] Dagan, 'The Utopian Promise of Private Law', *University of Toronto Law Journal* 66 (2016), 392 at 417.

I dissent from all three views. But obviously not from every aspect of them. As I have already said, I do not deny the great and constitutive importance of personal autonomy (and its associated freedoms) in the lives we lead today. I do not doubt that having extra options (objects of choice) is often valuable even when we do not pursue them (Voyiakis), and I do not doubt that there can be extra value in structuring valuable goals and relationships as options (Dagan). If I did, I could hardly have come out in Chapter 2 as an enthusiast for principles of legal toleration such as Mill's harm principle, and for rights held against the authorities such as those of freedom of speech, freedom of conscience, reproductive and sexual freedom, and freedom of movement. I say that I 'came out' but actually I have never hidden the fact, in any of my work, that in my politics I am an undaunted 1960s-style liberal. I do not plan to deny it now. Nor do I deny that many aspects of contemporary private law are coloured by distinctively liberal preoccupations like my own. Of course they are. And so they should be. I am only restoring these concerns to their proper parochial place. They bear on how to tailor to our contemporary needs a set of doctrines that have a more ecumenical and hence less ephemeral set of rationales and resonances. More ecumenical and less ephemeral because compatible, subject to some tailoring, with a far wider range of ideological outlooks and social conditions.

That does not mean, I hasten to add, that they are ideologically neutral. No norms or principles or doctrines are ideologically neutral, meaning even-handedly hospitable to all ideological outlooks. But some are more ecumenical than others. And what I have called the most durable features of private law are, as you would expect, more ecumenical than various more ephemeral features, such as the range of wrongs that are treated from time to time as tortious, or the range of legal relations that are at any given time contractualized.

The relative ephemerality of such features, recall, was a theme of Chapter 1. We noted the historical shift from strictly to loosely relational duties in the tort of negligence, a shift which both reflected and contributed to the rise in that tort's social importance. We also noted the still-ongoing shift towards contractual reductivism in respect of the law's treatment of various other strictly relational duties. These shifts represent accommodations of private law to changing social conditions in the late modern age. The law's doctrines have been tailored to the needs of people leading, or trying to lead, or being edged into leading, more autonomous lives. You may think, as I do, that late modern private law has tended to assume that people already possess such autonomy more than it has helped to nurture or protect them in securing it. You may also think, as I do, that late modern private law has a too-individualistic and too-voluntaristic picture of what an autonomous life would be like. (I expressed this in Chapter 1 by saying that contractual reductivism may augment but may also diminish our freedom.) And you may think, as I do, that late modern private law has therefore had very mixed fortunes in tailoring itself to the needs of late modern people. But be all that as it may, we are still talking specifically about the needs of late modern people. The basic interpersonal architecture of private law, the architecture of legal duties owed to particular others and reparative remedies for their breach and so forth, pre-exists them and could equally survive the end of their era. And there we see my dissent from the writings of Ripstein, Voyiakis, and Dagan (among many others), for whom the basic interpersonal architecture of private law is *essentially* an architecture of freedom.

2. The powers of the parties

It may strike you that I can get away with this dissent only by suppressing a key element of the basic interpersonal architecture of private law: namely, the extensive legal powers of the person who claims to have been wronged (the plaintiff) to initiate, maintain, and terminate court proceedings against the person whom she claims to have wronged her (the defendant). The authority of the court to tackle and resolve the dispute, in private law cases, is subject to the authority of the plaintiff. Don't I mean 'of the parties'? Aren't there also typically some powers of the defendant, e.g. the power to apply for an extremely unpromising claim to be struck out, and the power to apply for a stay, and the power to apply for leave to appeal? Yes, indeed. But the special feature of private law, procedurally speaking, is not that the parties to the proceedings have legal powers to initiate and in some circumstances to bring to an end the legal powers of the court. That

is true in criminal proceedings too, where one of the parties is
the State or the Crown or the Commonwealth, acting through
a prosecutorial official. There too the defendant may have important powers to apply for abandonment of the proceedings,
to obtain leave to appeal, etc. The special feature of private law,
procedurally speaking, is that the most extensive legal powers to
determine the powers of the court, those most akin to those of a
criminal prosecutor, lie with the very person who claims to have
been wronged. She is the plaintiff, a non-official who stands to
profit personally, whether financially or otherwise, from the outcome of the proceedings. Indeed, she is *meant* to profit personally
if her claim succeeds. A large and obvious conflict of interest is no
barrier, then, to having the draconian legal authority to bring the
court's authority to bear on the dispute, and to wield it against the
defendant. In the case of a civil plaintiff, neither the impartiality
of the judge, nor even the dispassion of the criminal prosecutor,
is legally insisted upon or socially expected. It is not even much
officially encouraged.

Thus, the legal powers of the plaintiff in respect of the conduct of court proceedings are, in most respects, less constrained
than those of the criminal prosecutor. First, the valid exercise of
the plaintiff's powers, unlike those of the prosecutor, does not
depend on their being exercised only in response to a complaint
or referral from another person or body, or only under a special licence or oath or warrant, or only for a particular reason, or
only taking account of a certain range of reasons. In many legal
systems, it is enough that the plaintiff issues, and serves on the
defendant, a comprehensible statement of claim. (More later on
the question of fees or deposits payable to the court at the time of
issue.) Secondly, a different matter,[6] the plaintiff has no legal duty
to exercise her legal powers at all, or to exercise them in any particular way if she does exercise them, including to exercise them
reasonably. (In some legal systems, however, she may have a duty
not to exercise them maliciously, meaning for no reason other

---

[6] On the contrast between invalidity (absence of power) and illegality (breach
of duty) see HLA Hart, *The Concept of Law* (Clarendon Press 1961) 27–41. Hart
concentrates on acts that are invalid but not illegal. However, the converse situation is also widespread. A good example is *Edwards v Ddin* (1976) 63 Cr App R 218.

than to upset or intimidate the defendant.[7]) That the conditions
for the valid exercise of the plaintiff's legal powers are few and
proforma, and that there are scant legal duties regulating their
exercise, could be summed up by calling them 'radically discretionary' powers.

Just how radically discretionary are the procedural powers of
the plaintiff seems to be poorly understood in wider public culture. People often complain, for example, that burglars are 'allowed' to sue householders for negligence in respect of injuries
that they, the burglars, suffered during their burglaries.[8] They
fail to realize that, with rare exceptions, anybody (recognized by
law as a person) is 'allowed' to sue anybody (recognized by law
as a person) for absolutely anything—where 'allowed' connotes
the legal power to do it, plus no legal duty not to. In this sense,
I am 'allowed' to sue a random restaurateur in a Welsh village
that I have never visited for the alleged wrong of serving peas on
a Tuesday. I am 'allowed' to sue NASA for the alleged wrong of
having a bad logo, the RSPCA for the alleged wrong of caring
too much about animals, and the BBC for the alleged wrong
of failing to make it snow in Brighton on Christmas Day 1943.
Clearly, I will not make it past the first ('striking out') hurdle with
any of these daft claims. But that is because, as compared with my
legal powers as plaintiff, the legal powers of the court are for the
most part non-discretionary.[9] The court has narrow legal powers
and many legal duties in dealing with whatever proceedings I may

---

[7] In *Willers v Joyce* [2016] UKSC 43, the UK Supreme Court confirmed that
the tort of malicious prosecution covers maliciously issuing civil proceedings. For
fear of encouraging 'satellite litigation', the court was at pains to stress that the tort
is of very narrow application. The companion tort of abuse of process, also rather
narrow, regulates the ways in which plaintiffs or defendants may exploit proceedings that are already underway.

[8] See e.g. Steven Morris, 'Burglar has right to sue Tony Martin, judge rules',
The Guardian (14 June 2003). The question of whether someone is 'allowed to take
[another] to court' is confused with whether the law will be on his side when he
does so. As if we could only sue if we would win!

[9] The discretion to issue or refuse injunctive relief (including an order for specific performance) is a notable exception. On why such relief is not available as of
right, even if it would be continuity-thesis optimal, see ch 4, s 5, as well as s 5 of
this chapter. For more detailed analysis, see David Winterton, *Money Awards in
Contract Law* (Hart Publishing 2015), esp ch 4.

launch, whereas I have wide legal powers and few legal duties in launching them. Most importantly, the court is duty-bound, in law, to assess my far-fetched claims on their legal merits. For me to have done the same would certainly have been prudent, given how much of everybody's (including my own) time and money and effort I am wasting, and given how that could come back to haunt me in a later order for the payment of the other side's costs in fending off my zany litigation. But costly or otherwise in the long run, there was nothing legally amiss in my issuing claims without the slightest legal merit—even if I gave no thought to their legal merit or indeed issued them in the face of strong advice that they were legally unmeritorious (barring malice on my part).

It must be the element of radical discretion here that invites an association with freedom. The plaintiff's powers are extremely permissively drawn; she has wide latitude for error. Is that not a typical liberal arrangement? Far from it. For the latitude she has to err is in exercises of authority over others—over the court and, through the court, over the defendant. Wide latitude to err in exercises of authority, especially authority exercised over and through officials, is a typical *illiberal* arrangement. It is not as if the plaintiff's errors are merely tolerated by the law, as when she makes an unsuitable friend or eats too much junk food or forgets her umbrella on a rainy day. No, her errors are positively supported and sponsored by the law. However stupid, she can dignify her stupidity with the authority of the court and foist it thereby on the defendant, not only at the stage of issuing the proceedings but also (where the proceedings are meritorious enough to progress) in how she handles them later, e.g. in the unaccountably tough conditions she sets for abandonment of her case, or in the disproportionately harsh mechanisms she chooses for enforcement of the court's judgment if she wins.

What might lead someone to think that such potentially oppressive authority has a distinctively freedom-based rationale? 'Trouble with rights-talk' is the usual explanation. The plaintiff claims to have been wronged by the defendant; she claims that the defendant did not do his duty towards her; she claims that he violated a right of hers. As I explained in Chapter 1, I regard all of these formulations as roughly synonymous. But many people, as I also noted in Chapter 1, read much more into the third formulation than into the other two. Having a right, as they see things, has extra implications beyond merely being owed a duty; that one's right was violated, correspondingly, has extra implications beyond the mere fact that one was wronged. Here are two extra implications that are often asserted or assumed.[10]

(a) It is in the nature of a right-based duty, some say, that the rightholder has a power to waive it or to license its breach by another. I may owe you a duty not to torture you, not to deny you a fair trial, not to deceive you, or not to bad-mouth you. But those are duties based on your rights, it is said, only if you also have authority to dispense with them, or to permit me to breach them. So there is no such thing as an 'inalienable right' if that is taken to mean that the associated duties of others do not bend to the will of the rightholder. In that way, we might say, all rights protect the freedom of rightholders to do without the (other) protections that their rights afford them.

(b) A right-based duty, some say, is an enforceable duty. If I owe you a duty but you are not permitted to make me do my duty, then my duty is not based on your right. The expression 'make me do my duty' here covers coercive measures you might use to bring me into line; depending on the content of my duty, it could also extend to substitutive action on your part to circumvent my non-conformity, e.g. by taking for yourself what I had a duty to give you. The permission to make me do my duty, in virtue of which you are designated a rightholder, could be a dispensation from what would otherwise be a duty you owe me not to make me do things (a 'negative' permission, the mere absence of duty), or it could be a licence to breach that duty (an 'affirmative' permission, one that can conflict with and override a duty). Either way, when I am an actual or potential violator of your rights, you may automatically help yourself to some relaxation of (what would otherwise be) *my* rights.

---

[10] Both are asserted, cautiously, in HLA Hart, 'Bentham on Legal Rights' in AWB Simpson (ed), *Oxford Essays in Jurisprudence: Second Series* (Clarendon Press 1973), 171, at 192–3. Hart sees 'many signs of the centrality of those powers to the conception of a legal right'. Although he carefully says 'legal right', his analysis is often applied to rights in general. Not totally unfair, as his thoughts about enforcement are echoed, in connection with moral rights, in HLA Hart, 'Are There Any Natural Rights?', *Philosophical Review* 64 (1955), 175 at 178.

To repeat: I do not think that either of these extra features, or indeed anything remotely similar, is built into the very idea of a right, even a legal right. That people are inclined to build them in is easy enough to explain. Idea (a) is borne of an equivocation painstakingly exposed by Wesley Hohfeld.[11] As well as being used in a strict sense to designate the beneficiary of another's duty, the word 'rightholder' can be used loosely to designate the party with the upper hand, so to speak, in a range of other normative relations. Sometimes it is used simply to mean 'holder of a normative power over another; person with authority'. This usage can lead people to think of rights as things that fall to be *exercised* by rightholders, which can lead them to read a normative power back into the relationship between a (strict sense) rightholder and the person who owes her a duty.

This is a simple case of conceptual slippage. As for idea (b), that seems to trade on what we might call a legalistic fallacy. The law says *ubi ius, ibi remedium.* That is a norm, a doctrine, a principle of particular legal systems or legal traditions. It says that when there is a right recognized by the law, a legal right, there ought to be a legal remedy for its breach. It is not a conceptual truth, and nor is it advanced as one. It does not say that nothing is a legal right *until* there is a legal remedy for its breach. In fact, it contradicts that proposition. If nothing is a legal right until there is a legal remedy, then the fact that something is a legal right could not be a reason to furnish a legal remedy. Nevertheless, the association of rights with remedies in the law is so intimate that it has often been read back into the very concept of a right. Rights, even outside the law, are thought to be equipped automatically with remedies for their breach. The problem is compounded by a vagueness in the idea of a remedy. As we know, there is some automaticity in this general neighbourhood. Where I breach a duty that I owe to you, I owe you a duty of repair without further ado. That repair would be, in a sense, a remedy. But it would not be a remedy in the relevant sense. It does not follow from the fact that I owe you a duty of repair that you enjoy any kind of permission to make

[11] Hohfeld, 'Some Fundamental Legal Conceptions as Applied in Judicial Reasoning', *Yale Law Journal* 23 (1913), 16.

me perform it, or for that matter a power to conscript others into making me perform it.

Since it does not follow, an additional argument for the existence of the permission, and for the existence of the power, is needed. Similarly, for the existence of any other permissions or powers supposedly enjoyed by any person to whom a duty is owed. It is no answer to say that—to your way of thinking, unlike mine—the existence of such extra normative incidents is dictated by the very concept of a right. Even if your way of thinking about rights were better than mine, the main implication would be that until the existence of each supposedly essential normative incident of a right to φ is defended, we have not defended the existence of a right to φ. Nor is it an answer to offer a defence of the legal doctrine *ubi ius, ibi remedium*. If that doctrine is sound, it follows that the law should not recognize rights to which it should not attach powers of enforcement. But that does not mean that there are no such rights. It only means that they should not be given effect in the law. Some may say that, if they are not to be given the effect in the law, they are not 'private law rights', and so are not relevant to our discussion. But that is question-begging. The question is whether there should be any 'private law rights', meaning rights that carry with them, as extra incidents, the extraordinary powers and permissions that are associated with the position of plaintiff in private law litigation. To work out the answer we need to ask why the (alleged) fact that a duty towards one was (or is about to be) breached should make one a suitable person to wield *any* new powers and/or permissions over *anyone*, never mind the radically discretionary authority that the private law plaintiff enjoys over the court, and through the court, over the defendant.

3. The enforcer

It would take us well beyond the natural ambit of this book to explore that last question in detail. Why? Because it is primarily a question about the *institutional arrangements* of private law. These have limited parallels in personal life. That is not because there is no justified role for authority or for coercion in personal life. Of course there is. Sometimes, even in the closest and fondest of relationships, a line must unilaterally be drawn, or an issue must unilaterally be forced. To your spouse you may have to say: 'No more boozing, or I'm leaving you.' To your best friend you may have to say: 'Face up to your problems; my patience is wearing thin.' To your grown-up sibling you may have to say: 'Go and talk to dad yourself, so that I don't have to be the one to tell him what you've done.' Repairs and apologies may also call for private enforcement. Recall the bickering children in *The Story of the Treasure Seekers*, already quoted in Chapter 4:

So Dicky said, 'Don't be disagreeable yourself, H. O. Let her alone and say you're sorry, or I'll jolly well make you!'

So H. O. said he was sorry. Then Alice kissed him and said she was sorry too; and after that H. O. gave her a hug, and said, 'Now I'm *really and truly* sorry.' So it was all right.[12]

Is Dicky justified in claiming the authority he does over his younger siblings, namely the authority to require an apology for wrongdoing? Perhaps. Is he justified in issuing a coercive threat to his little brother H. O. to get the apologetic plan off the ground? Perhaps. Is he usurping Alice's powers and permissions, as the (allegedly) wronged person, in doing so? You can certainly see how the identity of the enforcer might make some relevant differences. On the one hand, H. O. might not have been so easily mollified, and might even have been further provoked, if it had been Alice who had stood up for her rights, rather than Dicky who did it for her. On the other hand, Dicky's plan carried a risk of non-cooperation on Alice's part which would not have arisen had Alice been left to find her own solution. There are pluses and minuses in Dicky's assuming the role of peacemaker and there are plus and minuses in his abjuring it in favour of Alice herself. Notice, however, that the pluses and minuses all bear on what it would be reasonable for each of them to do in the circumstances. The justification for the use of authority or coercion, as the case may be, lies in the reasonableness of doing so. There is no reason to think that it would be in order for anyone, Alice included, to use authority or coercion *unreasonably* in extracting the apology she is owed.

<hr />

[12] E Nesbit, *The Story of the Treasure Seekers* (T Fisher Unwin 1899), 139.

Is there anything here resembling the powers and permissions of a plaintiff in civil proceedings? Not much. For the plaintiff is, as we saw, more or less exempted by the law from the demands of reasonableness. The plaintiff enjoys wide discretion about enforcement and about many other matters, discretion which is not surrendered merely because she is not, in a given case, the person best-placed to make the right moves.

But possibly this is a red herring. Maybe there is still a sense in which Alice has a special permission to demand and extract an apology from H. O. that is not shared by others. We need to notice two things. First, Dicky is Alice's older brother. Might his role be less akin to that of a mediator and more akin to that of a guardian *ad litem* in litigation involving children? Maybe he acts on Alice's behalf. If so the question is not whether she has permissions that he lacks. It is whether the two of them have permissions that are not shared by strangers—say, passing adults, who might be better placed than either of them to do a good job of requiring and extracting an apology. Secondly, as we have already noted, not all permissions are alike. An affirmative permission gives one extra licence, e.g. to breach a duty, or to act unreasonably.[13] A negative permission is merely the absence of a duty. Even though Alice and Dicky may not have affirmative permissions to enforce H. O.'s duty to apologize, might they lack a duty that a passing adult would have had, a duty, say, not to meddle in the disputes of strangers? If such a duty is owed to Alice, then what we have here is a right of Alice's in the strict sense. It is not, of course, her only relevant right in the strict sense. There is also her *primary* right, as we might call it, not to have been treated disagreeably by H. O. And then there is her *secondary* right, her right to an apology from H. O. Both are rights as against H. O.; he is the one with the associated duties.

But we might now think that Alice also has a *tertiary* right as against nearby busybodies (but probably not as against Dicky, and surely not as against H. O.) that they not usurp her in asserting or enforcing the right to an apology that she holds as

---

[13] These are what Joseph Raz calls 'exclusionary permissions' in Raz, 'Permissions and Supererogation', *American Philosophical Quarterly* 12 (1975), 161.

against H. O. This tertiary right does not give her (or Dicky acting on her behalf) any latitude to do anything beyond the limits of reasonableness. In that respect, Alice's position may well differ from that of the civil plaintiff. But maybe in another respect her position mirrors that of the civil plaintiff. Maybe we strangers owe it to Alice, as to a civil plaintiff, to let her— within limits—freely assert and enforce her own primary and secondary rights.

Why would we owe it *to her*, to Alice or to a civil plaintiff as the case may be? Respect for her own personal autonomy can't be the answer. That is not, I stress, because her autonomous actions of asserting and enforcing her rights would in turn invade the personal autonomy of the person who wronged her, namely H. O. or the defendant as the case may be. I assume that when a wrongdoer breaches his duty of repair, or indeed any other duty, the fact that he does so autonomously does nothing to redeem his breach. It follows that a narrowly tailored coercive action that does no more than secure performance of a duty—you may think that the coercion of H. O. is a good example—is not objectionable on the ground that it restricts the autonomy of the person coerced (which is not to say that it is not objectionable). But that is not the question. The question is: why should Alice or the plaintiff, personally or via a representative, be the one to wield the coercion, assuming that coercion is justifiably going to be wielded? Why not you or me? After all, our personal autonomy should be respected too. Why should Alice or the plaintiff enjoy this freedom to the exclusion of the rest of us, the rest of us who (the proposal goes) owe it to her not to muscle in on her assertion and enforcement of her rights? It is no answer to say that, when we muscle in like that, we are wronging her by usurping her role, and hence find ourselves in the same plight as H. O. or the defendant, pleading only worthless autonomy. For the very question is: Why would that count as wronging her? Why would standing up for her rights be her special role? Why would someone else taking the initiative count as a usurper?

The key thing to grasp is that respect for someone's personal autonomy, understood as a valuable constituent of her life, is not the only possible reason to protect her freedom of action on a particular occasion or in a particular domain—even to protect it by giving her a right. There are also the wider benefits of the freedom and of its protection by a right to be factored in. Here are some benefits that might help to justify a system in which civil plaintiffs take the lead, maybe even as of right, in asserting and enforcing their rights through the courts:

(i) Since the use of courts for the assertion and enforcement of rights is inevitably slow, cumbersome, stressful, and expensive, it may be better for the law to encourage, where possible, the use of other processes. Giving the plaintiff incentivizing options, including coercive ones, is an effective way to get the defendant to engage with the plaintiff's claim of wrongdoing and to face up to his or her reparative duties, if any. Many out-of-court settlements are coercively obtained using credible threats by the plaintiff of the further deployment of the law and its processes against the defendant. Such settlements are not to be defended and upheld on the ground that they are agreements freely entered into by the parties—for clearly they are no such thing. They are to be defended and upheld on the ground that they tend to secure the performance of a reparative duty by less wasteful means.

(ii) Where, notwithstanding (i), rights are destined to be asserted and enforced through the courts, prosecutorial officials may be more expensive, more erratic, less nimble, and/or less sensitive to the niceties of the situation than the plaintiff. For all of its blessings, dispassionate bureaucracy is not without its curses. The balance of blessing and curse may vary. Sometimes (e.g. when intimidation of the plaintiff is likely) the pursuit of a wrongdoer by a prosecutor may serve the person wronged, as well as the rest of us, better. Some generalizations about the optimal division of labour between these two models may be possible. There may be some types of cases which suit the litigation model better, and others better suited to the prosecution model.

(iii) Intervention in a dispute by a third party (official or not) is often counterproductive. Being relatively ill-informed and hence prone to clumsiness, the well-intentioned intervener often inflames, perpetuates and/or compounds the dispute, rather than helping to resolve it. But leaving the parties to the original interaction to work out their differences alone can also carry risks of escalation or impasse or worse. Ill-feeling between the parties often runs high. So it may well be a good idea for skilled third parties to participate in various ancillary roles—judge, mediator, bailiff, guardian, etc—to contain the various risks associated with leaving the parties to sort things out on their own.

(iv) Putting important decisions about the use of public authority in the hands of private litigants, defendants as well as plaintiffs, is one way among many of avoiding unhealthy concentrations of power in public officials and agencies. A plaintiff's freedom of action is, in this way, somewhat akin to a jury's freedom of action. Even when misguided, the plaintiff's freedom helps to confound the attempts of organs of government, including even the judiciary, to dominate the agenda concerning which alleged wrongdoers are called to account before the courts, which grievances receive public attention, which policies and doctrines are subjected to scrutiny and reform, and so forth. Although the fact of the plaintiff's freedom of action inevitably leads to selective upholding of the law, in the larger scheme of things it contributes to the flourishing of the rule of law by ensuring that the law and its institutions do not become a tool only of an oligarchy of officials.

This is not intended to be an exhaustive list. It includes some considerations which are of particular importance in the late modern age. At the heart of consideration (iv), for example, is a timeless worry about the perils of overmighty government, but one which nevertheless has extra salience today, given the heightened importance of personal autonomy as an aspect of living well. But in saying this, notice, we are thinking not about the autonomy of the plaintiff, but about the role that plaintiffs in general can play, by placing checks on public power, in protecting the autonomy of the rest of us. Like all the other listed considerations, this one emphasizes a public good that may be served by the plaintiff's tertiary right to assert and enforce her primary and secondary rights through the courts.

Should we worry that this tertiary right of the plaintiff supposedly rests for its defence on the contribution that its existence makes to one or more public goods? Is such a defence not inconsistent with the very nature of rights, existing as they do for the rightholder's benefit? Are they not 'considerations of policy ... inconsistent with corrective justice' because 'indifferent to the bipolar relationship of plaintiff and defendant'?[14] Not at all. It is not as if the plaintiff herself reaps no benefits. Her proposed tertiary right, on the contrary, exists to protect her against unremedied violations, by the defendant, of her primary and secondary rights. She is the right's principal beneficiary. The considerations of public good that I listed (together with many others that I did not list) are not alien, but subsidiary. They count in favour of the plaintiff's being the principal beneficiary of the right.[15] More precisely they count in favour of her enjoying a right as against the rest of us that, within limits, will make the assertion and enforcement of her rights as against the defendant mainly a matter for her, rather than a matter for us.

Interestingly, many of the same considerations also count in favour of her having access, as of right, to institutional arrangements to both facilitate and check her assertion and enforcement of her rights as against the defendant. The judicial system is such an arrangement. So perhaps the rest of us also owe it to her not to obstruct her access to the courts, e.g. by the levying of substantial court fees or security deposits or the like. Considerations (iii) and (iv) make a case for plaintiffs to have a right, as well as a power, to take their cases before a judge, or at least to have access to justice done by law, subject to the contrary force of consideration (i).[16] Whether or not the plaintiff's tertiary right goes that far, however, the point remains. Take any right that the plaintiff might be thought to have in respect of her assertion and enforcement of her rights as against the defendant, be it in the courts or otherwise, and be it publicly funded or otherwise. The public goods to which her having that right would contribute count in favour of her having that very right.

---

[14] Ernest Weinrib, *The Idea of Private Law* (Harvard University Press 1995). Here, I juxtapose phrases from pages 184 and 213.

[15] For detailed discussion of how this works, see Joseph Raz, 'Rights and Individual Well-Being', *Ratio Juris* 5 (1992), 127.

[16] Now you know why I sidelined the payment of court fees or deposits as conditions for the valid exercise of the plaintiff's legal power to commence proceedings. Typically, they do not detract from her legal power. They detract from her legal right to exercise her legal power. If (in error) no fee were levied by the court, the suit would remain legally effective. In England and Wales, see Civil Procedure Rules 1998, rule 3.7–3.7B (as amended 2017).

The situation is no different with, say, the right to freedom of expression. There each speaker gets the freedom to express himself, which brings more value to some potential self-expressors than it does to others. But thanks to the protection that the right gives to self-expressors taken one at a time, we all get to enjoy a vibrant and diverse public culture, the value of which helps to shape the right and give it the force that it has. Or rather, we do when the going is good. When the going is bad—say, when people use their freedom of expression mainly to threaten or abuse those with whom they disagree, thereby discouraging expressive experimentation—the case for the right to freedom of expression is correspondingly weakened. Perhaps, when that happens, the benefit to self-expressors themselves is no longer enough by itself to warrant the extensive protection they previously enjoyed under the right to freedom of expression. A reinforcing public good was needed to make up the difference; in its absence the scope and importance of the right recedes. We might worry about that recession, of course. We might mourn the right's decline. But then we are mourning the loss of the public benefits that made the right as important as it was. The right no longer deserves to be what it once was.

So let's not worry that the case for the plaintiff's tertiary right is partly based on public goods. Once it no longer serves those goods, it no longer deserves to be the right that it once was. Should we worry, however, that the case for it is instrumental, i.e. based on the good consequences of plaintiffs having the right? That may seem to be at odds with how the participants themselves see the right. The plaintiff tends to think—and the courts rarely disabuse her of the thought—that the reason why others, including the courts, are duty-bound to defer to her in respect of the pursuit of her action against the defendant, is that (so she alleges) *she was the one who was wronged and the defendant was the one who wronged her*. It is the Holy Grail of much theoretical work on private law to find a way of vindicating this thought. At one level it is not hard to vindicate. The plaintiff's (tertiary) right against the rest of us is a right to assert and enforce her (primary or secondary) right against the defendant. That the defendant was the one who wronged her is what she asserts when she asserts her secondary right to a remedy against the defendant, and the making of that very assertion is part of what her tertiary right protects. Since it is part of what her tertiary right protects it is true that, by drawing attention to it, she draws attention to a reason why others are duty bound to defer to her in respect of her action against the defendant. Her right is the reason! But that still leaves us wondering why she has that right. That is where, to my way of thinking, considerations (i) to (iv), among others, come in.

Those who seek the Holy Grail that I mentioned worry that considerations (i) to (iv) are somehow the wrong kind of reasons. They think that somehow the reasons why the plaintiff has the right should carry over the flavour of strict relationality from the reason that the plaintiff would typically give. Here, however, they repeat the sentimental mistake that Bernard Williams made when discussing 'she's my wife' as a possible reason for rescuing his wife.[17] This is the mistake that we exposed in Chapter 1 by drawing on the portrait of friendship in Steinbeck's *Of Mice and Men*. George and Lennie help each other because they are friends, not because they are well placed to help each other. That they are friends is a reason in its own right for them to help each other. But the reasons *why* their being friends is a reason in its own right for them to help each other include the fact that, when people are friends, they tend to be well placed to help each other. Williams dismissed such instrumental explanations of 'she's my wife' being a reason, but he was wrong to do so.

In the literature on private law, however, the sentimental mistake rides on the back of another. For the flavour of strict relationality in the plaintiff's reason, the reason she takes herself to have and of which the courts so rarely disabuse her, is anyway deceptive. The right that we are discussing here, the plaintiff's tertiary right, is not a right of the plaintiff against the defendant. It is a right of the plaintiff against the rest of us, minimally a right of deference, maximally a right of support, in her action against the defendant, of which the defendant's non-performance of his duties forms the subject matter. The defendant's duties are the primary and secondary ones that we discussed in previous chapters.

---

[17] Williams, 'Persons, Character, and Morality' in Williams, *Moral Luck* (Cambridge University Press 1981), at 18. For an amplification of the mistake, see Weinrib, *The Idea of Private Law* (n 14) 6, on how 'private law is just like love'.

The tertiary duty, by contrast, is no duty of the defendant. It is a duty of the rest of us. The tertiary right is principally a right against strangers to the litigation. If having such a private-law right against strangers to the litigation is 'inconsistent with corrective justice' then the correct conclusion is not that there is no such right. The correct conclusion is that there is much more to private law than mere corrective justice. There is also the whole business of (as some people like to call it) 'civil recourse' made available through the courts.[18]

In framing this section I have tried to remain tentative, even agnostic, about the existence of the tertiary right of the plaintiff. I only ever said that perhaps it exists. I have concentrated on the case for its existence, if it exists. You may suspect that the plaintiff's special position in the assertion and enforcement of her primary and secondary rights is better explicated in the way that I explicated it in section 2 of this chapter: in terms of powers and permissions, with no hint of a tertiary right. If true, that is no skin off my nose. The main payload of this section survives. Reasons (i) to (iv) also count as reasons for the plaintiff to have special powers and permissions, not enjoyed by others, in asserting and enforcing her primary and secondary rights.

I hope it is now slightly clearer what I meant by saying that there are aspects of private law's institutional arrangements that have limited parallels in personal life. Of considerations (i) to (iv), only number (iii)—the typical cack-handedness of third-party interveners—has direct application beyond institutional settings. The case for Alice's right to an apology as against H. O. to be asserted and enforced only at her behest is weak, as compared with the case for a plaintiff's right to reparative damages as against a defendant to be asserted and enforced only at her behest. And that is not, or not only, because Alice is still a child. It is also because she is not playing any significant institutional role. She is not playing a role in the administration of justice and

---

[18] The expression is owed to Benjamin Zipursky, 'Rights, Wrongs, and Recourse in the Law of Torts', *Vanderbilt Law Review* 51 (1998), 1 and is now associated with joint work that Zipursky has done with John Goldberg, notably in Zipursky and Goldberg, 'Torts as Wrongs', *Texas Law Review* 88 (2010), 917.

the maintenance of the rule of law in the way that plaintiffs do. What I earlier called a 'legalistic fallacy' leads many people now-adays to carry over the trappings of the plaintiff's institutional role into their personal interactions. They become indignant at Dicky-style interventions. They insist on plaintiff-like powers, permissions, and rights regarding the assertion and enforcement of their rights. They treat a wrong against them as if it were something that they own, like a house or a car—as if, barring emergencies, access to it were theirs alone to confer. They assume that if the law is justified in granting them such radical discretion as it does over such matters, that must be because they would already have (at least) such radical discretion were it not for the law.

We have already encountered a good example of such thinking in Chapter 1, the example of the self-defender, regarded by many as the owner of his own battle (and hence as having authority over others who would come to his defence).[19] That is a possible legal position, and maybe under some conditions a justified one, but there is no reason to think that anything remotely like it would obtain were it not for the law. Ironically, the myth that it would obtain, once widespread, can create extra pressures for the law to intervene. People become inclined to take the law into their own hands, regarding their hands as, so to speak, the natural hands for the law to be in, and the law of the land as a kind of usurper. Taking the law into their own hands, they make things worse by committing additional wrongs of their own. They fail to see that that the rights and permissions and powers of the self-defender, in the combination in which they take themselves to enjoy them, are partly justified by the way in which they are situated in a wider set of legal and polit-ical arrangements. The self-defender, although not necessarily an official, is in some ways an institutional actor. The case for her having a large role in managing her own defensive situation lies at least partly in the various advantages of organizing things that way in the law. Without that institutionalization she would not only be at risk of suffering more wrongs; she would be at risk of having less that she can legitimately to do to prevent

---

[19] See ch 1, s 6.

them. The case of the person who has already been wronged, and now seeks a reparative remedy, is no different. It is not only her ability to give effect to her rights and powers and permissions that would be diminished were it not for the law. The rights and powers and permissions themselves would be diminished, would have less force, were they not legally recognized. Institutionalization does not usurp her moral position; it constitutively improves it.

That institutionalization makes this kind of difference should not be a big surprise. In Chapter 2, we encountered the idea that the law often has to sharpen the world up for us. Our outcome-responsibility, which was the topic of our discussion back then, cannot be left as indeterminate in law as it is in personal life apart from the law. The same is true more generally regarding the allocation of authority, the granting of permissions, the assignment of rights, and so on. Sharpening up is not required only because we seek better guidance from the law than we can obtain without it. It is required also because once we have the law we have something extra that needs to be guided. The something extra is the institutional apparatus of the law itself, and the governmental arrangements of which it forms part. Once we have a legal system, and seek to use it to resolve our problems, we cannot but encounter questions about what role we are playing in the system when we do so. Many questions about the allocation of powers, permissions, and rights in litigation, as in many other contexts, take that form.

4. Putting it behind us

Many take that form, but not all. I have been emphasizing the plaintiff's role as asserter and enforcer of her reparative rights against the defendant. But I have said little so far about the plaintiff's authority *not* to insist on those rights, her power to waive the defendant's reparative duty or to license its breach. All we know so far is that the mere fact that the duty is owed to her does not *entail* that she has authority over whether it is to be performed. An argument is needed to link having been wronged with having such authority. I pointed this out a few pages ago, but I had already illustrated it earlier in the book.

Do you recall Larry David's misadventures with reparation, recounted in Chapters 3 and 4? Larry sent a cheque to Ben Heineman for the repair of his dented car; Marla later sent a cheque to Larry for the replacement of his stained jacket. In each case, the recipient of the payment later asserted a power ('it's my money') to determine that the duty of repair had been sufficiently performed by the delivery of the payment. The payer, however, insisted in each case on the completion of the reparative process. The car, said Larry, still had to be repaired; the jacket, said Marla, still had to be replaced. This insistence may seem a little fanatical, but it is by no means confused. That is how the comedy works: a really incisive question, pressed to a wild extreme by Larry, then—*touché!*—pressed to the same wild extreme against him. The incisive question is: why should the recipient be free to settle for anything less than the full performance of the payer's reparative duty? It is completely question-begging for the recipient to reply: 'it's my money'. Why is it the recipient's money? Why should she have the wide authority over its use that is associated with outright ownership? Such authority is quite an imposition on the would-be repairer. Recall that duties are the concern, first and foremost, of those whom they bind. The debt of non-performance lies on the duty-bearer's account. Perhaps someone to whom a duty of repair is owed sometimes has authority to relieve the duty-bearer of his debt, or indeed to dispense with his need to account. But there clearly needs to be a better reason than 'it's my money'.

Larry's case, where complete performance of a reparative duty is thwarted by the person to whom the duty is owed, is only a short step from the case in which a reparative offer is declined altogether. I don't mean the case in which a reparative offer is declined on the ground that no wrong was committed or no loss was occasioned ('you don't owe me anything'). I mean the case in which, although a wrong was admittedly done and a loss was admittedly occasioned, the cheque to cover the loss is left uncashed, or, more dramatically, returned to the wrongdoer ('I won't accept a penny from you'). This case may strike you as a long way from Larry's case because there is none of the scent of underhand dealing. The money is guilelessly refused. Yet the performance of the duty of repair is, as in Larry's case, thwarted by the person to

whom it is owed. It is thwarted at an even earlier stage, and even
more comprehensively, than in Larry's case. Returning the cheque
is the dramatic way to confirm that the thwarting is deliberate. To
a hardened litigator this may seem like a stroke of unbridled good
fortune: the wrongdoer is off the hook for the cash; his worries
are over. But in the real world (hah! so you thought *yours* was the
real world!), things are not so simple. To see why, consider the
case in which what is refused is not a reparative payment but an
apology. Again, I don't mean the case in which an apology is refused on the ground that no wrong was done ('you have nothing
to apologize for'). I mean the case in which an apology is refused,
even though a wrong was admittedly done ('I won't take "sorry"
from you').

The autobiographical story that Simon Wiesenthal tells in *The
Sunflower* helps us to think about such refusals.[20] On a work detail from Janowska labour camp, emptying clinical waste bins at a
military hospital in Lemberg, Wiesenthal is taken aside by a Red
Cross nurse and brought to the bedside of a mortally injured SS
officer, a young man named Karl S. The dying man has asked
for a Jew—any Jew will do—to be brought to his bedside in the
hope that he or she will grant him absolution, forgiveness, clem-
ency, on behalf of the unidentified Jews whom he has murdered
(or perhaps on behalf of Jewry at large: that aspect of the plea is
not particularly clear). What Karl S offers to Wiesenthal is not an
apology, exactly, but a frank confession. Yet his offering it, agrees
Wiesenthal, is an expression of true remorse for his admittedly
unjustifiable and inexcusable wrongs. Wiesenthal listens, but
cannot bring himself to speak. He exits and returns to his labour
without giving an answer. Although this is not what the dying
man seeks, it is also not quite a clean refusal. There is something
equivocal or evasive in his silence, and this fact haunts Wiesenthal
for his remaining days at Janowska, and still after liberation. His
camp buddy Bolek diagnoses: '[Y]our subconscious is not completely satisfied with your attitude at the time.' Wiesenthal's
reaction:

[20] Wiesenthal, *The Sunflower: On the Possibilities and Limits of Forgiveness* (2nd
edn, Schocken Books Inc 1997).

Was this true? Did my unrest come from my subconscious? Was this what drove me again and again to think about the encounter in the hospital? Why had I never been able to put it behind me? Why was the business not over and done with? That seemed to me the most important question.[21]

Wiesenthal finds himself, then, in an unwished-for posthumous entanglement. Karl S's death enters his dreams. After the war he finds himself taking a detour to visit the man's mother, claiming to bring her 'greetings' from her son's deathbed, and taking care not to 'diminish … in any way the poor woman's last surviving consolation' that her son had died a 'decent young man'.[22] He is drawn there in search of clues, not only to help him with the original question of how he should have responded to Karl S's plea, but also to help him with the now 'most important question' of why he is still dogged by that original question. He would dearly love to put all these questions to bed. The telling of *The Sunflower* is but another attempt to do so, juxtaposed as the story is (in book form) with a set of responses by prominent individuals with diverse insights into its subject-matter.

Karl S, to repeat, does not exactly apologize. There are some wrongs so heinous that no apology for them, however splendid, could ever rise above the level of a grotesquely feeble response; by apologizing one could only be underplaying the enormity and adding insult to injury. Nevertheless, the structure of Karl S's predicament mirrors that of an apologizer. To apologize one must find someone to apologize to. Until the apology is conveyed to an eligible recipient, it is not yet an apology. An eligible recipient is a person with the normative power to accept or reject one's apology, the authority to determine whether one's apology is a success or a failure. Refused or yet-to-be-accepted apologies are still apologies, and they may achieve something, but they do not yet achieve their apologetic aims. In the same way, the structure of Wiesenthal's predicament mirrors that of an apologizee: he has to decide whether to accept or reject, in his case with the added complication of uncertainty about his eligibility to do so. The element of equivocation or evasion in his silent departure comes

[21] ibid 81.   [22] ibid 94.

of the fact that, although it could be interpreted as a refusal, it could also be interpreted as a denial of authority to refuse.

Hence two layers of doubts. And two rival ways of looking at how to resolve them, reflected in Wiesenthal's later struggles with his conscience. Does he have a solemn duty towards Karl S, one that calls for dispassionate attention to the dying man's pleas and to the reasons for and against going along with them? Must he struggle with the competing imperatives of justice (the man is a monster; that he suffers now with his remorse is fitting) and humanity (the monster is a man after all; the pain of his remorse must be alleviated)? Or would allowing himself to be drawn into all this just be another expropriation of Wiesenthal's own life, yet another way in which his oppressors get to make his life theirs to toy with and dispose of at will? Karl S's is not of course a deliberate ploy to destroy his life, like the choice between her children delegated to Sophie in *Sophie's Choice*. Rather, Karl S shows a banal indifference towards Wiesenthal's life, proceeding from the wider disregard for Jewish lives to which he has been habituated by work in the SS. In that way, Karl S still betrays some of the attitudes that made it so easy for him to participate in the murders that he confesses. His remorse may be sincere but he is still very much the SS officer, for whom any Jew will do. Any Jew will do for murder, any Jew will do for expiation.

Wiesenthal's story has many layers of difficulty. Yet it is, at base, but a much-amplified and much-problematized version of the predicament in which we all find ourselves when we are on the receiving end of an apology, however run-of-the-mill. Let there be no doubt that I am the person to whom an apology is owed, and you are the person who owes it. Maybe, as in the William Carlos Williams poem 'This is Just to Say', I am the one whose sweet cold plums, saved for breakfast, you pilfered from the icebox.[23] An apology is the least I can expect. Even so, in a way, your apology is an imposition on me. By apologizing, you activate my authority, as the person wronged, to accept or reject your apology. Having this authority adds to my duties, or at any rate gives me a new decision to worry about: What am I to

---

[23] Williams, 'This is Just to Say' in Williams, *Selected Poems* (ed Tomlinson Penguin Books 1976), 72. Williams' plum-pilferer, although far removed from Karl S in the gravity of his wrong, has something interesting in common with Karl S. He confesses and asks for forgiveness, but never says the 'sorry' that the

do about your apology? Evading the decision is sometimes possible. If you apologize by letter I can leave the letter unanswered, hoping the situation will somehow resolve itself—a version of Wiesenthal's silence. As Wiesenthal's story shows, however, such evasion of my decision is no panacea. It may equally leave me afflicted with thoughts of unfinished business, a task poorly performed, loose ends, and rational remainders.

How afflicted I should be depends, naturally, on how much turns on the apology. But at the very least, this much always turns on the apology. Are you and I going to go on much as before, on our existing track or tracks, in spite of your wrong? Are we jointly going to treat the unrepaired, and in particular the irreparable, as if it had been repaired? Are we, for example, going to put the incident behind us, the one in which you repeated that salacious rumour about me? If so, apology accepted. But maybe the incident with the rumour is just the last straw, after years of inconsiderateness on your part. Maybe this is the rumour-mongering to end them all. In that case, I may decide, apology *not* accepted. No, we are not putting this behind us. Instead, I am putting you behind me. You are on your way out. At least, our relationship has shifted onto a new, more alienated, track. You have to hope that I soon come round to accepting your apology, or the two of us don't have much of a future. I am already starting to loosen our ties, if not quite yet cutting them.

These remarks on the case of your rumour-mongering presuppose that you and I are in a special relationship of some kind, as friends, or lovers, or colleagues, or something. It is interesting to reflect on how different things could be if you and I are strangers apart from the wrongful transaction. Whether we are strangers or friends, my accepting your apology is a way of putting the wrong behind us, a way of treating what went unrepaired as if it had been repaired. But at that point the two stories diverge. Between friends, putting the wrong behind us means sustaining,

---

title leads one to expect. The poem (which resembles a note on a fridge door) is apologetic but includes no apology. Is Williams reflecting on the difficulty of apologizing, or the insufficiency of doing so, or the presumptuousness of doing so, or what? Williams raises similar questions with a more challenging subject-matter in his poem 'Apology', ibid 28, which contains no (other) apology either.

or at least trying to sustain, our friendship. Between strangers, putting the wrong behind us often means—on the contrary—putting each other behind us, never seeing or hearing from each other again. After you carelessly knocked me off my bicycle by opening your car door onto the cycle lane, I want nothing to do with you. I was not injured but, trust me, you and I will never be friends. That being so, I should probably accept your apology. By rejecting your apology I am more likely to keep you in my orbit. The matter will not be closed. We may end up bickering about what was done by whom; I may have to deal with your repeated attempts to apologize, or to get me to accept your apology, perhaps leading eventually to escalation of hostilities; or I may find that, like Wiesenthal, I am haunted by the way things were left between us, and come to think of myself as somehow the one who now needs to make amends. An accepted apology, in short, is a conservative measure. It tends to preserve the relationship on its existing track between the giver and accepter. It is merely that the existing track of the relationship between friends is the friendship track, whereas the existing track of the relationship between strangers is the track of no relationship at all. Thank goodness, you and I may both think, that the little matter of the collision in the cycle lane could all be sorted out so quickly, so that we can forget all about it and about each other. An apology duly accepted, maybe an offer to cover the cost of the buckled bicycle wheel and the taxi home, and now, let us hope, you and I are done for good.

This is obviously a hugely simplified account of the interpersonal dynamics of apology. It suppresses many variables. The quality and timing of the apology, the gravity of the wrong, the intensity of the relationship, and many other factors can make a big difference. Yet the fundamental point remains that the power to accept or refuse an apology exists, when it does, primarily to allow the person wronged to preserve or alter the future shape of his relationship, if any, with the person who wronged him. If the apology is for a recent wrong, or a recently discovered wrong, it is already a tricky time for the two of them. The wrong has already changed things between them. It has thrown them together in a kind of unasked-for remedial collaboration, even if it has driven them apart in other ways. The wrongdoer, by the mere fact of her wrong if in no other way, has already disrupted the life of the person wronged. It is the wrongdoer's duty to put things back on track, so far as it can be done. Yet it is also an opportune time for the person wronged to reassess the affected aspects of his life, including his relationship with the wrongdoer. It is a good time for him to ask whether back on track is where things (including things with the wrongdoer) ought to be put, given what has changed, and in particular given what has been lost forever. It is an occasion for him to reassess some or all of his personal goals.

This is where his personal autonomy comes in. An autonomous person is one who confronts a range of possible goals as objects of choice, and who sets some aside in order to pursue others. True, we do not relate to our *prevailing* personal goals in that way. When certain goals are already ours, as I put it in Chapter 5, we cannot regard them as just possible goals among others. But sometimes we are put in a position from which we cannot but regard them that way. When our secure relationship with one or more of our goals has been made precarious, the question arises of where we are to go from here. Some goal we had hitherto is no longer straightforwardly a prevailing one. We no longer have the plums in the icebox, the ones we were going to eat for breakfast. At the other extreme, we have lost yet another friend or neighbour to an SS atrocity.[24] When we choose which way to go from here, rather than just drifting or being propelled by others, we act autonomously. If we take a valuable path, the fact that we took it autonomously adds extra value to our having taken it. Refusing an apology (or a repair) is a deliberate step, often an autonomous step, onto just such a path. One is declining to hold on to whatever one can rescue from the wrong, in favour of making a fresh start.

In the light of these remarks, it is tempting to look back on Wiesenthal's predicament in *The Sunflower* and to interpret it as follows. At Karl S's bedside, Wiesenthal is faced with a harsh dilemma of a kind faced by many victims of wrongdoing. The

---

[24] In recounting Karl S's confession, Wiesenthal digresses into the tale of a child he met in the Lemberg ghetto, called Eli, whose face he attaches in his imagination to one of Karl S's victims. See Wiesenthal, *The Sunflower* (n 20) 47.

humane reasons for granting Karl S the absolution he seeks conflict with no less (but no more) powerful reasons of justice to
refuse him. Wiesenthal is silenced by doubt, especially doubt
about his own standing to decide, and retreats. However, that retreat does not, as it turns out, save him from the dilemma. Far
from it. It leaves him with even more unconformed-to reasons,
a yet larger rational remainder, than if he had cleanly granted or
cleanly denied Karl S's request. He should have taken Jean-Paul
Sartre's advice: *il faut choisir*.[25] Had he cleanly chosen which way to
go, his autonomy in doing so would have lent extra value to the
path he took. It would have made it the *right* path for him to have
taken. There would still have been unconformed-to reasons in his
history, of course, but for the person he would have become, they
would have been less of a burden. For he would have been true to
the person that he made himself into by choosing, the just person
or the humane person as the case may be. Regretting the path not
chosen would then have seemed like the problem of an alternative
life, of a ghost with different goals.

This interpretation of Wiesenthal's predicament is not entirely
misguided. It begins well. There is, however, much to object to in
the way it ends. Let me mention a few objections.

First, the choice foisted upon Wiesenthal, like that foisted
upon Sophie, is between categorical reasons, not hypothetical
ones. That they apply to him is independent of his personal goals
(remember: any Jew will do!) and their rational hold over him is
correspondingly unaffected by any change in his personal goals.
That heightens the general point we made about apology as an
imposition. Even as he gives him the power of forgiveness, Karl
S adds to the Nazi sequestration of Wiesenthal's life, a creeping
consumption that has left him with neither room nor use for personal goals, at least beyond those of immediate exigency.

Secondly, Wiesenthal's dilemma, like Sophie's, is arguably one
in which he commits a wrong whatever he does. Arguably, he
not only has competing categorical reasons but competing duties
(categorical requirements). True, if he were to take a valuable
path, the fact that he took it autonomously would add extra value
to his having taken it. But arguably neither path open to him is

---

[25] Sartre, *La Nausée* (Gallimard 1938) 62.

valuable in the relevant sense. Each leads to wrongdoing and that wrongdoing is not made good by the mere fact that the other path leads to wrongdoing that is no less grave.[26]

Thirdly, even if presented with valuable options of which neither is rationally superior to the other, one should not regard one's own autonomous choice of one over the other as potentially tipping the balance in favour of it. If Wiesenthal were to take a valuable path, the fact that he took it autonomously (given the state of his existence, could he have done so?) would add extra value to his having taken it. But it would not give him any extra reason to take it. Compare: That I would eat tasty plums freely does not add a further reason on top of their tastiness for me to eat plums, even though my eating tasty plums freely would admittedly be better, *ceteris paribus*, than my eating them aimlessly, grudgingly, absent-mindedly, etc.

In these ways, and several others, *The Sunflower* ends up being a poor test case for the proposition that those who have been wronged are the ones to enjoy discretionary authority in respect of whether the wrong is repaired (or treated as repaired, as in the case of an apology). Not only is there the doubt about whether Wiesenthal is the right person to hear Karl S's deathbed plea; even if he is, as the above remarks show, he is thrust by Karl S more into the position of judge than that of plaintiff. His task, if he accepts it, is to get the decision about Karl S's benighted soul right on the merits, not to decide where he, Wiesenthal, is to go from here. Where can he expect to go, after a few more months of labour, except to his death in the gas chambers at Janowska?

The story of William Carlos Williams and the plums in the icebox (suitably elaborated) is closer to what we need. If Williams' plum-loving friend refuses Williams' apology, she chooses not to treat the irreparable aspects of the wrong he committed as if they had been repaired. She chooses to move on with her life. She chooses to move on, not in the sense of getting over the wrong (enjoying some replacement plums for breakfast, ideally bought by Williams, and then more of the same old

---

[26] On the value of autonomy put to wrongful use, see Joseph Raz, *The Morality of Freedom* (Clarendon Press 1986) 380. My remarks about autonomy in this chapter are influenced in several ways by Raz's insightful discussion around that page.

friendship). No, she chooses to move on in the sense of getting over Williams (distancing herself from this so-called friend who has been taking her for granted for years). In the terminology of Chapter 5, she chooses to let go of her relationship, rather than hold on to it. In the wake of serious or repeated wrongdoing, that choice may well be the right one. But even if it is not the right choice, the fact that it is chosen gives the rest of us something else to respect in it. We should respect the plum-lover's personal autonomy in the pursuit of valuable goals, and we should recognize that now—in the aftermath of wrongdoing—is an ideal occasion for her to exercise it, to reevaluate where she will find her value. Since she is the one whose existing pursuit of value was rendered precarious by the wrongdoer's actions, a fresh start vis-à-vis the wrongdoer is her prerogative. Thus, it is her prerogative—her discretionary authority—to eschew reparative and apologetic measures. Her cause of action is hers to pursue or abandon as she chooses.

5. Into the sunset, carrying the loot

It is one thing not to pursue one's cause of action, or to abandon its pursuit. It is another to pursue one's cause of action, to obtain reparative damages, and only *then* to choose new goals (or only then to let on that one has chosen new goals). That is the questionable situation with Heineman and his car: he chose to use the money provided by Larry for cosmetic surgery for his daughter, instead of using it to pay for repair of the car. Yes, his personal priorities had changed. But they had not changed because of anything Larry did to his car. So if he had substituted 'cosmetic surgery for daughter' for 'repair of car' on a list of expenses that he expected Larry to bear, even keeping the sum of money just the same, Larry would rightly have resisted paying. So we may wonder: how can it be in order to do the same thing secretly? When a tort plaintiff claims for the cost of replacing a faulty or damaged roof but uses the money instead for a three-week cruise, leaving the roof unrepaired, why is that not a breach of trust, or a deceit, or an abuse of process, or at any rate something such that the misapplied damages can now be recovered by the poor schmuck who paid them?

Some of the reasons we encountered in Chapter 3 are relevant here. We discussed some of the perils of requiring what contract lawyers call 'specific performance' of a duty upon its breach. Relations between the parties may have broken down thanks to the wrong, and expecting the two of them to collaborate now on a remedy may be inviting further and worse conflict. Even if it does not require much collaboration, insistence on *in specie* repair may threaten to heap new losses on top of those already suffered by the rightholder: disruptions, inconveniences, disappointments, and so forth. To these perils that arise when specific performance is insisted upon, we may add some extra perils that arise when specific performance is insisted upon *by a court*. There is a serious risk of perpetuating the litigation or generating satellite litigation. One of the attractions of placing conflicts before the courts is to bring them to a decisive resolution. That an award of money damages is the only remedy for wrongdoing available to the plaintiff *as of right* is a key part of the scheme for assuring the finality of court decisions. It creates an occasion for the court to assert that its work is done, and to rule out further inquiry. So far as the law is concerned, the repair is effected when the money reaches the plaintiff, never mind whether the plaintiff spends it on what he said it was for, or how long he takes to do it, or whether he can do it at lower cost than allowed for by the court so that he ends up with money to spare, or whether he can now only do it at higher cost so that he ends up out of pocket.

There is also another consideration, which was only hinted at in Chapter 3. The example of Larry and Heineman was useful because the next best thing to Larry's not having damaged Heineman's car was clear, and indeed (we gathered) agreed between them. It was the repair of the car. That was the continuity-thesis-indicated solution and it fixed the amount of money (we gathered) that Heineman expected from Larry and that Larry paid to Heineman. But suppose the collision had been more serious and, as well as damaging Heineman's car, Larry had injured Heineman in such a way that he would never be able to drive again. What would be the continuity-thesis-indicated solution now? That is not so clear. In such a case, it might have been reasonable for Heineman to say, from the outset: 'I don't need to get the car repaired. What I need is a different kind of car, suitable for a wheelchair, plus the cost of a driver to ferry me around.' Or: 'I don't need to get the car repaired. What I need now is money to pay for accessible taxis and trains.' Or: 'I don't need to get the car repaired. I'm never going on the roads again after that terrible experience. What I need is a new way of living without moving around. I need an adapted home that is also my office and I need money to cover the cost of having everything and everyone brought to me there.' It is not only that we would need a great deal of extra information to decide which of these, if any, is the continuity-thesis-indicated solution. There are also going to be indeterminacies that cannot be resolved by any amount of information, thanks to the wide-ranging effects that Larry has had on Heineman's life. The collision, as we have now reimagined it, has thrown much up into the air at once. Putting it more technically, Larry's reasons for not having left Heineman in a wheelchair are many, and while sometimes they may all point the same way in respect of what would count as the next best thing for Larry to do, sometimes they point on different ways. Sometimes they point in different ways even for Heineman. Even he cannot be expected to settle what his new life is to be before he is leading it, and in time to have Larry pay for it. The reasons for going one way rather than another are incommensurable in the abstract and only gradual changes in Heineman's personal goals, as he adapts to his new lack of mobility, will yield a best way forward for him.

This consideration problematizes the law's quest for finality. To secure finality, the law has to face the plaintiff with a choice at the point of litigation. Which life is the one for you? The plaintiff may say: 'I can't choose right now. I'd rather not exercise my autonomy like this. I don't want to choose a future. I want to see how it all unfolds, feeling my way as it does.' The court understandably declines to let things drift like this indefinitely. Its reason is not that it prizes the plaintiff's autonomy and wants to give it special play whether the plaintiff likes it or not. Its reason is that it needs to be able to envisage the plaintiff's life after the wrong, whether autonomously chosen or otherwise. That the plaintiff must envisage and plump for a future life at the point of litigation is a necessary evil, borne of the need to get the whole business authoritatively cleared up. Hence, limitation periods for commencing litigation, and time limits for completing various steps within litigation, and no scope to return to court for re-assessment of damages if, after a while, the future goes differently from the one that the plaintiff plumped for, however short-sightedly, in his statement of claim.

Doesn't there come a point at which the destructive effect that the defendant's wrong has had on the plaintiff's previous life is so pervasive that the right thing for everyone to do is to think about the plaintiff's future from scratch, from *tabula rasa*, without regard to its continuity with his past? I am not so sure. It seems to me that this question can be recast, and should be recast, as a question arising within the scope of the continuity thesis, not going beyond it. So recast, the question is whether the next best thing to do, given the plaintiff's terrible losses, is not to attempt to piece any remnants of her old life back together again, but rather to enable her to make a fresh start. It does not seem to me that the continuity thesis has run out at this point. We are not thinking about a fresh start *instead of* the next best thing. Rather, we are thinking about a fresh start *as* the next best thing. The continuity thesis applies, but its application is afflicted by radical indeterminacy. That radical indeterminacy surfaces when we ask: Which fresh start? How ambitious, how durable, how active, how challenging, how comfortable, how sociable, how autonomous, how satisfying to the plaintiff, and so on?

Applying the continuity thesis at this point, one ends up thinking about how the plaintiff's future life, although unrecognizably different in its ingredients from the life she led before, could nevertheless be *as good as* the life she led before. The 'as good as' relation between the future and the past provides the requisite element of continuity. In working out what would qualify as a life as good as the one that the plaintiff had before, however, one is hamstrung by the fact that there is no natural transitive metric for comparing overall quality of life. There are various dimensions of goodness that compete for attention and leave us, at best, with intransitive rankings of possibilities. By way of transitive overall metrics, there are only artificial proxies, mainly those cooked up, for better or for worse, by economists. The law needs to resort to one of these proxies if it is to impose the kind of determinacy that is needed in the cause of legal finality. It tends to use something like the following proxy: a life as good as the one

that went before is a life *no more expensive* than the one that went
before. That constraint is most clearly visible in the rules about
mitigation of damage, which allow the court to check, for reasonableness, a plaintiff's ability to be too experimental or lavish
or careless in getting back on his feet at the defendant's expense.
We could call this the 'bottom line' proxy. It is an extremely
crude proxy. There are many objections to it. But at least the law
recognizes that it is only a proxy. How does it recognize this?
By letting the plaintiff decide how to spend the award of damages. That is not primarily an act of deference to the plaintiff's
autonomy. It happens to augment the plaintiff's autonomy, but
the primary rationale for it is not to augment the plaintiff's autonomy, but to enable the law to draw a line under its own in-
volvement. Even in cases where a fresh start for the plaintiff is not
inevitable, it may well be indeterminate whether a fresh start for
the plaintiff would be better than an attempt to pick up the pieces
of her old life. And even where it is not indeterminate whether
it would better to pick up the pieces, it may be indeterminate
which pieces it would be better to pick up. And these indeterminacies may shift over time such that what is determinate or indeterminate at the start of litigation may be more or less so at the end,
and then more or less so again a year later, and so forth. The law
needs all of this to be confronted by someone else. It appoints the
plaintiff to be the one to do most of the confronting: by electing
whether to sue, by electing what losses to claim in his writ,
by electing what remedy to settle for out of court, by electing
whether to enforce an award of damages made by the court, and
finally by electing what to do with the money once it has been
paid. Kudos to Larry David for noticing that this laissez-faire attitude is an institutional necessity, not a liberal ideal. So kudos to
him for querying Heineman's attempt to carry the same attitude
over into reparative life outside the law. True, personal autonomy
matters. True, Larry should (therefore) try to be more tolerant
of other people's moral errors. It is probably not worth making
a big fuss about this error and ruining Heineman's lunch. But it
is an error: Heineman is wrong to think that, once the money is
paid, it is simply his money to be spent as he chooses. That is the
legalistic fallacy again. Heineman's position is one illicitly carried
over from the law into personal life. Its defence, when defensible,

depends on the importance of finality in litigation, not on respect for Heineman's autonomy. The value of Heineman's autonomy tells in favour of Larry's laying off Heineman a little, but it does not tell in favour of its being acceptable for Heineman to spend the money Larry paid him on something else.

In this respect as in various others, it is misleading to say, as Robert Stevens says: 'The starting position of the common law is based upon a premium placed upon our freedom to choose how we live our lives.'[27] The *starting position* of the common law, rather, is this: that the continuity of our lives is to be protected; that, in pursuit of our valuable personal goals, we are to enjoy security against others to whose actions we are vulnerable, or with whom we have special relationships. Sure, the value of our choosing our personal goals for ourselves often makes a difference. Sometimes—as with its rampant contractualization of our relationships—the law gets carried away. It credits value even to valueless freedom of choice. But that does not alter the fact that, in the defining features that were my focus in this book, private law is less a conferrer of choice than a conserver of value. We should not think the less of private law for this. Without security, as Orwell showed in *Nineteen Eighty-Four*, we have not only no freedom, but no life. The big questions for private law are always: Whose security is to be protected? Against whom? In what way? I wish that private law's record of answers were better. But I did not make it my main task in this book to appraise private law's record of answers. My main task was to show you the big questions to which private law—in its fundamentals—attends. And to persuade you that those questions are not that different—not as different as many think—from the big questions of personal life.

---

[27] Stevens, *Torts and Rights* (Oxford University Press 2007), 9.

NAME INDEX

SUBJECT INDEX

Printed and bound by CPI Group (UK) Ltd, Croydon, CR0 4YY